GHETTO REVOLTS

The Politics of Violence in American Cities

Joe R. Feagin · Harlan Hahn

The Macmillan Company, New York

Collier-Macmillan Publishers, London

10017337?1

T LC72080914

Introduction

In the fall of 1970 the attorney general of the United States
gave an important address to a Heritage Groups Conference in
Washington, D.C., in which he discussed and evaluated the
attacks on the American system made by various groups in recent
years.[1] He began his analysis with a statement that the increased
use of "civil disturbances" by various groups was a phenomenon
that "has no justification whatever in a society having the machinery for peaceful debate and orderly change." The attorney
general explicated his contention by citing the Bill of Rights,
the system of laws and courts, the electoral mechanisms, and the
checks and balances of federal and state governments as the
machinery he had in mind. Arguing that no group could justifi-
ably use violence in the name of reform and social change, he
further implied that historically collective violence has not played
a significant role in shaping or changing the arrangements of
wealth and power in American society. After calling the attention
of his audience to the fact that the national government was still
moving to increase the repressive capabilities of existing law
enforcement agencies, the attorney general concluded with the

[1] John N. Mitchell (address presented at the Heritage Groups Conference, Republican National Committee, Washington, D.C., October
2, 1970). The quotes are taken from a Department of Justice press
release.

assertion that too little was being said about what is right with the American system:

> Let's talk about the political system by which the people rule, through elected representatives, and by which change is effected through debate and ballot.
> Let's talk about the economic opportunity for the individual to reap a growing reward for his talents in terms of living standards for himself and his family. Such opportunity is far greater here than in any other country in the world.
> Let's talk about the educational system—again, the greatest in the world—which gives a person the basic tools he needs for the best use of his abilities.[2]

Doubtless, from the perspective of members of established white groups, including the attorney general (in this case a wealthy Wall Street lawyer), arguments such as these appear accurate and eminently reasonable. From this viewpoint the wealth and power of established groups were secured by means of individual effort and the utilization of the machinery for peaceful change; and the members of these groups tend to view the deprivation, poverty, and the powerlessness of minorities as being essentially determined by the flawed character of minority individuals, not by the flawed character of an unjust society. Moreover, since powerholding groups have inculcated their goals and values in dominant American institutions, including not only the law and the courts but also electoral politics, they have a vested interest in urging dissident minorities to trust in the doctrine of "opportunity for the individual" and to rely on "the machinery for peaceful debate and orderly change."

However, since in the last decade thousands have participated in collective violence, it seems obvious that many Americans have taken a different view of the justifiability of violence in the

---

[2] Ibid., pp. 7–8 of the press release.

Introduction

quest for social change. A basic question being raised in many of these outbreaks of collective violence—it seems to us—has been the very one which the dominant perspective intentionally ignores: What do minorities do when they cannot make significant gains by utilizing the traditional machinery such as electoral politics and the legal system?

Few would argue with the contention that among the most significant outbreaks of collective violence in recent years have been the revolts which took place in and around the hundreds of black ghettos strewn across the fabric of urban America. The central focus of this book is on these dramatic events—particularly the riots that occurred in the years between 1962 and 1970. The conceptual and empirical scope of our effort will generally be restricted to recent ghetto riots within the United States, although we will depart from this central concern to examine the historical background of the black movement to collective violence and to assess in the conclusion certain developments in the ideologies and tactics of black Americans as we move into the seventies. Thus in the chapters that follow we will attempt to suggest answers to such important questions as: What has been the history of collective political violence in America? How many times and in what places did ghetto riots occur? What was the role of various factors, including police actions, in the precipitation of ghetto revolts? What theories have been offered to explain the emergence and evolution of rioting? Was there a conspiracy behind the riots? Were those who revolted drawn primarily from the riffraff in black communities? What was the reaction of government authorities during and after the occurrence of rioting? What did the riots accomplish for black Americans? In delineating answers to these and other critical questions we will attempt to bring some order to the burgeoning literature on ghetto rioting. While most of our analysis is necessarily *tentative* and *exploratory*, a basic task will be to examine systematically much of the research material that has recently appeared.

As we will note in several of the chapters which follow, there are serious weaknesses in the existing empirical literature on ghetto riots, including that which has developed in the various social sciences. A number of important questions about black revolts as yet remain unanswered or inadequately answered because of the paucity of available data. While much popular and some social science writing has concentrated on the flamboyant or colorful aspects of violence, too little attention has been given even to such basic issues as the number of riots, trends over time in the character of ghetto violence, and the specific types of establishment action taken in the wake of rioting. Particularly neglected have been the ghetto riots that occurred in the years between 1969 and 1971, and even those that took place after the assassination of the Reverend Martin Luther King, Jr., in the spring of 1968, have received much less attention than one might have expected, given their magnitude. For example, since many observers have contended that there was a precipitous decline in ghetto rioting after 1967, the year during which massive rebellions broke out in the cities of Newark and Detroit, analysis of data on the years after 1967 would appear to be extremely important. Thus sketchy data, which are only now becoming available (February 1972), suggest that the number of race-related riots may not have decreased systematically between 1967 and 1971; in fact, by some measures of rioting the years 1969 and 1970 saw a notable increase.[3] Even a cursory glance at data such as these points to the need for much additional empirical analysis and research in regard to ghetto riots.[4]

[3] See Jane A. Baskin et al., "The Long, Hot Summer?" *Justice Magazine,* February 1972, p. 18.

[4] The literature provides a lengthy list of terms for the ghetto events studied here: riot, hostile outburst, turmoil, revolution, rebellion, insurrection, uprising, revolt, violent protest, ghetto violence, urban conflict, civil disorder, upheaval, civil disturbance. Decisions on which of these to use can be difficult and often reflect interpretations of events. "Turmoil," "disorder," and "hostile outburst" suggest less purposiveness than we believe was usually present and de-emphasize political meaning. Terms such as "revolution" have generally been used to describe larger-scale collective violence than has so far been

Introduction

In regard to the theoretical literature on collective behavior we have in this analysis generally stressed those interpretations and explanations which have been utilized or developed in the process of interpreting recent rioting on the part of black Americans. While we are here giving emphasis to descriptive analysis and middle-level generalizations about the background, emergence, character, and consequences of ghetto revolts, it is not our intention to discount the importance of broader conceptual or theoretical analyses. There is indeed a need for new and well-developed theoretical perspectives in the area of collective behavior analysis. However, it is our suspicion that too much emphasis has been given at this early stage of social science research to highly abstract and complex theories of collective behavior and too little attention to carefully collecting descriptive materials and analyzing them to determine the basic patterns that appear.

In conclusion, a brief outline of the chapters in this book, and the basic questions with which they deal, may aid the reader in grasping the arguments that follow. Chapter 1 reviews a variety of popular and social science theories and explanations which have been utilized in examinations of the collective violence that occurred in urban ghettos. The importance of the idea of marginality in many conceptualizations is explored, and some exploratory notes directed toward developing an alternative view of riots are offered. Conceiving of ghetto riots as politically meaningful acts in a struggle between powerholding groups and powerless blacks on the urban scene seems to be a promising and suggestive framework for interpreting the recent

---

involved. Other terms in the list—"rebellion," "uprising," and "revolt" —are compatible with the perspective adopted in this book and have been utilized. Each suggests that the violent events took place within a critical social and political context. "Riot," by far the most widely used word, seems to fall in between. One can speak of rioting "against" something, thus pointing to the power structure context. Because of its ubiquitous presence in the literature, we will often use the term "riot" in this book, although we usually construe the term as more or less synonymous with "revolt" or "uprising."

shift by black Americans in the direction of collective violence. Chapter 2 examines the historical emergence and character of collective violence in America as used by a number of dissenting groups, particularly collective violence aimed at altering or maintaining existing arrangements of power and authority. Questions are also raised in regard to the place of the United States among contemporary nations in the frequency and magnitude of collective political violence and in regard to the rank of the most recent decade in the history of American violence. Chapter 2 concludes by painting in broad strokes the history of the black struggle for self-determination prior to the 1960s and briefly examines the first instances of collective violence on the part of black Americans in that decade. Chapter 3 focuses on a series of basic questions about ghetto revolts in the decade of the sixties, particularly on the number of riots, the definition of a riot, and the conditions underlying the emergence of rioting. Chapter 4 proceeds to examine additional important questions about ghetto rioting, focusing on the final precipitating events which triggered rioting and the pattern or stages of rioting which seemed to recur. The reactions of authorities in riot situations are also examined.

Chapter 5 begins a three-chapter examination of the aftermath of rioting and analyzes the reactions to riots by federal, state, and local agencies. The character and functions of government riot commissions are analyzed, followed by an examination of the reform and repressive actions taken by government authorities and private agencies in the wake of rioting. Chapter 6 continues the analysis of riot aftermath issues, assessing the views on riots of black urbanites in several postriot surveys; particular emphasis is given to a survey of local resident reactions to the massive 1967 Detroit riot. Ghetto resident attitudes on the causes, character, and effects of rioting are examined. Chapter 7 concludes the study of the consequences of ghetto revolts with a brief examination of an apparent trend in black communities toward an increased emphasis on self-determination and black power. Ghetto rioting in hundreds of cities, the resurgence of

Introduction

black consciousness, the growing sense of personal efficacy, and the drive for community control all appear to be part of a mutually reinforcing trend in the black struggle. A conclusion briefly discusses the probable future of the black quest for self-determination.

A Postcript. In most undertakings of this character, authors have received aid and support from more persons than they can possibly thank in a brief postscript such as this. But we would especially like to thank our editor, James J. Carroll, Jr., for his patience and guidance, which were essential to the final completion of this project; Gideon Sjoberg, James Button, Robert Lineberry, Ted Robert Gurr, and David Perry, for their useful comments on various portions of the manuscript; and Clairece Feagin, for extensive aid in typing the several drafts of the manuscript.

J. R. F.
H. H.

CONTENTS

Introduction   **iii**

Chapter 1   Theories of Urban Violence:
                 Critiques and Proposals   1
The Backdrop of Black Urbanization   3
Popular Explanations of Urban Violence   6
Social Science Explanations of Collective Violence   12
Some Ghetto-Specific Explanations   24
Some General Problems   28
*Notes Toward an Alternative Theory of Ghetto Vio-
    lence*   31
An Aside   46
Conclusion   47

Chapter 2   The Background and Context of Recent
                 Ghetto Violence   57
Political Violence in American History   60
Conflict in American History: Some Specific Examples   62
Vigilantism   66
Agrarian Violence   68
Labor Violence   69
Collective Violence Among White Ethnic Groups   72
White Violence Against Nonwhite Americans   77
The Political Tactics of Black Americans   81
The Fifties and Early Sixties   91
*Conclusion: Collective Violence Before Harlem and
    Watts*   94

Chapter 3   Ghetto Rioting in the Sixties: Some Basic
                 Questions   99
How Many Riots?   101
Underlying Conditions   109

CONTENTS

Black Perspectives and Underlying Conditions   124
The Issue of Shifts in Black Perspectives   126
Conclusion   134

Chapter 4   The Development of Ghetto Riots: Precipitants and Patterns   141

Final Precipitating Incidents   142
A Chain of Events?   149
The Critical Role of the Local Police   151
The Developmental Trajectory of Ghetto Riots   159
Information Transmission and Riot Development   167
The Later Stages of Rioting   172
Official Actions in Ghetto Riot Situations   183
Conclusion   197

Chapter 5   The Aftermath of Rioting: The Establishment Response   199

Remedies for Ghetto Violence: Some Broad Perspectives   200
An Age of Riot Commissions   205
Who Serves on Riot Commissions?   210
On the Operation of Commissions   212
Commission Findings and Recommendations   216
The Significance of Commissions   224
The Government Response to Riots: Law Enforcement and Reform Measures   226
The Law Enforcement Response: The National Level   227
The Law Enforcement Response: The State Level   233
The Law Enforcement Response: The Municipal Level   235
Social and Economic Reform: The National Response   239
Social and Economic Reform: The State Response   248
Social and Economic Reform: The Local Response   250
Conclusion   260

Chapter 6   Ghetto Resident Views in the Aftermath of Riots   263

The Detroit Uprising   264
Opinion Surveys of Ghetto Residents   265

Contents

The Causes and Character of Ghetto Riots   268
Perspectives on the Use of Violence   275
Views on the Police   283
Some Other Views   286
Conclusion   294

Chapter 7   The Continuing Struggle for Black Power   297
Rioting and the Struggle for Black Power   300
The Meaning of Decentralization   304
Advocates of Community Control   306
An Aside on Federalism   317
The Prospects for Community Control   322
Conclusion   328

Index   333

CHAPTER

Theories of Urban Violence: Critiques and Proposals*

Among the events that have focused increased national attention on the problems of urban areas, perhaps the most important have been the hundreds of ghetto riots that erupted in the major cities beginning in the early 1960s. As Americans became alarmed by the mounting tide of collective violence, many began to display a growing, if ephemeral, interest in those black Americans who participated in the ghetto upheaval. Riots dramatized both the complex problems that now confronted American cities and the urgent need for solutions to these problems. Hence the outbreak of ghetto violence and the plight of urban areas came to be regarded as highly interrelated; it became virtually impossible to discuss one of these topics without considering the other.

Although this interpretation may have been useful in directing public concern, for a brief period at least, toward the unmet needs of the cities, it also seemed to yield some unfortunate consequences. It appeared to imply a causal relationship between certain commonly discussed conditions in the cities and the occurrence of rioting. Since many believed that the riots were inspired by pressing problems within the urban community, they

* This chapter is a substantial revision and expansion of a paper we presented as "Theories of Urban Violence" at the Conference on Political Micro-Violence, University of Texas (Austin), March 1971.

naturally were susceptible to the view that the apparent decline in collective violence on the part of black Americans also reflected a corresponding reduction in the seriousness of those problems. As a result, the predominant reaction of Americans to the widely heralded, if inaccurately proclaimed, cessation of ghetto violence at the end of the sixties betrayed unmistakable signs of relaxation rather than of reform.

Even more fundamentally, the connection between the problems of cities and the problems of collective violence discloses critical theoretical and empirical weaknesses in existing discussions of both subjects. In large measure an adequate understanding of collective violence in urban areas is dependent on an understanding of the process and consequences of urbanization. Social scientists appear to be highly vulnerable in this regard. Not only had they failed to devote serious consideration to the role of collective violence in American society prior to the ghetto riots of the 1960s, but they also had acquired a perspective on urbanization and urban problems that embodied an unusual assortment of misconceptions and questionable assumptions. Since the available literature reveals a paucity of information on collective violence in America's urban areas, and since an adequate comprehension of this subject seems contingent on a satisfactory understanding of urbanization, including the urbanization of black Americans, these deficiencies pose fundamental obstacles to the comprehensive understanding of ghetto riots.

Perhaps one of the most critical errors in prevailing assessments of city life and structure is the general tendency to view the urban scene in pathological terms, true of both public and academic perspectives. Problems in urban areas are often seen in terms of a vivid organic metaphor: urban society is viewed as a "sick" society. Complex social phenomena are seen as symptoms of a basic "sickness in the center of our cities,"[1] just as a fever is

---

[1] The phrase is from one of the first governmental reports on a ghetto riot. Governor's Commission on the Los Angeles Riots, *Violence in the City—An End or a Beginning?* (Los Angeles, 1965), p. 2.

one of the symptoms of bodily illness. Thus, ghetto riots have been seen as symptomatic of some deeper malady requiring the immediate invocation of curative, if not surgical, powers. The flaw in this approach does not lie in its rhetorical appeal; such language may be necessary to convince others to initiate constructive action. Yet there is always the danger that people may begin to take the analogy too seriously. Both urban problems in general, and the occurrence of ghetto rioting in particular, have been perceived not only as unhealthy but also as quite abnormal. Consequently, the belief that urban riots are a manifestation of a pervasive sickness may prompt the conclusion that either it can be corrected by strong palliatives, quarantined by repression, or dismissed as atypical.

The purpose of this chapter, therefore, is to review conventional assumptions about the nature of the urbanization and adaptation of black Americans and to examine existing theories of collective violence that appear to be grounded in these and related assumptions. In addition, an attempt will be made to present an alternative view of urbanization that emphasizes the structural rather than the pathological nature of cities and to develop a different framework for the examination of urban riots.

The Backdrop of Black Urbanization

One of the most significant features of the American urbanization process has been the large-scale trek northward by millions of black southerners, beginning in earnest in the second decade and accelerating in later decades of the twentieth century. Pushed by the declining situation in southern agriculture and pulled by the war-spurred industrialization of northern and western cities, impressive numbers of black southerners crossed regional lines—one of the most massive migrations in American history. Relatively early in this migrating process, the public image of both the migrants and their impact on the cities of destination was exaggerated into a predominantly threatening and pathological portrait. To illustrate, grossly exaggerated images of black

3

migration to the St. Louis area laid the foundation for the white-dominated East St. Louis riot in 1917, in terms of deaths the most serious of all twentieth-century riots.[2] The entrance of black citizens into many urban areas was marked by white attacks of this type and, less often, by retaliatory responses.

A common view of this urbanization process focuses on the profound disorganizing effects on black migrants.[3] In line with much of the literature on migrants in general,[4] black migrants have been viewed as uprooted from the traditional rural milieus to which they had become accustomed. They were suddenly thrust into a strange environment with new obligations and customs. They were cut off from the restraining and integrating effects of traditional social controls, resulting in the troubling phenomena of social isolation, anonymity, and deviance—developments commonly associated with urban migration.

The influx of black migrants into the destination cities appeared to contribute significantly to the growth of urban problems. As growing numbers entered northern cities, there were increases in various highly touted indices of social pathology, such as welfare expenditures, family instability, juvenile delinquency, crime rates, radical agitation, and eventually collective violence. All of these problems, therefore, were easily attributable to the

---

[2] Elliott M. Rudwick, *Race Riot at East St. Louis* (Carbondale: Southern Illinois Press, 1964).

[3] See, for example, Governor's Commission on the Los Angeles riots, *Violence in the City;* U.S. Departmet of Labor, Office of Planning and Research, *The Negro Family: the Case for National Action* (Washington, D.C.: U.S. Government Printing Office, 1965); E. Franklin Frazier, *The Negro Family in the United States* (Chicago: University of Chicago Press, 1939).

[4] See William Kornhauser, *The Politics of Mass Society* (Glencoe, Ill.: The Free Press, 1959), especially pp. 145–150; Philip Hauser, "The Social, Economic, and Technological Problems of Rapid Urbanization," *Industrialization and Society,* ed. Wilbert E. Moore and Bert F. Hoselitz (The Hague: Mouton, 1963), pp. 210ff.; Clark Kerr et al., *Industrialism and Industrial Man* (Cambridge: Harvard University Press, 1960).

wrenching experience that was produced by the skill-less character of these southerners, by the translocation from a rural to an urban environment, and by the impersonality and malaise that allegedly characterized ghetto life. Since this image of the plight of the black migrant and of the ills of urban America was widely accepted both by the general public and by academic analysts, it seemed to form a natural benchmark for the development of theories of collective violence. The rapidity of the social changes black Americans had endured seemed to be responsible for the instability and pathological conditions that had emerged in cities. Consequently, significant departures from the "normal" order of urban life, even collective violence, seemed to be understandable in this context. Although this interpretation has frequently portrayed black migrants in essentially negative and even paternalistic terms, it has been widely accepted as an adequate explanation of emerging urban problems.[5]

Basic to this account of the process of urbanization and to many existing theories of urban violence, therefore, is the concept of marginality. Thus the black resident of ghetto areas is often viewed as functioning outside the prevailing normative system of the cities. He is in many ways an unassimilated alien, an outsider, a man whose prevalent antisocial behavior could be explained because he had not been able to achieve a niche in the conventional framework of city life. Moreover, his state is frequently pictured as one of normative conflict or anomie; he is caught between the standards of the old rural order and those of the urban scene. He is no longer committed to traditional rural norms and values, but not really a part of the urban framework either. In fact, for many explanations of urban problems and of ghetto violence, the characterization of the ghetto

[5] For discussion of research indicating that black migrants are less likely than natives to participate in crime, see Charles Tilly, "Race and Migration to an American City," *The Metropolitan Enigma*, ed. James Q. Wilson (Cambridge: Harvard University Press, 1968).

dweller as a marginal man appears to be crucial. How else can one explain the dramatic increase in social deviance and criminality that has accompanied the movement of black migrants into the cities? How else would it be possible to interpret the willingness of many ghetto residents to defy the established social norms that restrain the resort to violence? For many observers, therefore, the assumption of marginality in theories of collective violence seemed undeniable.

Although the theories and explanations that were developed to explain ghetto riots have been so numerous that any effort to catalog them is almost certain to be incomplete, many of the major approaches we have examined seem to have at least one basic concept in common. Explicitly or implicitly, they accept some version of the assumption of marginality: that participants in ghetto riots were uprooted from old social controls and were not fully integrated into the normal or accepted order and processes of city life. As a result, the tension or strain suffered by a people who had migrated from a rural southern milieu to an urban northern locale is a distinguishing feature of many theories of collective ghetto violence.

Popular Explanations of Urban Violence

Perhaps the one interpretation that embodied this theme most explicitly was the first explanation offered by public officials after the initial outbreak of violence in major American cities. Immediately after the explosion of riots in New York and Los Angeles in 1964 and 1965, mayors and other public spokesmen advanced the proposition that the rioting had been sparked by the enormous wave of recent black migrants from the South, who had sorely taxed the resources of the city and whose unfamiliarity with urban life led to a wrenching culture shock; migrants were seen as quite unprepared for the rigors of city life. In fact, this interpretation received official approval in one of the first government reports, the report of the Governor's Commission on the 1965 Watts riot:

Theories of Urban Violence: Critiques and Proposals

Many have moved to the city only in the last generation and are totally unprepared to meet the conditions of modern city life. At the core of the cities where they cluster, law and order have only tenuous hold; the conditions of life itself are often marginal; idleness leads to despair and finally, mass violence supplies a momentary relief from this malaise.[6]

In a more sinister form, a somewhat similar theme was struck by numerous public officials and many private citizens who attributed the rioting to the work of outside agitators—Communists, or other alien radicals who had migrated to the ghetto community with the specific aim of arousing an otherwise contented rank and file to engage in acts of violence against duly constituted civic authorities. This is an age-old American theory of collective disturbance, perhaps first manifest during the Revolutionary War period. Witness one of the earliest assessments of ghetto rioting made by the acting Mayor of New York after the Harlem riots in the summer of 1964:

I would like to point out however, that anyone who has been on the scene—and I've had first hand reports from people outside the Police Department too—will tell you that the whole operation, the whole rioting operation, is directed toward the so-called fringe groups, including the Communist Party and some of the more radical groups, and not involving the rank-and-file persons living in the Harlem community.[7]

The agitator interpretation even received federal recognition in the passage by Congress of riot-related legislation, including the bill prohibiting the interstate travel of persons for the purpose

[6] Governor's Commission on the Los Angeles Riots, *Violence in the City,* p. 3.

[7] Quoted in the *New York Times,* July 22, 1964, p. 18. For similar comments on extremists made by the Los Angeles police chief and the attorney general of California after the 1965 Watts riot, see the *Los Angeles Times,* August 17, 1965, p. 15.

of inciting others to riot (see Chapter 5). Although these perspectives differ considerably in characterizations of the motives of the riot instigators and in estimates of the numbers involved, both ascribe the problem to external sources, to outsiders or to persons who are not really assimilated into the predominant norms of the urban community. Such views contain important advantages for incumbent city officials. Although many acknowledged that their own areas had problems that required assistance from other sources for their amelioration, community leaders could preserve the image of an essentially harmonious local community. The basic source of the trouble, therefore, was not to be found among long-standing and well-established residents of the city, an otherwise tranquil and satisfied populace.

While interpretations attributing the blame for violence to recent migrants or to external agitation continued to enjoy widespread popularity, these views were soon joined by yet another individualistic explanation that also focused upon the personal characteristics of the riot participants. This view was what social scientists have termed the "riffraff" or "rotten apple" theory of rioting.[8] From one riffraff perspective, the major groups of people involved in the upheavals were hoodlums, vandals, and other criminal elements. One of the first and particularly influential statements of this riffraff theme can be found in the FBI report to President Lyndon Johnson on nine 1964 riots, which gained national newspaper attention in the fall of 1964.[9] This explanatory perspective possessed many similarities to the approaches emphasizing external influences. In each case the instigators and

[8] Joe R. Feagin, "Negro Riot Participants: 'Rotten Apples' or Otherwise Law-abiding Citizens?" (Riverside, Calif., May 1967), typewritten; Robert M. Fogelson and Robert B. Hill, "Who Riots? A Study of Participation in the 1967 Riots," *Supplemental Studies for the National Advisory Commission on Civil Disorders* (Washington, D.C.: U.S. Government Printing Office, 1968), pp. 217–244.

[9] Quotes from this hard-to-get FBI report can be found in John D. Morris, "FBI says Riots Had No Pattern or Single Leader," *New York Times,* September 27, 1964.

the participants in the riots are described as external to the mainstream of the urban community. Neither recent migrants nor criminals, hoodlums, and similar groups could be described, from this perspective at least, as persons who were fully acculturated to the predominant norms and values of the community. Furthermore, the riffraff explanation had distinct advantages for the civic leaders who widely espoused it. Civic leaders argued that this troublesome fraction of the populace was quite small and did not detract from the "exemplary race relations" and harmony of the general community.[10] Thus civic authorities could easily dismiss the sentiments of these groups. Moreover, from this point of view, the outbreak of rioting did not necessitate a radical change in existing city leadership. Although this account of the characteristics of rioters and causes of the rioting has been labeled the "rotten apple" or "riffraff" theory, perhaps a more accurate label for such interpretations would be the "fearsome strangers" theory. Often the initial explanations of rioting provided by local officials and other public spokesmen centered on these threatening segments of the population, segments that most people either did not know or did not like. Such groups appeared to be both mysterious and ominous; but these alien elements were not seen as contradicting the prevailing image of internal social tranquillity and order. The threat that they posed to the peace and tranquillity of the city, therefore, could easily be controlled by strong repressive measures.

Because they focus specifically upon the individual characteristics of the rioters, the theories of ghetto rioting that attempted to characterize the participants as recent migrants, agitators, or riffraff are the most capable of disproof. Social science researchers employing various techniques for identifying participants in the riots have generally found that those ghetto residents actively involved in the riots did not typically or disproportionately possess the characteristics that had been commonly attributed to

[10] The phrase in quotes is from a statement of Mayor Sam Yorty after the 1965 Los Angeles riot. *Los Angeles Times,* August 18, 1965, p. 16.

9

them.[11] For example, arrest data indicate that rioters were more likely than the noninvolved to have been born in the North; and available data indicate that long-term residents of ghettos were more likely than recent migrants to participate. It seems that it takes some time in the city to develop the inclination to riot. In addition, several investigations by government commissions and agencies, including the FBI, have failed to uncover any evidence that the riots had been instigated by organized conspiracies or by outside agitators from other cities who had been imported for the specific purpose of inciting violence.[12] Available studies also suggest that people who were active in the riots were no more likely to have extensive records of criminal convictions than young black adults living in the areas where violence exploded.[13] On a wide range of personal attributes or characteristics, the participants in the riots appeared to be generally representative of the ghetto community as a whole, at least of the adult males in their twenties and thirties. The overwhelming weight of the evidence, therefore, has failed to support the interpretations that portrayed the riots as the work of alien, threatening, or atypical elements in the ghetto population.

Yet another popular explanation of ghetto violence, an individualistic one having elements in common with the theories we have just examined, was the "wild youngsters" theory. Some of the first city officials to comment on ghetto riots stressed this argument. Again witness the acting Mayor of New York after the 1964 Harlem and Bedford-Stuyvesant riots in his assessment of the reasons for the rioting:

[11] Feagin, "Negro Riot Participants"; Fogelson and Hill, "Who Riots?"; Nathan S. Caplan and Jeffery M. Paige, "A Study of Ghetto Rioters," *Scientific American,* **219** (August 1968), 15–21.

[12] *Report of the National Advisory Commission on Civil Disorders* (New York: Bantam, 1968), pp. 201–202; Governor's Select Commission on Civil Disorder, *Report for Action* (State of New Jersey, 1968), p. 142; Morris, op. cit.

[13] See Fogelson and Hill, "Who Riots?"; Feagin, "Negro Riot Participants."

And of course a lot of young kids who have nothing better to do and get great fun and delight out of throwing a bottle or a stone at a policeman or anyone else.[14]

This "wild youngsters" theory was also one of the first explanations of ghetto rioting in the 1960s and set the tone of much that followed. Indeed, it was only a few months later that the influential FBI report to President Johnson on the 1964 riots emphasized this argument, actually using the terms "young punks," "school dropouts," and "drunken kids."[15] This interpretation generally emphasized two major characteristics of the rioters: their age and their youthful propensity to engage in destructive acts because of their excitable nature or their natural rebellion against the constraining influences of the social order. Here again we have fearsome strangers invading adult society, this time from below. One of these contentions was susceptible to relatively direct examination. While some evidence indicated that decreasing age was related to activity in the riots, participation seemed to be most prevalent among men in their twenties and early thirties.[16]

The second portion of the "wild adolescents" theory concerns motivation and thus is less amenable to proof or disproof. Like the theories that stressed the individual traits of the rioters, however, it suggests a purposelessness and a lack of direction in the behavior of rioters. According to this view, the violence was not provoked by specific social, economic, or political grievances; nor did it present a determined effort to ameliorate those conditions. Furthermore, the description of rioting merely as an expression of adolescent rebellion also seems to rest on the assumption that the rioters were not adequately integrated into the prevailing

[14] Quoted in the *New York Times,* July 22, 1964, p. 18
[15] Morris, "FBI says Riots Had No Pattern or Single Leader."
[16] The data are not broken down so that this can be precisely assessed; but from our review of the available data this appears to be true for most serious riots. Fogelson and Hill, "Who Riots?", pp. 234–235; Feagin, "Negro Riot Participants."

social system. In this case, however, the source of the maladjustment was defined less as a product of social and economic circumstances than as a function of the failure of youth to recognize or respect the need for regulations on social behavior. The characterization of riots as a youthful rampage, therefore, also seemed to contain an implicit premise that the rioters were marginal young men—marginal not because of their social and economic circumstances but because of their inadequate socialization into the world of adult responsibilities.

Social Science Explanations of Collective Violence

The characterization of the rioter as a person who was marginally assimilated or unassimilated into the prevailing norms of the urban scene, however, was not limited to those interpretations that sought to explain the violence in terms of the individual characteristics of the participants. This assumption also seemed to permeate a large number of other explanations and theories that had a different focus and origin. Perhaps the most important are the theories of collective violence that began to appear in the literature of the social sciences. Unlike the earlier accounts, these propositions did not focus exclusively upon the attributes of individual riot participants. Instead, they frequently attempted to explain the origins of the violence as a function of broader forces to which the rioters had been subjected; they interpreted the violence less as the action of specific groups or segments of the population than as the outcome of a social process that had placed the riot participants in a frustrating or tension-producing position from which violent disruptions might be an expected result. Unlike the individualistic and personalized explanations of ghetto violence propounded primarily by public officials, the subsequent interpretations of the riots were provided by social scientists, many of whom had earned reputations for expertise in the collective behavior field. Consequently, the interpretations of the ghetto riots proposed by social scientists deserve careful scrutiny.

Theories of Urban Violence: Critiques and Proposals

One of the most commonly accepted points of origin for the scholarly investigation of urban violence emerged from certain traditional sociological theories of collective behavior. Until the 1960s social science could claim few systematic studies of collective violence going beyond the level of classification and typologies. With Smelser's pioneering *Theory of Collective Behavior*, however, came a new concern among social scientists for the causes, sources, and stages of development of collective behavior, including collective violence.[17] Although studies such as Smelser's have yielded important, and elaborate, frameworks for investigation of collective action, perhaps the most central concept in many such social science theories is the notion of tension or strain. Violence participants, including ghetto rioters, are viewed as engaging in collective violence as a result of their exposure to unusual or highly potent pressures or serious malintegration. Most commonly, some type of social change leads to tension or strain; the change can take a variety of forms, such as urbanization, migration, a shift in unemployment, or economic decline.[18] As a result of these wrenching experiences, and given conducive conditions such as the breakdown of social controls, certain individuals, typically those experiencing the greatest tension, participate in collective behavior. The resulting collective behavior has often been seen as deviating from the established norms; consequently, it is often portrayed in terminology suggesting irrationality or inappropriateness, as contrasted with what is regarded as normal or orderly institutionalized behavior.

A variation on this collective behavior theory is related to ideas in what is often termed "mass society theory." This approach gives great emphasis to the lack of effective social controls or binding networks, usually combined with the idea of tension or frustration. The social constraints commonly operative in relation to other individuals are thought to be ineffective. Migrating or uprooted individuals, in particular, are viewed as highly

[17] Neil J. Smelser, *Theory of Collective Behavior* (New York: The Free Press of Glencoe, 1963).
[18] See ibid., pp. 1, 74ff.

13

susceptible to manipulation because of their presumed lack of local affiliations and religious or group loyalties. This perspective emphasizes the reactive response to strain by individuals who have few social ties and nothing to lose.[19] Ghetto rioting, thus, is seen as a hostile outburst by social isolates.[20]

A few perceptive critics have noted that the assumptions implicit in many such theories frequently lead to explanations of collective behavior that portray such activity, implicitly or explicitly, as deviant, abnormal, or irrational.[21] A certain kind of malintegrated individual is seen as choosing peculiar or bizarre strategies of action, based on exaggerated views of the situation, because of his exposure to stressful pressures emanating out of relatively sudden social changes.[22] Such theories of collective be-

[19] On social isolation and ghetto riots, see James A. Geschwender, Benjamin D. Singer, and Richard D. Osborn, "Social Isolation and Riot Participation," an unpublished manuscript (University of Western Ontario, n.d.), p. 14; for general mass society views see Clark Kerr et al., *Industrialism and Industrial Man* (Cambridge: Harvard University Press, 1960), pp. 200ff.; William Kornhauser, *The Politics of Mass Society* (New York: The Fress Press of Glencoe, 1959), pp. 74ff.; Eric Hoffer, *The True Believer* (New York: New American Library Mentor Books, 1951), pp. 44ff.

[20] Other theorists have emphasized the breakdown of social control, not in the sense of social isolation or the lack of social networks, but in the sense of the inability of local authorities to handle the collective disorder. This element has been given emphasis both in traditional collective behavior discussions as well as in recent treatments of ghetto riots. See Morris Janowitz, *Social Control of Escalated Riots* (Chicago: University of Chicago Center for Policy Study, 1968).

[21] Elliott Currie and Jerome Skolnick, "A Critical Note on Conceptions of Collective Behavior," *The Annals,* 391 (September 1970), 34–45; see Smelser's reply in Neil J. Smelser, "Two Critics in Search of a Bias: A Reply to Currie and Skolnick," *The Annals,* 391 (September 1970), 46–55.

[22] One of the best discussions of social science theories can be found in Jerome H. Skolnick, *The Politics of Protest* (New York: Simon and Schuster, 1969), pp. 329–339. For an example of this tension approach applied to ghetto riots, see Morris Janowitz, "Patterns of Collective Racial Violence," *Violence in America,* ed. Hugh D. Graham and Ted R. Gurr (New York: Bantam, 1969), pp. 412–444.

havior often appear to be designed to explain forms of conduct that represent a marked departure from the theorist's view of what is normal or ordinary. Yet this view makes the problematical assumption that there is a definable pattern of human conduct which can be classified as orderly and organized and can be contrasted with forms of behavior that are easily classified as disorderly and disorganized.

Even more important, the basic presuppositions encompassed by these theories of collective behavior seem to contain many of the root concepts of marginality that are embodied in popular explanations. Nearly by definition, an individual subjected to severe social strain inducing him to engage in violent activities is depicted as a marginal man. He is somehow not protected, or not fully protected, by the common social safeguards that would otherwise shield him from disruptive influences; he is vulnerable to overpowering social forces that impel him to supposedly extreme forms of behavior such as violence. From this point of view, one of the most disturbing sources of tension to which an individual can be exposed is the process of sudden or telescoped social change such as the transplantation of a person from a placid rural environment to an industrialized urban milieu. In fact, in many descriptions of collective violence, the unsettling effects of rapid urbanization are accorded a prominent role among the forces that may produce the intense tension underlying the development of collective violence. In the alien and impersonal world of the city, the rural migrant is assumed to suffer from a strong sense of anxiety that may provoke him to engage in socially disapproved behavior. Hence, interpretations of ghetto riots founded upon these sociological appraisals of collective behavior seem to have much in common with popular individualistic assessments of those events. Even though they emanated from different sources and embodied different theoretical aims and concepts, both perspectives seemed to be grounded in the assumption that the riots were the products of marginal men who acted outside the normal perimeter of acceptable social or political behavior. To the extent that this assumption is accu-

15

rate, of course, these theories may provide a useful explanation of the violence. But to the extent that this assumption is inadequate or incomplete, such theories may not only fail to achieve these goals, but they may also promote serious misconceptions in the existing understanding of these events.

Moreover, a very serious misconception about collective violence emerges from the prevailing emphasis in many social science analyses on one side of the collective behavior situation: the focus on the marginal groups and the situations of strain and tension in which they find themselves. Yet collective violence, including ghetto riots, inevitably involves at least two sides, two formations of antagonists: one the dispossessed, and the other the agents of the state, fronting as it were for the powerholding groups in the society. The agents of the state play a much more important role in the recurrent phenomenon of collective political violence than many analyses suggest. If one is enamored of a strain approach, then the focus should also be on the strain those groups in power are experiencing. The role of the civil authorities and the power groups controlling them is not just one of conduciveness or of social control but also one of precipitating and inaugurating collective violence, and one of channeling violence once it has begun. We will return to this argument at a later point.

Yet another interpretation of ghetto violence that emerged from the social sciences employed the now common theme of alienation. Although this concept also is derived from a well-established tradition in social thought, it has as yet not been fully developed in relation to collective behavior. The idea of alienation has encompassed a variety of meanings and has been used in numerous contexts to explain popular reactions to established authorities ranging from the defeat of referendum issues to full-scale acts of insurrection. The term has become so broad that it has been assigned definitions extending from a vague feeling of political powerlessness to a pervasive sense of general estrangement from one's environment. Perhaps the only common element that can be divined from the many conceptions of alien-

Theories of Urban Violence: Critiques and Proposals

ation is again the underlying premise of marginality. A person who is alienated presumably stands apart from others; he feels cut off from society and generally unable to control events around him.[23] His sense of isolation ultimately is transformed into deep and chronic feelings of withdrawal and disaffection that may eventuate in outbursts of violence. Although a much more focused and specific concept of alienation might conceivably be used in the development of a comprehensive political theory of violence, in the vague senses of common usage it seems to obscure the possibility that ghetto rioting arose from a background of specific political grievances. Moreover, documenting the presence of alienation in a given population does not provide an explanation of why those attitudes might result in the outbreak of collective violence rather than in some other form of resistance.

Although interpretations of ghetto rioting based on tension, isolation, and alienation theories of collective behavior attracted some adherents in the flurry of research interest in the 1960s, perhaps the "easiest and by far the most popular explanation of social violence"[24] emphasized the psychodynamics of frustration and aggression in human beings. Although frustration-aggression theories vary greatly in complexity, the central concepts can be stated in relatively simple terms. Given the requisite conditions, an individual whose basic desires are thwarted and who consequently experiences a profound, chronic sense of dissatisfaction and anger is likely to react to his condition by directing aggressive behavior at what is perceived as responsible for thwarting those desires, or at a substitute. The greater the perceived importance of the desires and the more comprehensive the checking, the more vigorous the aggressive response. Recent analysts

[23] See H. Edward Ransford, "Isolation, Powerlessness, and Violence," *Racial Violence in the United States,* ed. Allen D. Grimshaw (Chicago: Aldine, 1969), pp. 434–446.

[24] Leonard Berkowitz, "The Study of Urban Violence," *Riots and Rebellion,* ed. Louis H. Masotti and Don R. Bowen (Beverly Hills, Calif.: Sage Publications, 1968), p. 39.

have given particular emphasis to aggression as a reaction to frustration seen as the blockage of ongoing goal-directed behavior, rather than to aggression seen as an aspect of instinctual human behavior.[25] Arguments grounded in the concepts of frustration and aggression, therefore, attempt not only to examine the process by which frustration induces discontent and anger but also to provide some indication of the likely response of the frustrated. Moreover, an extension of this conceptualization also might provide some indication of the target of aggressive action, presumably those individuals or groups responsible for the frustration.

In many important respects, a well-developed sociopsychological model of the frustration-aggression type provides a framework for the examination of urban violence more comprehensive than some of the other explanations previously discussed. And it certainly provides a more penetrating psychological analysis than the quasi-psychological explanations of some prominent observers of recent turbulence, some of whom like Schlesinger see America's violent way of life as attributable to "the destructive impulse"; explanations in terms of the "darkest strains in our national psyche" do not lead us very far in understanding the origin or nature of collective political violence.[26]

Yet there are some basic weaknesses in the common frustration-aggression approaches to collective violence. By using terminology connoting instincts or chronic inner conflict and by focusing on the psychodynamic forces that shape human behavior, frustration-aggression theorists frequently divert attention from a thorough examination of the broader societal forces that shape the situations of individuals and of the groups to which they belong. Moreover, frustration-aggression theories taken alone point to possible sources of the dissatisfaction lying behind individual acts of violence, but they do not indicate how or why individual dissatisfaction becomes collective and how or why that collective

[25] Ibid.
[26] Arthur Schlesinger, Jr., *Violence: America in the Sixties* (New York: Signet, 1968), p. 31.

discontent eventuates in collective aggression. Missing too in many frustration-aggression explanations is a discussion of why the aggression is directed outward rather than inward and why it frequently focuses on the real source of the frustration rather than a substitute. Certainly light can be shed on collective violence, including ghetto rioting, from the frustration-aggression point of view, but major gaps remain. Utilizing the sociological approaches, it is at least possible to suggest social forces such as rapid social change, urbanization, or value conflict—forces that may have been responsible for generating group discontent, and ultimately collective violence. By concentration on the internal or individual mechanisms, the frustration-aggression approaches tend to discourage the systematic raising of fundamental questions about the social context.

Yet another problem with frustration-aggression analyses is that anger and consequent aggression can occur without the postulated frustration. For example, a black youth may throw a rock at police because he has just seen a pregnant woman beaten and dragged to a police car, because the situation violates his "learned standards of justice and right," not because of frustration in the sense of blockage of his own goal-directed activity.[27] Furthermore, according to frustration-aggression approaches, the type of frustration endured by an individual participating in collective violence seems to differ from the normal stresses and strains of everyday life; it is frustration that leads to aggressive behavior. While most persons in a society are compelled to endure frustration, the sort of frustration that is implied by the frustration-aggression hypothesis seems to be substantially more intolerable by virtue of its resulting in aggressive conduct. Those subjected to this type of frustration are in an unusual position compared to people whose frustrations can be directed to nonaggressive outlets.

Although frustration-aggression explanations often do not de-

[27] Peter A. Lupsha, "On Theories of Urban Violence," *Urban Affairs Quarterly,* 4 (March 1969), 289.

vote much attention to identifying the social forces responsible for placing people in the frustrating position, they do suggest that individuals subjected to the frustration that produces aggression occupy a somewhat distinctive status. Thus the model of frustration-aggression is also similar to theories that derive their fundamental assumptions from an image of the marginal man. Presumably persons exposed to the type of frustration leading to aggression are not as fully integrated into prevailing normative routines of life as those who are not buffeted by this kind of frustration or those who can manage or control such frustration in nonaggressive ways. Furthermore, a serious question might be raised about whether or not frustration-aggression approaches assume the abnormality of the behavior studied. They suggest that he who reacts to frustration with aggressive behavior is in a separate psychological category from those who react in other ways.

The basic postulates of the frustration-aggression perspective appear to be closely related to another psychological approach widely used in studying collective violence. This is the relative deprivation perspective. To begin with, most relative deprivation approaches leap immediately and inexplicably to the collective level; individuals frustrated by relative deprivation are no longer as important as the collective frustration generated by various discrepancies in the situations of social groups. Moreover, the concept of relative deprivation has taken a number of different forms, depending on the particular type of discrepancy emphasized. In looking at the situation of black Americans in the 1960s, some have emphasized discrepancies in the status of black rioters compared to other reference groups within black communities.[28] Other analysts have stressed the objective deprivation revealed in black socioeconomic levels examined relative to whites, usually noting a decline in the relative position of blacks prior to the ghetto uprisings.[29] Yet others have emphasized the

[28] Caplan and Paige, "A Study of Ghetto Rioters," 20.

[29] James C. Davies, "The J-Curve of Rising and Declining Satisfactions as a Cause of Some Great Revolutions and a Contained Rebellion,"

Theories of Urban Violence: Critiques and Proposals

"revolution of rising expectations," arguing that the actual socio-economic gains of blacks have not been accumulating with sufficient rapidity to satisfy rapidly rising expectations.[30] And this approach is often connected with an emphasis on the declining objective socioeconomic situation of blacks relative to whites.[31] A severe reversal after a period of sustained advance, Davies has argued, is particularly conducive to collective violence.[32]

One of the most sophisticated theories of collective violence, propounded by Ted Gurr, places heavy emphasis on the concept of relative deprivation, interpreted to mean a state of mind where there is a discrepancy between what men seek and what seems attainable.[33] The greater this discrepancy, the greater their anger and their propensity toward violence. Frustration is no longer seen as the blockage of present goal-directed activity, but as anticipated frustration, frustration engendered by discrepancies between what is realistically attainable given the social context and what is sought.[34] Indeed, Gurr opts for a version of the "revolution of rising expectations" argument in explaining the emergence of ghetto riots; that is, although aspirations of black Americans have been increasing dramatically in recent years, their perceived capabilities to secure the goals they desire are increasing less rapidly.[35] The want-get gap, therefore, is also

---

Violence in America, ed. Hugh D. Graham and Ted R. Gurr (New York: Bantam, 1969), pp. 716–725.

[30] Thomas F. Pettigrew, *Racially Separate or Together?* (New York: McGraw-Hill Paperback, 1971), pp. 148–152. See also Thomas F. Pettigrew, *A Profile of the Negro American* (Princeton, N.J.: Van Nostrand, 1964), pp. 192–193.

[31] Pettigrew, *Racially Separate or Together?* pp. 147–149.

[32] Davies, "The J-Curve of Rising and Declining Satisfactions," pp. 690ff.

[33] Ted Gurr, "A Causal Model of Strife," *When Men Revolt and Why,* ed. James C. Davies (New York: The Free Press of Glencoe, 1971), pp. 293–313.

[34] Lupsha, "On Theories of Urban Violence," 288.

[35] Ted Gurr, "Urban Disorder: Perspectives from the Comparative Study of Civil Strife," *Riots and Rebellion,* ed. Louis H. Masotti and

increasing, at least as perceived by those who engaged in rioting.

Basic to most theories of relative deprivation is the idea that there is a relationship between the willingness of particular groups to engage in violence and their status or position in society. Consequently, this approach not only suggests some of the basic sources of sentiments that lead to collective violence but also hints strongly that the structural features of a society play a role in spawning such sentiments. Yet, while relative deprivation theories seem at this point in time to offer one of the most sophisticated approaches to explicating ghetto violence, they also reflect some serious deficiencies.

One of the critical problems is the lack of specificity of the referent. Relative to what? The referent used in the measurement of relative deprivation has varied widely in different studies, and the exact nature of the referent or the discrepancy is sometimes only vaguely specified. Relative deprivation theories also share some of the problems of their cousins, frustration-aggression theories. Again the relationship between individual deprivation and collective deprivation is frequently assumed rather than explicated and the linkage between collective deprivation and collective violence is usually left weakly developed. Also, there is the thought-provoking suggestion that "anger can occur without one's being frustrated or deprived."[36] Persons can react in violent fashion to an affront to their learned values, their sense of what is right and just, without any personal sense of deprivation.

In many relative deprivation arguments there is also the problem of vaguely specified declining objective conditions. While many have used the argument of declining socioeconomic position of blacks vis-à-vis whites prior to the emergence of ghetto riots to explain collective violence, few have carefully examined the trends in these socioeconomic conditions.[37] Indeed, there are

---

Don R. Bowen (Beverly Hills, Calif.: Sage Publications, 1968), pp. 51–67.

[36] Lupsha, "On Theories of Urban Violence," 288–289.

[37] See Ted R. Gurr, *Why Men Rebel* (Princeton, N.J.: Princeton University Press, 1970), p. 54; Pettigrew, *Racially Separate or Together?*

available data that indicate that, relative to whites, blacks were making significant strides by the 1960s. Particularly difficult to demonstrate would be the sharp reversal in conditions just before riots, postulated by Davies, Gurr, and others as significant in the emergence of black violence. While we do not intend to suggest a Pollyanna view of ghetto conditions, particularly in the absolute sense, it is clear that black Americans generally made socioeconomic gains relative to whites before the emergence of serious riots. To illustrate, nonwhite median income as a percentage of white increased systematically from 53 percent in 1961 to 63 percent in 1968; this measure reflects a relative gain;[38] between 1950 and 1961 the yearly percentage figures fluctuated up and down with no clear declining trend discernible. The period also saw a decrease in the number of black poor and no increase in the relative seriousness of the chronic black unemployment problem.[39] In addition, research on variations in deprivation levels as related to riots has so far offered little support for relative deprivation approaches which stress discrepancies in objective socioeconomic conditions. One careful empirical study of variations in objective relative deprivation found that, when size of black population in the cities was controlled, there was no association between measures of relative deprivation, such as the ratio of nonwhite median income to white median income, and the number of ghetto riots (see Chapter 3).[40] At the very least, these data suggest the conclusion that those who rely heavily on increases in deprivation to explain the collective violence recently

---

p. 148; Davies' evidence on this point is quite weak. Davies, "The J-Curve of Rising and Declining Satisfactions," pp. 722–725.

[38] Bureau of Labor Statistics, *The Social and Economic Status of Negroes in the United States, 1969* (Washington, D.C.: U.S. Government Printing Office, 1970), pp. 14–15.

[39] Ibid.

[40] Seymour Spilerman, "The Causes of Racial Disturbances: A Comparison of Alternative Explanations," *American Sociological Review,* 35 (August 1970), 627–649; Seymour Spilerman, "The Causes of Racial Disturbances: Tests of an Explanation," *American Sociological Review,* 36 (June 1971), 427–442.

characteristic of growing black ghettos need to re-examine their position.

Just as other theories examined previously have imputed a socially marginal position to persons who engage in violence, there may also be a variant of this marginality assumption in some deprivation theories. Persons active in a riot are viewed as materially deprived in relation to some contrasting group; in the case of black rioters the standard is often white urbanites or the white middle class. Their deprivation becomes an indication of their social or cultural marginality, of unique distinctiveness.

Some Ghetto-Specific Explanations

Although the relatively general social science theories of strain, alienation, frustration-aggression, and relative deprivation certainly provide more sophisticated models for interpreting violence than the statements of public officials focusing on the riffraff or migration characteristics of rioters, when they have been applied to ghetto riots, they do not seem to have adequately incorporated an awareness of the wide-ranging social and political significance of racial discrimination and segragation, both in its institutional and individual forms. Although some of these theories are certainly broad enough to incorporate a comprehensive treatment of the pervasiveness of racism in relation to ghetto violence, they have tended to divert attention from this issue. Perhaps in recognition of this problem, a number of more specific interpretations have been developed by social scientists and other professionals influenced by social scientists. Each of these explorations includes a greater awareness of the impact of racial discrimination and segregation on black Americans living in encapsulated ghettos.

In one of the most widely publicized interpretations of ghetto rioting, the National Advisory Commission on Civil Disorders concluded that "white racism is essentially responsible for the explosive mixture that has been accumulating in our cities since the end of World War II."[41] By attributing the blame for ghetto violence to the pernicious effects of an ideology of racial superiority, the Commission succeeded, where other interpretations seemed to fail, in drawing an explicit relationship between the external effects of racial bigotry on ghetto communities and the outbreak of rioting. Yet, while giving attention to problems of race prejudice and discrimination, the Commission did not probe many of the interactive implications of their assertions about the causal role that white racism played in the development of ghetto rioting, specifically with relation to the political settings of American cities. Moreover, this causal judgment of the Commission, as well as its promising recommendations for programs to alleviate the plight of ghetto residents, did not appear to result in massive public support for the verdict or in determined political efforts to implement its proposals (see Chapter 5). By stressing the pervasive and insidious effects of attitudinal racism—the stress emphasized in the mass media—the Commission perhaps confronted the white public and governing officials with a problem that was so overwhelming and so amorphous that it would have paralyzed the national will for action, even if other restricting factors had not been present.

There are at least two additional interpretations of ghetto violence that also seem illuminating, both of which focus specifically on the American racial situation. These two approaches, the "new ghetto man" view and the "riot ideology" perspective, reflect attempts at lower-level generalizations based on actual data collected in the 1960s in urban ghettos. Indeed, building an adequate explanation for ghetto violence may well necessitate this type of working from the ground up.

Some commentators have attempted to explain the outbreak of violence by noting the recent emergence of what they term "the new ghetto man."[42] According to this interpretation, the

[41] *Report of the National Advisory Commission on Civil Disorders,* p. 203.

[42] Nathan Caplan, "The New Ghetto Man: A Review of Recent Empirical Studies," *The Journal of Social Issues,* **26** (Winter 1970), 59–74.

eruption of riots is related to the growth of a new set of values and self-perceptions in certain segments of the ghetto population. According to this view, the conduct of most members of society is affected by a normative structure that assigns a higher value to the maintenance of social order than to the venting of aggression or violence; therefore, the outbreak of ghetto violence reflects a growing feeling that attaches greater importance to the visible and physical expression of dissatisfaction than to the external sanctions that have traditionally inhibited such displays. This shift in attitude toward violence in turn reflects a shift in conceptions of Negro life and potential, major changes in the direction of increased black consciousness and a feeling that one can shape his own destiny, coupled with a rejection of the passive acceptance of ghetto conditions characterizing the past.[43] From this perspective, then, socialization into black consciousness and militancy has become a distinctive and extraordinarily important characteristic of urban ghetto communities in the United States, presumably for the last two decades. Perhaps, too, as a part of this general process there has been a shift in black political socialization.

According to the "riot ideology" point of view, the outbreak of ghetto violence was inspired and perpetuated by a developing riot ideology among black Americans—a view of riots which sees them as protest, as a legitimate and productive way of making demands on the existing authority structure. This argument is partially based on several postriot surveys which found that a large proportion of ghetto residents, as well as riot participants, discussed riots in protest terms. In his relatively brief development of this intriguing conception Tomlinson has emphasized the view that a riot ideology gradually emerged in the activist

---

[43] Ibid., pp. 70–71. This argument meshes well with recent data on system-blame perspectives among blacks. See John R. Forward and Jay R. Williams, "Internal-External Control and Black Militancy," *The Journal of Social Issues,* **26** (Winter 1970), 75–92.

segment of the ghetto population and spread easily among less sophisticated ghetto residents.[44] Others have elaborated this approach to include the development of riots from the early 1960s into the 1970s. In this view the first riots were actually hostile outbursts, but were also crucibles in which the riot ideology was born, an ideology which in turn led to more "creative rioting."[45] Rioting seemed to bring gains, even if they were limited gains. With the spread of the belief that rioting represented a significant and utilitarian instrument of protest ("the demonstration effect") came an increasing likelihood of more riots, given an appropriate riot situation and precipitating event.[46] Consequently, a major advantage of this perspective, in contrast to frustration-aggression or relative deprivation explanations, is that it points toward viewing riot participants as political dissidents, toward the interactive relationship—crucial to the development of ghetto rioting—between the existing authority structure and the black community. Yet the view of rioting as a type of protest may convey the impression that the violence was designed only to attract the attention of public officials and to arouse them to action. Although this intention apparently represented one of the objectives of rioters, it did not appear to exhaust their goals. Ghetto rioting reflected more than a strong hope that the political system would respond peacefully and favorably to black needs and demands. Rather, rioting appeared more as a desperate and con-

[44] T. M. Tomlinson, "The Development of a Riot Ideology Among Urban Negroes," *Racial Violence in the United States,* ed. Allen D. Grimshaw (Chicago: Aldine, 1969), pp. 226–235.

[45] James A. Geschwender, "Civil Rights Protests and Riots: A Disappearing Distinction," *Blacks in the United States,* ed. Norval D. Glenn and Charles M. Bonjean (San Francisco: Chandler, 1969), p. 407. This point is emphasized in regard to the historical spread of rioting in Lupsha, "On Theories of Urban Violence," 292. See George F. Rudé, *The Crowd in History* (New York: Wiley, 1964); E. J. Hobsbawm, *Primitive Rebels* (New York: Norton Paperback, 1965).

[46] See Gurr, *Why Men Rebel,* p. 173; Ulf Hannerz, *Soulside* (New York: Columbia University Press, 1969), p. 170.

certed effort to compel political authorities to change not only their policies but also to force alterations in the process by which those decisions are made.

Admittedly, each of these relatively limited and ghetto-specific explanations of collective violence suffers from underdevelopment when compared with other theories, such as relative deprivation approaches. Yet they do have several advantages over previously discussed perspectives in at least two major ways: (1) they point toward the wide-ranging, perhaps distinctive, significance of racial discrimination and segregation in shaping the development of collective behavior among black Americans; and (2) they point up the interactive character of relationships between black Americans and white authorities in urban ghetto settings.

Some General Problems

Having reviewed a number of theories and perspectives devised to explain collective violence, and before proceeding to some suggestions for an alternative framework for viewing ghetto rioting, let us briefly recapitulate and summarize what we consider to be the serious weakness in the common approaches to collective violence. Certainly, many of the theories applied to ghetto rioting have important explanatory power; many contribute to understanding ghetto rioting. Yet most make assumptions that should, at the very least, be carefully and rigorously investigated, not simply accepted as a matter of conjecture and assumption.

Perhaps one of the basic weaknesses of many approaches to ghetto riots is that they explicitly or implicitly opt for a reactive rather than a proactive view of collective actions taken by black Americans.[47] Violence is not viewed as reflecting any specific ob

---

[47] A similar argument is made with regard to opposition to police violence by William A. Gamson and James McEvoy, "Police Violence and Its Public Support," *The Annals,* **391** (September 1970), 97–110.

jective or goal; it is perceived as a response to a set of adverse circumstances and conditions that impel people to engage in what is portrayed as unusual or aberrant conduct. The immediate conditions that produce violent actions often are depicted as a state of social and personal disequilibrium, usually seen as resulting from relatively significant social changes. Although the various theories proposed to interpret urban violence assume different forms, many seem to have key concepts in common. To oversimplify somewhat, many seem to assume a sequence of events that might be depicted as follows: social change → frustration or tension → aggressive release of frustration or tension. According to this basic formulation, therefore, those who undergo intensive social changes such as rapid urbanization, economic recession, or declining conditions relative to a critical reference group will be subjected to extreme strain or tension that eventually, perhaps inevitably, is released in a display of aggression such as collective violence. Such a view of disequilibrating events is often coupled with the notion of a breakdown in traditional social controls or the weakening of traditional normative restraints. We do not mean to suggest that all explanations of collective violence explicitly assume this pattern; in some perspectives it is only implicit. In other explanations only part of the sequence is given considerable emphasis, or the sequence is lacking entirely. But the sequence does seem to be a common feature of both general theories of collective behavior and of explanations focusing specifically on ghetto rioting.[48] As a result of some preceding series of sudden and dramatic events, people are placed in a position in which they are subjected to pressures resulting in personal disequilibrium, ultimately resulting in the eruption of some type of aggressive behavior.

Moreover, frequently underlying many existing explanations

[48] This analysis has been influenced by the work of Charles Tilly. See Charles Tilly, "Revolutions and Collective Violence" multilithed (Ann Arbor: University of Michigan, 1970). See also Chalmers Johnson, *Revolutionary Change* (Boston: Little, Brown, 1966), pp. 59–82.

of ghetto riots—particularly popular explanations—is the idea that the persons who engaged in rioting can be found at the edge of society. They are not fully assimilated into the norms of the prevailing social system, or their aberrant behavior is not as strongly influenced by commonly accepted social values as is the conduct of others. Such assumptions facilitate the interpretation of events of collective violence as marked deviations from "normal" forms of political expression. From such a perspective, ghetto rioting reflects action that took place outside the confines of the prevailing social and political system; therefore, in the minds of many observers it was necessary to identify the external sources of violence. As a result, these assumptions permitted the maintenance of an image of societal order that excluded the use of collective violence as a legitimate tactic and that might be disrupted only by a small segment of the population located on the lunatic fringe of that order.

As a result of these various assumptions, ghetto violence has frequently been viewed as nonpurposive, meaningless, or a temporary outburst of aggressive release. Perhaps this is a natural consequence of the dominant assumptions and orientations of many theories. Since the principal origins of the violence are ascribed to situations that produce psychodynamic tensions or frustrations, the fundamental assumptions of the theories seem to exclude the possibility that the riots were purposeful or rationally related to relatively well-defined aims or objectives. In some explanations there is a recognition that ghetto violence was centered primarily on those perceived as primarily responsible for the discontent. Yet the major targets of the violence or the effects that many rioters apparently sought to accomplish do not appear to form a crucial feature of many violence theories proposed thus far. Nor is the crucial role of authorities, interacting with those challenging their authority, given much play in these existing theories, particularly prior to the stage of riot control and suppression. As a result, it was easy for many to conclude that the riots represented random, generally unintentional, or apolitical behavior rather than purposive and political activity.

Notes Toward an Alternative Theory of Ghetto Violence

Hence, there appears to be a need for a thorough re-examination of existing theories as they apply to collective violence in general and ghetto violence in particular. An appropriate point of departure for such a re-examination might be the environmental context within which ghetto rioting has occurred. Much of the literature on the process of black urbanization distorts the picture by giving far too much emphasis to the impersonal, dehumanizing, and disorganizing aspects of the movement of rural settlers to an industrialized urban milieu. There are other features of this process that are equally deserving of attention and that apparently contributed to the eventual outbreak of ghetto violence. As increasing numbers of black migrants from the South entered urban areas in the North, they congregated in relatively confined and tightly bounded sectors of the cities.[49] Newly arrived black residents in a northern city were not free to locate at any place in the community; their choices were severely limited by the prevailing discrimination, both individual and institutional, that divided the city into distinctive black and white areas.[50] Thus geographic residential segregation became one of the most crucial and continuing social facts both for black residents and for cities in which they reside. A comprehensive understanding of the social, economic, and political implications of ghetto encapsulation seems an essential prerequisite for the study of black America.

The separation of black and white inhabitants into sharply divided sectors, therefore, had important consequences for the subsequent social and political development of metropolitan areas and eventually for the outbreak of urban violence. In the first place, the migration resulted in the concentration, for the

[49] Evidence on the extreme segregation of black Americans can be found in Karl E. Taeuber and Alma F. Taeuber, *Negroes in Cities* (Chicago: Aldine, 1965).

[50] On the important role of institutional racism, including banking and real estate patterns of discrimination, see John H. Denton, *Apartheid American Style* (Berkeley, Calif.: Diablo Press Paperback, 1967).

first time, of very large numbers of black Americans in tightly bounded areas; this became particularly significant for second- and third-generation black urbanites. At least as important, too, was the fact that the concentration of black urbanites promoted an important degree of informal and formal interaction. Confronted with similar problems and faced with omnipresent prejudice and discrimination, and drawing on previous social ties, ghetto residents developed extensive social networks and patterns that were restricted primarily to the black community and that did not encompass a large number of informal contacts with whites. In contrast to the widely circulated and accepted image of disorganized and atomized black migrants set adrift in an alien urban setting, there is much evidence indicating that a protective web of kinship and friendship enveloped most black migrants in the destination cities, actually influencing the pattern of migration and facilitating the integration of black southerners into the urban milieu.[51]

According to the available evidence we have surveyed, the interdependence and relationships that emerged in urban ghettos continued and promoted a substantial degree of social cohesion and communalism in most ghetto neighborhoods, conventional pathological theories notwithstanding.[52] Moreover, as a result of

[51] Tilly, "Race and Migration to an American City," pp. 147ff.; see also Charles Tilly, *Migration to an American City* (Newark, Del.: University of Delaware Division of Urban Affairs and School of Agriculture, 1965).

[52] Joe R. Feagin, "The Kinship Ties of Negro Urbanites," *Social Science Quarterly,* 49 (December 1968), 660–665; Joe R. Feagin, "A Note on the Friendship Ties of Black Urbanites," *Social Forces,* 49 (December 1970), 303–308; Joe R. Feagin, "The Social Ties of Negroes in an Urban Environment: Structure and Variation" (unpublished Ph.D. dissertation, Harvard University, 1966); Leonard Blumberg and Robert R. Bell, "Urban Migration and Kinship Ties," *Social Problems,* 6 (Spring 1959), 328–333; Nicholas Babchuk and Ralph V. Thompson, "The Voluntary Associations of Negroes," *American Sociological Review,* 27 (October 1962), 647–655; Kathryn P. Meadow, "Negro-White Differences among Newcomers to a Transitional Urban Area," *The Journal of Intergroup Relations,* 3 (Autumn 1962), 320–330.

Theories of Urban Violence: Critiques and Proposals

the circumscribed nature of their associations, with relatively infrequent interpersonal ties with whites on an equal-status basis, and as a consequence of the omnipresent discrimination they faced, black urbanites tended to develop common perspectives. The relative homogeneity of problems, and of viewpoints on social and political goals, in black communities often equaled and perhaps surpassed that of the white population. This solidarity provided the basis for substantial organization to advance the collective interests of the black ghetto, or significant segments thereof. Unlike the white segment of the population which was frequently divided by sharp socioeconomic, ethnic, and other cleavages, as well as by diverse problems and interests, many black communities seem to have generated a growing sense of unity and purpose.

Furthermore, this urbanizing situation of black Americans might be viewed as a process of group mobilization, broadly taken.[53] Moving from the relative isolation and traditionalism of the rural milieu, over the last few decades ghetto blacks have been part of a general group mobilization process whose underlying goal is to break into the American system: increasing the number of black persons in encapsulated urban areas, thereby increasing the number of available participants in civil rights and other group activities; accelerating the growth of material resources such as money and weapons; developing important formal organizations and leadership; strengthening old social and communication networks and building new ones; building black solidarity and consciousness. While these processes can produce phenomena that work at cross-purposes, and they have often been decelerated by the activities of whites, they have generally increased the resources available to urban black communities and to subgroups within those communities. Thus it is extraordinarily

[53] We are here extrapolating on the basis of provocative ideas on mobilization in Amitai Etzioni, *The Active Society* (New York: The Free Press of Glencoe, 1968); and Charles Tilly, "Revolutions and Collective Violence."

important to view Negro migration in terms of its generation of large encapsulated black communities.

The mounting numbers of black migrants segregated in numerous cities in the North and South, coupled with growing cohesion and organization, thrust them into urban politics, into the ongoing competition between various urban groups.[54] Unless the meaning is otherwise clear from the context, the terms "politics" and "political" hereafter should be construed in the broadest sense as referring to competition for power and influence between distinctive social groups within a given sociopolitical system. In the urban setting "politics" can be seen as including jockeying for influence and control over the existing governmental structures and also competition for influence and control in other major institutional sectors, including the economic, welfare, and educational sectors.[55] Once tradition-bound, isolated, and relatively lacking in power in rural areas, in recent decades black Americans have become an active competitor for power on the urban scene. Not that black Americans are unique in this regard, for numerous white immigrant groups entering the city in prior decades similarly struggled to gain power. Yet at a relatively late stage in the development of American cities, black citizens were thrown into contention with other important segments of the urban community for the rewards and benefits that could be provided by full political participation. With growth in numbers and the stirrings of mobilization of resources, the black community emerged as a force to be reckoned with.

However, in pursuing their political interests, including attempts to move government to meet their needs, black urbanites

[54] Hereafter we will frequently use the term "group" broadly to refer to the various class, ethnic, and other groups with common interests jockeying for power and legitimate authority in urban settings, similar to Gamson's use of the term "solidary group." See William A. Gamson, *Power and Discontent* (Homewood, Ill.: Dorsey Press, 1968), pp. 34–35.

[55] We have been influenced in our image of the urban political situation by Gamson, *Power and Discontent,* and Tilly, "Revolutions and Collective Violence."

confronted major obstacles, including some important barriers not encountered by earlier white ethnic groups with similar aspirations and goals. The migration and encapsulation of black Americans not only resulted in a framework for potential and actual group mobilization but also presented a golden opportunity for previously established white groups to exploit black urbanites in a new, neocolonial fashion. First-generation black urbanites and their descendants faced the obstacles of traditional racism and discrimination, as well as a new series of incursions by whites aimed at exploiting encapsulated ghetto residents for their own purposes. Many of these exploitative activities were for economic purposes. There was the raid on the ghetto pocketbook in the form of exploitative ghetto merchants, including many whites who operated ghetto businesses long after their own families had moved out. These whites profited from the restricted consumer situation of an encapsulated people.[56] White landlords and other real estate groups bent on taking advantage of profits in a restricted situation moved into ghettos, or expanded their operations.[57] Moreover, ghetto land was sometimes coveted by city authorities who by the process called urban renewal removed black urbanites from valuable land, profiting as a result.[58] This white in-migration only made the economic situation more difficult, for black mobilization was already hampered by the declining supply of low-skilled jobs, jobs that had greatly facilitated the emergence of earlier ethnic groups.[59] Important too is a rec-

[56] *Report of the National Advisory Commission on Civil Disorders,* 274–277; Richard E. Rubenstein, *Rebels in Eden* (Boston: Little, Brown, 1970), p. 124.

[57] Rubenstein, *Rebels in Eden,* p. 122; William K. Tabb, *The Political Economy of the Ghetto* (New York: Norton Paperback, 1970), pp. 12–20.

[58] Chester W. Hartman, "The Housing of Relocated Families," *Urban Renewal: People, Politics, and Planning,* ed. Jewel Bellush and Murray Hausknecht (Garden City, N.Y.: Doubleday Anchor Books, 1967), pp. 315–353.

[59] See *Report of the National Advisory Commission on Civil Disorders,* p. 278.

ognition that many governmental resources and benefits remained in the hands of white-dominated politicians and machines. These nonresidents of ghettos controlled, to cite one important example, many jobs important on the ghetto scene, including the positions of policemen, postmen, school officials, and teachers.[60]

Neocolonial intrusions into the economic side of ghetto life, however, were not the only obstacles black urbanites faced. City fathers, and the powerholding groups lying behind them, were concerned with rising crime rates and looked toward the burgeoning ghettos in their midst. Their reactions to crime resulted in new police invasions of ghetto life, for example, in the form of preventive patrolling.[61] Indeed, some analysts would argue that the ghetto situation has parallels to that of many underdeveloped countries caught in the vise of colonialism.[62] Critical aspects of colonialism have been economic and governmental subjugation. In both cases the black residents of urban ghettos found themselves and their movement to political self-determination hemmed in by white powerholding groups.

Moreover, particularly because racial distinctions were more visible and more salient to large masses of white voters and leaders than other community cleavages, the efforts of black Americans to achieve their objectives by means of traditional electoral and party politics frequently united white groups.[63] Often when a particular issue gained recognition as a "civil rights issue" or as a proposal of primary interest to the black community, heterogeneous forces in the city—such interest groups as the Irish, Italians, the WASP business community, the unions—abandoned their internecine squabbles and united against the black community. The conventional process of coalition founda-

[60] Rubenstein, *Rebels in Eden,* p. 125.

[61] President's Commission on Law Enforcement and Administration of Justice, *Task Force Report: The Police* (Washington, D.C., U.S. Government Printing Office, 1967).

[62] See Tabb, *The Political Economy of the Black Ghetto,* pp. 23–24.

[63] See *Report of the National Advisory Commission on Civil Disorders,* pp. 279–280.

tion in electoral struggles commonly collapsed when the race question was injected. Indeed, a clear sign of the significance of an emerging group is the response of groups already in power and the civic authorities which are ultimately under their control. Unified resistance of formerly antagonistic groups to black demands signifies the emergence of a real threat by blacks to seize a share of urban power.[64]

Significantly, the white immigrant groups that entered the cities between the Civil War and World War II came when the then existing economic system required much unskilled labor. Coupled with other factors such as the development of urban machine politics, such economic resources enabled white immigrant groups to become, together with big business and earlier WASP groups, powerholders within the framework of the urban political system. As a result, it is this coalition which has resisted so vigorously the claims for power by the millions of blacks establishing communities in cities a few decades later. Hence, the broadly based coalition of urban powerholders often includes not only big business, but also unions and the white immigrants, in varying political arrangements. Yet by the time large ghettos were springing up all over the North the redistribution of power which occurred in the first half of the century had slowed dramatically. Because of opposition of entrenched interest groups, black citizens usually failed to achieve either representation in city government that was proportionate to their numbers or the enactment of major programs to alleviate their most pressing problems, nor were they able to penetrate in a significant way the economic and welfare institutions of the cities.

Nor is it surprising that existing powerholding groups resisted the entrance of a new group of have-nots into the system. In addition to a natural inertia manifested by ruling groups in most societies, there was the additional problem of a less expansive economy. Acceptance of black Americans into the power arena would mean a significant reallocation of certain basic economic

[64] Rubenstein, *Rebels in Eden,* pp. 91–92.

resources available. In addition, the admission of black Americans would mean a change in the rules for admission to the ruling coalition, providing a precedent for the entry of other powerless nonwhite minorities into the powerholding arena.

Given this background, the prospects of attaining more than token racial progress through traditional party and machine politics increasingly seemed remote to the growing numbers of black urbanites.[65] As a result, black citizens in the North as well as in the South were forced to utilize other methods in promoting their objectives. One such tactic involved the use of the legal process. By seeking to obtain redress of grievances through the courts, black Americans gained a number of significant, if in several ways limited, judicial victories in such areas as residential covenants and public accomodations.[66] But the victories were frequently hollow. The implementation of judicial decrees required administrative or economic support that was often absent; court decisions had an effect on legal rights, but they often exerted little pressure on the distribution of political benefits, particularly on the urban scene. Changing the allocation of major urban resources so that they would be used to the advantage of black Americans seemed to require alternative tactics.

Another technique widely employed by black citizens was verbal persuasion. For several decades blacks have attempted to demonstrate, through the sheer force of argument, the debilitating effects of racial discrimination and to arouse the conscience of the white public. Indeed, several major reports and research studies documenting the conditions of black Americans were spurred by this effort. Yet such efforts were not very successful. A principal problem was the refusal of white groups to recog-

[65] See the discussion in Chuck Stone, *Black Political Power in America* (rev. ed.; New York: Delta, 1970), pp. 116ff.

[66] Inge P. Bell, *CORE and the Strategy of Nonviolence* (New York: Random House Paperback, 1968), pp. 6–7; Richard Bardolph, ed., *The Civil Rights Record* (New York: Thomas Y. Crowell, 1970), especially pp. 233ff.

nize the distinctive effects of racial bigotry and discrimination; or, if they did recognize discrimination, to propose renewed individual efforts as the preferred remedy.

As a result, black citizens began to make increasing use of techniques designed not only to gain increased prominence for black grievances but also to force white groups into a negotiating situation. Black protest activity in the North and South began to take the form of mass marches, picketing, sit-ins, and other civil disobedience tactics. With a few isolated precedents in the fledgling demonstrations of the 1930s and 1940s in the emerging ghettos in Chicago and Harlem, the civil disobedience movement escalated in the late 1950s and early 1960s, marking an important new direction in the black struggle for power. The sit-in movement in Greensboro, North Carolina, was organized and aggressive, outside traditional party politics, and focused indirectly on the economic camp of the enemy. As these tactics yielded modest successes, the movement increased in size and significance in the urban North and South.[67]

The result was often a type of bargaining process: demonstration, coercive government response coupled with some type of negotiations, on occasion, significant gains from the negotiations, then demonstration again. Indeed, the avowed intent of nonviolent demonstrators and their leaders was to force whites into negotiations aimed at altering the distribution of power and resources. To illustrate, in *Why We Can't Wait* Martin Luther King emphasized that the intent of demonstrations was to force a community "which has constantly refused to negotiate" to face the issue and negotiate with the demonstrators, "to create a situation so crisis-packed it will inevitably open the door to negoti-

[67] St. Clair Drake and Horace R. Cayton, *Black Metropolis* (New York: Harper Torchbooks, 1962), Vol. I, pp. 88–113; Bell, *CORE and the Strategy of Nonviolence,* pp. 12–17; John Hope Franklin, *From Slavery to Freedom* (New York: Random House Vintage Books, 1969), pp. 623–624; Arthur I. Waskow, *From Race Riot to Sit-In* (Garden City, N.Y.: Doubleday, 1966), pp. 225–234.

ation."[68] The shock and threat of disruption generated by black actions began to pressure powerholding groups which valued civic tranquillity to negotiate and even to begin to show signs of a willingness to relinquish some power.

Such nonviolent tactics were by no means limited to the South. Militant tactics, sponsored by groups like the Congress of Racial Equality (CORE) and even the National Association for the Advancement of Colored People (NAACP), spread throughout northern cities. Activities were escalated against housing and employment and school discrimination; stall-ins, job blockades, economic boycotts occurred in numerous northern cities, including San Francisco, Boston, Philadelphia, and New York.[69] Nevertheless, the increasing use of civil disobedience and other nonviolent tactics did not produce a thoroughgoing amelioration of conditions in ghetto communities, most conspicuously perhaps in ghettos of the urban North. Black urbanites continued to suffer from significant underrepresentation in important decision-making councils, governmental and otherwise. And even though the passage of civil rights legislation prompted by the movement began to establish a legal basis for black equality, such legislation could do little to precipitate a major redistribution of resources and power.

Thus the collective violence that began to occur in cities in the early 1960s occurred against a backdrop of various politically motivated activities on the part of black Americans. Indeed, as the forms of nonviolent expression increased in number and intensity, they were increasingly referred to as "violent" demonstrations rather than as nonviolent or protest demonstrations. Underlying much of the thought during this period seemed to be the notion that these events contained a potential for violent confrontation.

Seen from the point of view of a minority attempting to move

[68] Martin Luther King, Jr., *Why We Can't Wait* (New York: Signet, 1964), especially pp. 79–80.
[69] Bell, *CORE and the Strategy of Nonviolence,* pp. 13–15; Waskow, *From Race Riot to Sit-In,* pp. 236–246.

Theories of Urban Violence: Critiques and Proposals

up in a political system, collective violence historically appears to be one of the last alternatives utilized in their struggle for power. However, if we were to conclude these notes on collective violence with such a statement, it would be quite inadequate. Collective violence involves more than a dissident minority. Other questions must be raised. For example, where does collective political violence typically occur? It occurs where major shifts in power are occurring, or where there is increasing pressure for such shifts, within a given political system. Indeed, Dahrendorf has reminded us that it is the differential and unequal distribution of power and authority in a society that invariably gives rise to far-reaching social conflicts, including collective violence.[70] And Charles Tilly has emphasized that, viewed historically, collective violence has been part of the regular and normal political life of all nations—part of the process by which competing vested interest groups maintain power, gain power, or lose power in the process of jockeying for influence and control over governmental and other social institutions.[71] Consequently, Tilly's definition of collective political violence is suggestive in this regard:

An instance of mutual and collective coercion within an autonomous political system which includes violence to persons or property and threatens the existing control over the organized means of coercion within the system.[72]

This definition points up the problematical nature of focusing only on emergent or challenging political minorities. The em-

[70] Ralf Dahrendorf, *Class and Class Conflict in Industrial Society* (Stanford, California: Stanford University Press, 1959), pp. 165, 210–217.

[71] Charles Tilly, "Collective Violence in European Perspective," *Violence in America,* ed. Hugh D. Graham and Ted R. Gurr (New York: Bantam, 1969), pp. 1–3, 37–41.

[72] Charles Tilly, "Methods for the Study of Collective Violence," *Problems in Research on Community Violence,* ed. Ralph W. Conant and Molly A. Levin (New York: Praeger, 1969), p. 28.

phasis on mutual coercion points to the involvement of power-holding groups or governmental agencies which represent them, commonly in the form of police forces, in collective violence. Moreover, critical to the development of mutual and collective violence is the threat that the actions of the emergent minority pose to the control of existing powerholding groups, particularly with reference to the means and use of coercion.

In contrast, many recent popular and scholarly analyses of collective violence, including assessments of ghetto rioting and guerrilla activities, see "violence" solely in the actions of those trying to alter the existing structure of power, rather than in the activities of those defending established order.[73] Terms like "order," "disorder," and "violence" have usually been defined in the political process itself. The definitions of those in power tend to prevail in determining which actions represent order and which disorder. However, from the alternative perspective, the police forces which suppressed ghetto rioting were also engaged in collective violence, as governmental agents for those interest groups attempting to maintain their power and control in American cities.

Moreover, the question of why this type of collective behavior occurs should be answered both in terms of the emerging minority and in terms of the existing powerholders and the governmental agents representing them. On the one hand, collective action on the part of an emerging group trying to move up in a political system is certainly not uncommon in the histories of nations, taking a variety of forms running from electoral politics, to the politics of civil disobedience, to the politics of violence. Collective violence on the part of have-not groups frequently occurs after other alternatives have been tried, if not exhausted, and have not produced significant shifts in the distribution of power. American history, as we shall see in a later chapter, is re-

[73] Skolnick is one of the few to give some emphasis to this point. *The Politics of Protest*, pp. 4–5. See also Rubenstein, *Rebels in Eden.*

plete with examples of emerging groups that engaged in collective violence in the struggle for power. On the other hand, both the development and timing of collective violence is greatly affected by the actions of powerholding groups and governmental authorities, particularly in their responses to alternative political tactics used against them and their willingness to relinquish power. Moreover, collective violence also occurs at the behest of those in power—usually through the means of governmental agents such as the police or armed forces—in an attempt to recapture a monopoly over the means of coercion and force.

In many respects, therefore, the rioting which erupted in America's black ghettos in the 1960s—and is still occurring at the time of writing—represents what we would term the "politics of violence." Such a perspective helps explain the timing of collective political violence at the end of decades of civil rights struggle. Black Americans had not been successful in achieving their principal objectives through the political processes of voting, parties, or machine politics. Nor had they fulfilled their goals through rhetoric or nonviolent activities such as sit-ins and demonstrations. Given the presence of a coalition of white interest groups unwilling to restructure the extant pattern of racial subordination, to growing numbers of black Americans the prospects of achieving major advances through nonviolent tactics must have seemed increasingly dim. As a result, violence emerged as the ultimate alternative for many, to be engaged in regardless of the personal consequences. The ghetto rioting that erupted in hundreds of cities represented a concerted attempt to achieve political objectives that had not been gained through other means. Such rioting does not represent simply random and senseless destruction lacking meaning or purpose (as some would define "riot"), nor does it represent a full-scale rebellion or revolution seeking to overthrow the national government. If the urban violence of the 1960s fits any of the neat categorizations evolved in the historical analyses of collective violence, it might best be seen as insurgency, or perhaps as insurrection against local political arrangements and authorities by those lacking the status of a formal belligerent.

In one sense, ghetto rioting might be perceived as a continuation of the type of collective bargaining which developed in earlier nonviolent efforts, as a way of disrupting the affairs of the existing political system in the hope that negotiations would result.[74] Seen as a method of redressing popular grievances, of influencing governmental authorities, and of forcing a shift in the distribution of power and resources, rioting in a communal context has a long history. During the eighteenth and early nineteenth centuries, urban areas in England and elsewhere were in some cases nearly governed by a type of collective bargaining by riots that continued for many years before these areas were placed under the surveillance of organized police forces.[75] It is interesting that "politics" is often presented as though its essence were peaceful negotiation and interaction, while violence is frequently seen as the antithesis of politics. Yet collective violence has frequently created the situation in which those in power were forced to take political dissidents seriously and therefore were pressed to negotiate.[76] From this perspective, ghetto rioting means a new group is acting for themselves, is demanding recognition and negotiation, is trying to force an entrance; counterviolence by civic authorities indicates a clear recognition of the seriousness of the black threat to the political status quo.

Mutual and peaceful influence may be most typical of interaction between stabilized groups or coalitions of relatively equal power. In a political system where it is very difficult or impossible, for whatever reasons, for an emerging interest group to secure a place in the sun, to secure a nonviolent transfer of power

[74] See the discussion of political bargaining in H. L. Nieburg, *Political Violence* (New York: St. Martin's Press, 1969), pp. 56–61.

[75] Hobsbawm, *Primitive Rebels.*

[76] Matthew Stolz, "A Speculation Concerning Politics and Violence" (unpublished paper presented at the annual meeting of the Western Political Science Association, Seattle, Washington, March 1968).

Theories of Urban Violence: Critiques and Proposals

from existing groups, significant negotiation may well be "un-likely unless the weak can threaten to disrupt and therefore dam-age the social order which the powerful value."[77] At the very least, ghetto rioting, and types of guerrilla activity, generate a situation where those in power were forced to take black America seriously. Significantly, negotiations on a variety of matters actu-ally occurred during and after a number of major ghetto riots; indeed, in some cities organized groups in the midst of rioting—for example, the Malcolm X Society in Detroit—submitted a list of demands to be negotiated with white authorities.[78] Subse-quent to the riots, concessions were won from existing authorities in a few cities, although the ultimate results of the rioting in regard to negotiation are difficult to assess. In many ways, per-haps, the attempt at forcing negotiation failed.

The characterization of ghetto violence as an act of political disruption, however, is not intended to imply that it was con-sciously viewed in the same way by all those who rioted. The motives of black riot participants were doubtless varied. To some extent the collective violence may have encompassed the motives of earlier nonviolent protest demonstrations: that of focusing public attention on problems in the hope that ameliorative ac-tion would be forthcoming from conscience-stricken whites. For some the rioting may have been viewed as an attempt to seize authority and control over an area, to chase whites from their midst, even for the brief period of time before the law enforce-ment arm of the government restored complete control. For others it reflected the hope of forcing local authorities to bar-gain, to participate in negotiations. For many more it meant expropriation of economic goods and property, or the destruc-tion of the property of those guilty of exploitation. Taken sin-gly or in concert, such motives or objectives, and still others,

[77] Ibid., p. 13.
[78] See *Report of the National Advisory Commission on Civil Dis-orders,* p. 112.

45

influenced the behavior of the rioters, even though some may have been only dimly aware of these objectives, caught up as they were in the indignation and exhilaration of a moment of political assertion. Yet all of these motives are consistent with the basic goal of seeking the fulfillment of aspirations viewed as broadly political. Moreover, the interpretation of rioting as the politics of violence and disruption does not preclude the possibility that there was a recognition among some rioters that the rioting was an act of desperation that might not succeed in attaining lasting goals.

An Aside

Perhaps it will clarify the argument we are making with regard to ghetto rioting if we make explicit some questions which may have occurred to the reader. An important set of questions is related to the issue of point of view or perspective. Do we mean ghetto riots were political from the point of view of the rioters, from the point of view of the powerholding groups and government the rioters were challenging, or from the point of view of observing social scientists trying to assess the importance of rioting? We are here arguing that riots were political from all three perspectives. Although it is difficult to assess directly the motives of ghetto rioters, what survey evidence there is on the expressed views of rioters indicated that they were quite critical of existing power arrangements in ghetto areas, particularly economic and governmental arrangements. Furthermore, their motivation can be inferred in part from the groups they challenged and the targets they commonly attacked: ghetto merchants and their property, police and their property.[79] Their attack was on accessible representatives of certain important centers of power controlling their destinies. Their actions may not have been as focused on government buildings and higher level government officials as some other recent demonstrations on the American

[79] Ibid., pp. 112–116.

scene, but they were often intensely political in the targets attacked, in their attempt to remove hated examples of outside oppression and exploitation.

In addition, black rioting was political in that it was seen by white interest groups and civic authorities as a serious threat to white power and control in cities, including control over the means of coercion. The magnitude of the coercive and other reactions of authorities clearly reflected the perceived importance attached to ghetto rioting, in contrast to, for example, the perceived importance of the sometimes violent upheavals after football games. From the viewpoint of social science observers, perhaps the most important way in which ghetto riots were political is in terms of their place and occurrence in the recent struggle of black Americans to move up in the American structure of power, particularly on the urban scene. Thus ghetto rioting is intimately related to the attempts of blacks to move out of the grip of the neocolonialism characteristic of the ghetto, to remove the control of modern-day white carpetbaggers over their lives. In their struggle to gain control over their destinies blacks have, as we have pointed out before, used a variety of tactics running from electoral politics to the politics of violence. Moreover, based on a retrospective examination, we would also argue that ghetto riots were political in terms of their consequences. As a result of the rioting, subsequent significant political developments took place, ranging from the local and national response of study commissions and general legislative action to specific programs that came to ghettos as a result of the rioting.

Conclusion

This interpretation of ghetto rioting as the politics of violence has some advantages over the other theories we discussed earlier. Initially, the politics of violence approach does not encompass assumptions about the negative effects of urbanization, about criminality and disorganization, or about social marginality that permeate other theories. When riots are viewed as another type of political action—as reflecting the emergence of a new interest group on the urban scene—blacks participating in a riot need not be seen as the victims of unusual, sudden, or abnormal social pressures. Indeed, conventional formulations emphasizing marginality, disequilibrium, tension, or frustration seem less useful for explanatory purposes than, or subordinate to, the ideas of encapsulation, ghetto organization, mobilization, and political competition among interest groups in urban areas.

A politics of violence perspective also meshes well with certain pertinent data about riots and rioters turned up by a variety of riot studies, data which are problematical for other theories. To illustrate, the political perspective fits well with what we know about black mobilization in cities, the growth in numbers, resources, and organization; for example, one study of the major riot in Detroit found that most rioters not involved in the initial precipitating incident learned of the riot by means of interpersonal communication networks, not as some theorists might predict through the more impersonal means of the mass media.[80] Such a tantalizing finding points to the importance of the hitherto neglected informal social networks in ghetto areas, and consequently the role of such networks in the developmental phases of ghetto rioting, and does not support theories tied closely to assumptions of anonymity, social isolation, and the breakdown of social control.

In addition, the political perspective fits well with data indicating that most rioters were relatively long-term residents of ghetto areas not recent migrants caught in the alleged disorganizing experience of migration.[81] It may well take time residing in the political framework of an urban setting to develop a riot orientation. Thus the outbreak of rioting reflected the fundamental fact of urban segregation and the emergence of group political identity. Rioting was probably occasioned less by

[80] Benjamin D. Singer, Richard W. Osborn, and James A. Geschwender, *Black Rioters* (Lexington, Mass.: Heath, 1970), p. 44.

[81] See *Report of the National Advisory Commission on Civil Disorders,* pp. 128–135.

the impersonal, anomic, or psychologically stressful conditions of urban life than by the concentration of large numbers of black residents in distinct sectors of the city, by their frequent inter-action, by their developing cohesion and political consciousness, and ultimately by their mobilization for militant political action. This view, therefore, facilitates the linking of ghetto riots to closely related, and similarly motivated, black actions on a col-lective basis before and after the riots, ranging from electoral politics, to nonviolent organization, to black power and local control movements; it encompasses a recognition of the influences exerted by the electoral and civil disobedience forms of political expression that preceded rioting.

Some alternative theories of violence see rioting as a relatively blind and lashing-out response to tension or frustration. Yet one of the most salient features revealed in much of the riot litera-ture is that the urban rioters' action was taken in furtherance of the long-standing objectives. This politics of violence approach, therefore, not only encompasses a designation of the major source of the violence (the inability to attain important political objec-tives by other means), but it also suggests a reasonable explanation of the actual recipients of much of the wrath of ghetto rioters (those authorities and representatives of institutions heavily im-plicated in the failure to grant blacks power). Accessible repre-sentatives of governmental and economic authority, the police and local merchants were among the principal objects of attack during ghetto rioting. Indeed, the principal types of behavior engaged in during riots—hurling stones and epithets against authorities, challenging the police, violating curfews, looting and burning ghetto stores, sniping and assault on white authorities and civilians—all have been seen as reflecting relatively specific grievances resulting from the framework of institutionalized in-equality of power along racial lines.[82] (It is also noteworthy that in one study of 15 northern cities grievance level was found not

[82] Robert M. Fogelson, *Violence as Protest* (Garden City, N.Y.: Dou-bleday, 1971), pp. 79–103.

to differentiate between riot and nonriot cities; apparently in all cities the grievance level exceeds the requisite threshold.[83])

Approaching ghetto rioting from a framework emphasizing groups with different and competing interests also provides a more satisfactory perspective on the role of civic authorities in fostering and channeling the emergence and development of violent protest. Remarkably, this interaction issue has been given little attention by many who have theorized about riots. Viewing ghetto riots as events in an urban power struggle not only points toward an ongoing interaction process between those bent on gaining power and present powerholders, before as well as after the outbreak of rioting, but also suggests that the riot-related actions of government authorities—including mayors, city councils, police, the National Guard, and federal troops—directly represent the wishes of powerful established groups adamantly opposing the emergence of blacks on the political scene. These authoritative actions represent far more than the commonly expressed concern for "law and order" intimates. Interest groups forming the present ruling coalition in most urban areas, including the business community, the WASPs, white immigrant groups, and labor unions, rule in part through governmental authorities charged with reducing black political pressures.

It is clear that the interaction of ghetto residents with key representatives of urban powerholding groups goes back well before the emergence of ghetto rioting in the early 1960s. Various commission reports and research studies have stressed, for example, that prior frictional interaction between police and ghetto residents has played a crucial role in the sometimes lengthy process of riot precipitation. This is particularly true in regard to the more serious riots.[84] Historically, violence on the part of dis-

[83] Peter H. Rossi and Richard A. Berk, "Local Political Leadership and Popular Discontent in the Ghetto," *The Annals,* **391** (September 1970), 111–127.

[84] See *Report of the National Advisory Commission on Civil Disorders,* p. 120.

sidents challenging established authority has often been provoked, stimulated, or accelerated by the violent actions of civic authorities. One important study of thousands of collective violence incidents in Western Europe found that most violence on the part of rioters and demonstrators grew out of initially nonviolent group actions and the retaliatory responses of the authorities.[85] Indeed, the series of events leading to many ghetto riots, including the final precipitating incident, often involved government-sanctioned police violence used against ghetto residents—violence perceived as illegitimate by subsequent gatherings of black demonstrators. And in many riot situations the events following on the immediate precipitating incident were initially limited and nonviolent protest reactions to specific police behavior. Some riots even emerged out of relatively peaceful rallies and protest demonstrations over the actions of authorities.[86] Although the data are sketchy, in many settings the actions of authorities, including violence on the part of police or National Guard, seem to have stimulated or escalated the violence of rioters.

One tactic of powerholding interest groups and their governmental representatives is to exaggerate the threat of a new interest group trying to move up in the political system. In the current American context, the actions of a group of blacks milling around in an intersection will often be considered violent and as necessitating massive police force or violence, while a massive response by the police in injuring or even killing dissidents will generally not be considered collective violence.[87] Yet the number of repressive agents present—police and soldiers—could logically be a critical factor in the development or severity of any instance of collective political violence. But the role of police forces in violence has usually been viewed in the reverse:

[85] This research is summarized in Tilly, "Revolutions and Collective Violence."

[86] See *Report of the National Advisory Commission on Civil Disorders,* p. 121.

[87] See Skolnick, *The Politics of Protest,* pp. 5–7.

the more severe the riot the greater the number of repressive agents needed.[88] However, such a formulation underestimates, perhaps seriously, the role of civic authorities and the agents in participating in and in shaping collective violence. Actually, the overwhelming majority of personal casualties in ghetto riots were black civilians—not policemen, soldiers, or other agents of power-holding groups. The repressive agents inflicted the most bodily damage.[89] Moreover, for the 1967–1968 riots at least, it seems that the larger the number of repressive agents from outside the city—the National Guard and federal troops—the larger the number of riot-related deaths of ghetto residents.[90] In addition, in the report of the President's Commission on Civil Disorders, data charts relating the level of rioting to police, National Guard, and federal troop involvement point to the conclusion that the involvement of major forces of troops did not immediately reduce the level of ghetto resident violence.[91] At the very least, it is obvious that the role of civic authorities, and the violence they used against dissidents, have received relatively little attention in the riot literature, beyond attempts to decide whether or not the responses of authorities were swift or efficient enough to quench the rioting responses of ghetto residents.

Furthermore, conspiracy theorists have emphasized the planning of outside agitators in explaining the re-emergence of collective rioting. Yet evidence for this is nonexistent. Such an explanation has even been rejected by prominent investigating bodies, as we pointed out earlier in this chapter.[92] Perhaps of much greater importance in the development of rioting has been

[88] See Tilly, "Revolutions and Collective Violence," p. 20.

[89] *Report of the National Advisory Commission on Civil Disorders,* p. 116.

[90] Lemberg Center for the Study of Violence, "April Aftermath of the King Assassination," *Riot Data Review* (Boston, 1968), pp. 59–77 (mimeographed).

[91] *Report of the National Advisory Commission on Civil Disorders,* pp. 581ff.

[92] Ibid., p. 201.

Theories of Urban Violence: Critiques and Proposals

the planning by civic authorities. For example, one analysis of cities with ghetto riots in the 1960s suggested that the presence of a special riot plan prepared by city authorities and their police forces correlated highly and positively with riot severity. Such data point to the argument that riot preparation by authorities may well be related to the development and escalation of ghetto riots.[93] The alternative explanation, that city authorities consistently anticipated the severity of the rioting which eventuated, seems less likely.

Viewing ghetto riots as politically disruptive acts in a continuing politically motivated struggle between competing vested interest groups on the urban scene, therefore, seems the most promising and suggestive framework for a comprehensive understanding of recent shifts in the direction of collective violence. Instead of treating the prevailing social and political system as a given that cannot be altered, or as an irrelevant context, this orientation makes that structure accountable for the lion's share of causality lying behind collective violence. Violence did not result primarily from the failure of ghetto residents to adjust satisfactorily or normally to the tensions or strains imposed on them in an urban context to which they were unaccustomed. Rather, in the main, collective violence was occasioned by the failure of the existing urban political system to respond adequately to their desires and aspirations, to allow them a proportionate role in the urban structure of power. Ghetto rioting, therefore, reflected an attempted reclamation of political authority over ghetto areas and a type of political recall, not necessarily of specific public officeholders, but of the entire political apparatus that had failed to grant a reasonable share of the political pie to ghetto residents. Collective political violence may well represent the ultimate act of popular sovereignty. In a tradition that dates back in this country to the revolutionary period, and even before in

[93] Jules J. Wanderer, "An Index of Riot Severity and Some Correlates," *American Journal of Sociology,* 74 (March 1969), 500–505.

the lengthy English tradition of popular violence, collective violence becomes one of the ultimate weapons of any people whose political aspirations remain significantly unfulfilled after other alternatives have been tried.

Whether or not these actions represented an effective method of promoting black goals over the long term is rather difficult to assess at this point in time. Yet it seems clear that ghetto rioting did at least produce a momentary retrieval of significant power for those engaged in the rioting. For a brief period of time, until the authority of external coercive agencies was restored, the perspectives and policies sanctioned by the groups on the streets constituted the ruling and coercive majority in ghetto areas. As a result, the political emergence of black Americans on the urban scene was made conspicuously evident. This collective violence did not emerge as a sweeping revolutionary movement for a number of reasons, but it did mean revolutionary home rule for a moment. Eventually, as it became clear, the forces of suppression available to the white authorities would make any attempt to wrest permanent political control from existing authorities by force extraordinarily difficult.

Unlike many alternative theories of violence, therefore, this politics of violence perspective emphasizes that the rioting of ghetto residents represented a demand to change both the outcomes of day-to-day decisions and the overall decision-making process itself. The dissidence generated by the failure of the processes of city government and electoral politics to satisfy the demands of black Americans yielded a growing recognition that this failure was not produced solely by the intransigence of those public officials in office at any one point in time. There was also a critical flaw in any political structure, including governmental arrangements, that prevents an emergent minority within its midst from securing the political goals they seek. Thus the outbreak of ghetto violence and the subsequent growth of demands for self-determination, community control, and the decentralization of political authority were more than coincidental. Both during the ghetto riots themselves and in the movement for com-

CHAPTER 1

munity control that accompanied later riots, black Americans seemed to be pressing a demand for significant powers of self-governance and for the right to control their own lives and destinies.

The Background and Context of Recent Ghetto Violence

Among the most important side effects of the ghetto rioting in the 1960s was the recognition by social scientists, if not by the general public, that we know relatively little about the history and character of collective violence in America. This is true whether the focus is on the distant past or on recent decades. Indeed, the editors of a recent volume reproducing some of the first studies of American violence concluded that the volume was the first "attempt to link the historical and comparative dimensions of research on the subject of group violence in America, and all we have proposed is a tentative, partial synthesis."[1]

While the main thrust of our book is intentionally limited to analysis of the theoretical and empirical literature on recent ghetto riots, in an attempt at a broader perspective on this violence, in this chapter we will examine the general background and context of ghetto rioting: historical and contemporary, international and national. Utilizing much of the limited available literature, we will briefly touch on the international setting, then examine the historical background of collective violence on the part of various groups in American history, then concentrate on

[1] Hugh D. Graham and Ted R. Gurr, "Conclusion: The Commonality of Collective Violence in the Western Tradition," *Violence in America,* ed. Hugh D. Graham and Ted R. Gurr (New York: Bantam, 1969), p. 819.

the development of politically oriented collective behavior among black Americans.

The International Setting

Is the United States a uniquely "violent society"? Is its cultural system adequately characterized as a distinctive "culture of violence"? Certainly, the rising crime rates, college upheavals, assassinations, and ghetto uprisings of recent years have given credibility to the suggestion that the United States is somehow distinctively different from other nations in regard to violence. Yet much recent public discussion of this culture of violence issue has been far too limited, focusing almost exclusively on recent American experience. Indeed, only a handful of scholars have attempted comparative studies of violence, particularly collective violence with political overtones.

However, the research that has so far been published indicates that by most measures the United States is not the most politically violent of contemporary nations. That dubious honor is reserved for certain countries such as Indonesia, Bolivia, Argentina, and the Union of South Africa, varying somewhat with the type of measure one chooses. Examination of political turbulence between 1948 and 1965 found that among 84 different countries, using measures of the severity of political instability, the United States fell at the middle position on the continuum of violence.[2] When the measure used was the sum of scaled instability events for each country, the United States ranked nearer the top, 14th among the 84 nations. Such a discrepancy in rank is a function of the measure used and indicates that, while the United States has seen much political turbulence in terms of distinct events in the postwar period, none of the events reached the highest levels

[2] Ivo K. Feierabend, Rosalind L. Feierabend, and Betty A. Nesvold, "Social Change and Political Violence: Cross-National Patterns," *Violence in America,* ed. Hugh D. Graham and Ted R. Gurr (New York: Bantam, 1969), p. 154.

of strife, such as *coup d'état* or civil war; the political conflict that Americans have experienced in the last few decades never attained the level of overturning the national political institutions. However, the same cross-national study, examining the sixties, did suggest that political violence has apparently increased somewhat in recent years in the United States.[3]

Furthermore, another researcher, examining political strife in over one hundred nations between 1961 and 1965, came to a similar conclusion. By his calculations, the United States ranked, in terms of the total magnitude of civil strife, only 24th among the 114 nations studied, although for that recent period the United States ranked first among major Western countries.[4] Thus, by any measure the United States has not been the most violent nation in the world. But for the most recent decade of the sixties, existing research suggests that the United States has been among the most conflict-ridden Western countries. Needless to say, such exploratory studies as these indicate the great need for further historical and cross-national research, particularly for the years preceding the last two decades.

Yet it seems clear that most countries in the postwar world have experienced conflict involving collective violence with important political overtones, with the exceptions numbering perhaps less than a dozen. As a result, insofar as the idea of a culture of violence is a useful notion at all, it would seem to apply to most twentieth-century countries, rather than to the United States taken alone. Most societies have experienced collective violence in the normal operation of the political process; indeed, civil strife generated as a result of competition for power and influence among varied interest groups, involving force and violence and counterviolence, has bypassed few modern countries for more than brief periods.

[3] Ibid., p. 672.
[4] Ted R. Gurr, "A Comparative Study of Civil Strife," *Violence in America,* ed. Hugh D. Graham and Ted R. Gurr (New York: Bantam, 1969), pp. 575–578.

CHAPTER 2

Political Violence in American History

Even if one can demonstrate that the United States is not unique among contemporary nations in frequency or magnitude of collective political violence, still, some might argue that the violence of the 1960s, particularly the ghetto riots in that period, resulted in by far the most violent decade in American history. Can such an argument be substantiated? In the light of the relevant information beginning to emerge, it appears that the answer to this question would be in the negative, depending again on the index of violence chosen.

Accordingly, one important study of the place of political violence in America, for the period 1819–1968, discovered that the most recent decades were generally not the most politically violent in American history, although their exact rank among the decades in this period varies with the index chosen. For example, using deaths resulting from political conflict as an index, the three most recent decades (1939–1968), when compared with the four preceding three-decade periods, ranked low, only fourth among the five periods.[5] When a death index was computed taking into account population size and available newspaper space, the most recent three-decade period dropped to the lowest rank. Using a different index, injuries resulting from political violence, the most recent three-decade period ranked second, significantly below the 1909–1938 period, even when adjustments were made for population size and newspaper space. Yet another index based on the actual number of violent events reported in the sampling of major newspapers over this 150-year period—the data being tabulated in this case for each decade between 1819 and 1968—revealed that the most recent decade surveyed had the greatest number of violent events of any decade. However, when the necessary adjustments were made for population size and newspaper space, its rank again fell to a lower position among

[5] Sheldon G. Levy, "A 150-year Study of Political Violence in the United States," *Violence in America*, ed. Hugh D. Graham and Ted R. Gurr (New York: Bantam, 1969), pp. 84–100.

the 15 decades. Interestingly, the most violent decade in terms of politically violent events per 100,000 population was the 1879–1888 decade.

One need not rely solely on statistical analyses based on newspaper coverage to conclude that the nineteenth century saw much collective violence. Several observers of the American scene in the nineteenth century were quite impressed by its violent character. To cite one typical example, in 1833 Senator Henry Clay was said to have commented that "We are in the midst of a revolution." Michael Chevalier, a perceptive Frenchman who spent the years 1834–1836 studying the basic institutions of this country, wrote a series of letters on his experiences. In one such letter he comments on Senator Clay's remarks:

> These words have often been repeated by others. More recently, since the scenes of murder, outrage, and destruction which have been exhibited through the United States, both in the slaveholding states, and in those in which slavery does not exist, in the country as well as in the towns, at Boston, the republican city *par excellence,* as well as at Baltimore . . . [with] the title of *Mob Town,* good citizens have repeated with grief: "We are in the midst of a revolution."[6]

Chevalier proceeds to recount numerous instances of collective violence in the 1830s: group lynchings of Negroes, destruction of houses in Philadelphia, and the burning of a Catholic convent in Massachusetts. Another English analyst, who spent several years in America in the same period, was also impressed by the resort to collective violence:

> The mobbing events of the last few years are celebrated; the abolition riots in New York and Boston; the burning of the

[6] Michael Chevalier, *Society, Manners, and Politics in the United States,* translated from 3rd Paris ed. (New York: Augustus M. Kelley, 1966), p. 385.

61

Charlestn [*sic*] Convent; the bank riots at Baltimore; the burning of the mails at Charleston; the hangings by Lynch-law at Vicksburgh; the burning alive of a man of colour at St. Louis; the subsequent proceedings there towards the students of Marion College; and the abolition riots at Cincinnati.[7]

Martineau also suggests that the membership of the mobs was generally not comprised of the lower classes, but of gentlemen: "The mobs of America are composed of high churchmen . . . merchants and planters, and lawyers."[8] On the whole, then, the most recent decades in American history have seen a great deal of political upheaval, but they have by no means been uniquely violent years in the history of internal struggle in the United States.

Conflict in American History: Some Specific Examples

Consequently, collective violence with political overtones has been part of the warp and woof of the American fabric since the seventeenth century, perhaps even a little before. Surprisingly, no definitive attempt has been made to analyze the scope and history of this collective political violence, to sort out the various interest groups using violence, or to catalog the types and consequences of such collective violence for the dissidents or established powerholding groups. However, one exploratory attempt to develop a typology of American violence, suggests that a meaningful distinction might be made between (1) negative violence unrelated to "constructive development," and (2) positive violence related to "popular and constructive movements."[9] On the

[7] Harriet Martineau, *Society in America* (New York: AMS Press, 1966), Vol. I., p. 162.

[8] Ibid., p. 164.

[9] Richard M. Brown, "Historical Patterns of Violence in America," *Violence in America,* ed. Hugh D. Graham and Ted R. Gurr (New York: Bantam, 1969), pp. 45–83.

one hand, one finds included in this category of negative violence such conflictual events as lynchings, violent crimes, racial violence, urban riots, and assassination. On the other hand, positive violence encompasses such phenomena as the Revolutionary War, the Civil War, and vigilante violence in the western frontier towns. Police, labor, and agrarian violence are also included in this latter category.

Yet one major difficulty with this suggestive classification is that the designation of a given group's collective violence as related to, or unrelated to, "constructive developments" may reflect a premature and problematical value judgment on the part of the historical observer, since the degree of constructiveness will vary with the position of the analyst. What is seen by the participants as "constructive" and "positive" collective action may well be seen by the established authorities as "destructive." For example, as Hobsbawm has pointed out, even small bands of bandits, viewed negatively by authorities and some historians alike as "criminals," have in the history of Europe played an important protest role.[10] Banditry is described by Hobsbawm as a primitive type of organized social protest; in many areas bandits were viewed as constructive by the "poor, who consequently protect the bandit, regard him as their champion, idealize him, and turn him into a myth."[11] Conceivably, the same may be true with regard to urban rioters or other groups classified in the "negative" category.

As we have previously suggested, in Chapter 1, it seems that a more satisfactory way of viewing much collective violence on the part of distinctive groups with differential interests is from a perspective focusing on their position in or out of the existing structure of power, at a given point in a society's history and at a specific level of that society. Initially influenced by the approaches of analysts such as Dahrendorf and Gamson to expect

[10] E. J. Hobsbawm, *Primitive Rebels* (New York: Norton Paperback, 1959).
[11] Ibid., p. 13.

collective struggle where interest groups come into conflict over power arrangements, we subsequently found Tilly's classification to be suggestive. Thus, one can view the emergence of group violence in America in terms of the following positions of groups with reference to powerholding: (1) groups attempting to acquire power, (2) groups trying to maintain their existing power, and (3) groups losing power.[12] Technically, of course, this typology points to political situations and shifts in which collective *action* is likely to occur, and not necessarily to types of collective violence. However, it is in such situations that the probability of collective violence significantly increases. In looking at the development of collective behavior, the critical role of another group, governmental authorities and agents usually representing established interest groups against challengers, should not be overlooked.

Utilization of this type of classification frees one from some of the problems of a value-laden typology of "positive" and "negative" violence. In the first place, one is no longer committed to evaluating the constructive character of collective behavior. Second, one has a few clues as to where and why collective violence typically occurs. Inclusion, for example, of urban riots in the 1960s with lynching under negative violence unrelated to constructive developments is problematical, not only because of the evaluative dimension, but also because it lumps violence at the hands of a group beginning to acquire power together with a distinctively different type of collective violence used by groups concerned with maintaining their position in the existing structure of power.

The history of the American political system has been replete with instances of distinctive social groups, including those distinguished by race and ethnicity, moving up into the structure

[12] Charles Tilly, "Collective Violence in European Perspective," *Violence in America,* ed. Hugh D. Graham and Ted R. Gurr (New York: Bantam, 1969), pp. 37–41.

of power at the expense of, and often over the strong resistance of, other groups. Historically, collective political action, whether nonviolent or violent, has arisen in situations where certain groups perceive themselves as losing rights which were once theirs, as in many of the agrarian uprisings, or where emergent groups are attempting to achieve rights or force the granting of rights which they see as justly theirs but so far denied, as in the labor movement in America. And established groups, such as businessmen in frontier communities, have engaged in collective action to maintain their position. In this struggle for power, tactics have varied along a continuum running from the use of electoral mechanisms and party politics to various kinds of actions involving collective violence.

Which distinctive groups with special interests have resorted to collective violence in their struggle to maintain or improve their positions in the structure of American society? A comprehensive answer to this important query might well fill numerous volumes, for the number of groups involved in conflict with political overtones would ultimately be calculated in hundreds or thousands, depending upon the number and organization of individuals used as defining characteristics. Almost by definition, in the review of collective political violence which follows we will exclude small-scale instances of violence such as family feuds, dueling, and individual crimes of violence. Moreover, a truly comprehensive review of collective violence in America would necessarily give much greater attention to violence at the behest of established groups and governmental authorities than we give in the sections which follow—in part a consequence of weaknesses in the available literature.

Thus it is not our intention here to review in any detail the history of collective political violence in America, an important task at this time yet to be accomplished. Our purpose here is twofold. First, we will demonstrate that a variety of groups in American history have resorted to violence in their struggles to regain, maintain, or improve their positions within the existing structure of power. Second, we will show in particular that various ethnic groups have utilized, or been subjected to, collective violence with obvious political overtones. From the lengthy list of interest groups which have resorted to collective violence, ranging from urban Protestants and white southerners to Irish Catholics and Appalachian farmers, we have selected certain groups in four divergent categories: (1) vigilantes, (2) farmers, (3) workingmen and unionists, (4) ethnic-immigrant groups.

Vigilantism

Apparently a rather distinctive American type of collective violence, vigilantism originated in the eighteenth century as a way of controlling or competing with so-called "outlaw" elements and other predominantly lower-class groups in outlying areas. Vigilante groups early resorted to violent tactics, including lynching and whipping, in establishing, maintaining, or re-establishing the control of certain interest groups in frontier or back country areas. Identifying vigilante groups in terms of their frontier determination to "take the law into their own hands" and relatively organized character, one analyst reports that between the eighteenth and the early twentieth centuries there were well over three hundred identifiable bands of vigilantes, the most violent period being the decades between 1850 and 1880.[13] Over these centuries, violence-oriented formations resulted in at least seven hundred recorded deaths and numerous other casualties.

Perhaps most important from a violence-as-politics perspective is the fact that vigilante movements, particularly on the moving western frontier, often reflected a conflict for power between the lower classes, including outlaw elements, and the middle and

[13] Richard M. Brown, "The American Vigilante Tradition," *Violence in America*, ed. Hugh D. Graham and Ted R. Gurr (New York: Bantam, 1969), p. 154.

upper levels of new communities. In their violent actions typical vigilante groups reflected a consensus of the presumably white and Protestant substantial citizens—the large landowners, the leading businessmen, the more affluent farmers and ranchers—on controlling those challenging them from the lower classes, including "outlaws" and "riffraff" and on establishing the proper values with regard to property and order in those classes. Indeed, vigilante groups were often led and populated to a significant degree by members of the higher classes. These vigilante leaders wished to maintain or "reestablish the three-level community structure (in which they would be dominant) and the values of life and property that supported it."[14]

In some cases vigilante groups used violence simply to maintain their established position vis-à-vis outlaws and the lower classes who were beginning to challenge their control, as in many frontier areas of the West. In other cases, well-to-do citizens banded together and engaged in lynching and other types of violence to re-establish positions which they felt they were losing or had actually lost to other special interest groups. A good example of this latter situation was the position of certain white groups after the Civil War, during the Reconstruction period. White vigilante movements under the leadership of men of affairs, such as the various cells of the Ku Klux Klan, engaged in reactionary violence, attempting to establish a pre-Civil War arrangement, in conflict with the increasing power of blacks, some groups of poor whites (varying with the region), and—to a lesser extent—white northerners. One excellent study of the rise and fall of the Klan concluded that the aim of the Klan after the Civil War was to restore order, to return Negroes to the fields and "the pre-war leaders to their former seats of power." The process of acquiring lost political power was a bloody one: "Although Klansmen were occasionally hurt, the death toll of Negroes and Republicans probably ran close to a

[14] Ibid., p. 176.

67

thousand."[15] Thus, politically and economically, the Klan had a significant effect.[16]

Yet other reactionary vigilante movements occurred in urban areas outside the South, variously directed by middle- and upper-class Protestants against mobilizing immigrant or ethnic groups, such as Irish Catholics and Jews. A striking example of the use of force to re-establish a mobile group's political position can be seen in the San Francisco Vigilance Committee of 1856, which was composed of old American Protestant businessmen who struggled violently to regain control of local government from a machine dominated by Irish Catholic workingmen.[17]

Agrarian Violence

Not only have the business, landholding, and professional citizens of the South and West resorted to collective violence when necessary, but less well-to-do farmers and workingmen have also engaged in collective violence to protect or extend their group interests and rights as they perceived them. Indeed, numerous agrarian uprisings occurred between the late seventeenth century and the twentieth century. Certain groups of farmers in the western sections of their colonies, or states, often found themselves losing power to East Coast cities and legislatures, which passed new tax laws and other legislation contrary to the interests of debtor farmers. To some extent farmers in these western sections were reacting to the increasing urbanization of the colonies (or states) and the trend toward centralization of institutions. In such a situation, the desire to return to earlier, less complex arrangements, in which farmers had fewer taxes and more control over their land, is explicable, but in a fundamental sense reactionary. However, for many debtor farmers the critical issue was

[15] David M. Chalmers, *Hooded Americanism* (Chicago: Quadrangle, 1968), p. 2.
[16] Ibid., p. 14.
[17] Brown, "The American Vigilante Tradition," p. 197.

68

continuing powerlessness in the face of continuing exploitation by external economic interests.

Collective violence was part and parcel of attempts by farmers to secure or regain their rights. In their struggle they frequently cited the very justification used for the American Revolution.[18] Nathaniel Bacon's farmer movement in seventeenth-century Virginia resulted in the burning of Jamestown. Subsequently, the New Jersey land rioters directed violence against land companies; the New York antirent groups engaged in violence against landlords; Shays' rebellion in Massachusetts against land foreclosures resulted in the disruption of court sessions; the famous Fries and Whiskey uprisings by Pennsylvania mountain men and farmers were against new federal taxes.[19] Later, the nineteenth-century night rider movement in California was directed against railroad land buyers and was typical of agrarian movements in this period against established authorities or other agents in a struggle for control over land. As a consequence of violent conflict, these heterogeneous agrarian groups were sometimes successful in securing greater control over their areas, if only for short periods of time—until the militia or troops restored the control of colonial or state authorities.

Labor Violence

Nor have American workingmen refrained from violence in their struggle for increased power, economic and otherwise. And threatened owners and managements have been responsible for a significant share of labor violence. Accordingly, Taft and Ross

[18] Martin S. Reichley, "Federal Military Intervention in Civil Disturbances" (unpublished Ph.D. dissertation, Georgetown University, 1939); Brown, "Historical Patterns of Violence in America," pp. 71–73; Jerome L. Skolnick, *The Politics of Protest* (New York: Simon and Schuster, 1969), pp. 11–12.

[19] See Leland D. Baldwin, *Whiskey Rebels* (Pittsburgh: University of Pittsburgh Press, 1939); William W. H. Davis, *The Fries Rebellion, 1798–1799* (Doylestown, Pa.: Doylestown Publishing Company, 1899); Marion L. Starkey, *A Little Rebellion* (New York: Knopf, 1955).

have summed up their detailed analysis of labor violence in America: "The United States has had the bloodiest and most violent labor history of any industrial nation in the world."[20] Documentation of this assertion can readily be seen in the recorded figures for one brief but important three-year period in the labor-management struggle. In the three years 1902–1904, at least 198 persons were killed as a result of strike- and lockout-related labor violence, and nearly 2,000 were injured. Total figures on the numbers killed in labor-management altercations are difficult to secure because of the weakness or bias in reporting. However, conservative estimates indicate that at least seven hundred persons were killed in this bloody political struggle since the late nineteenth century, while the number of injured probably reaches into the tens of thousands.[21]

Not that collective violence was openly advocated as a tactic by emerging worker organizations and unions. However, in spite of this formal eschewing of collective violence as a tactic, the use of less violent but militant tactics such as strikes and picketing by worker organizations sometimes resulted in private guard and police attacks on strikers. In retaliation workingmen engaged in violence against the guards or police and private property. Particularly important as triggering events were the illegal, and sometimes violent, attempts of worker pickets to prevent the entrance of strikebreakers (or materials) into company plants, followed by violent police actions, actions intended to force the opening of plants with nonunion strikebreakers. Not only were local police often involved on the side of owners or management in labor disputes, but forceful surrogates such as the National Guard and federal troops were also utilized on at least 160 different occasions in the struggle against workingmen.[22] Thus

---

[20] Philip Taft and Philip Ross, "American Labor Violence: Its Causes, Character, and Outcome," *Violence in America,* ed. Hugh D. Graham and Ted R. Gurr (New York: Bantam, 1969), p. 281.

[21] Ibid., p. 380.

[22] Ibid., pp. 380–383. Reichley, "Federal Military Intervention in Civil Disturbances," passim.

much employer violence was accomplished at the hands of governmental agencies in control of the organized coercive means, while the violent actions of unionizing workers were illegal and forcefully opposed by governmental agents.

Consequently, examination of labor-management disputes leading to collective violence again emphasizes one extraordinarily important point about much collective violence in American history—its mutuality or interactive character. Nonviolent or violent, attempts by workers to increase their power in local economies were usually viewed as threatening by established groups of businessmen and property owners, whose representatives even inaugurated much violence. In addition, the organized actions of working-class Americans were often seen as threatening, not only to economic control, but to control over governments as well.[23] In point of fact, the growth of electoral organization tied to working-class groups as increasingly linked to the weakening of control of owners and managers over government.

That the emergence of organized workingmen as a significant powerholding group in industrial and urban settings came only after a lengthy history of worker-management warfare can readily be illustrated by enumerating some of the more important clashes. A comprehensive list might well include the following major events: (1) the 1877 railroad strikes in Maryland, Pennsylvania, New York, Ohio, and New Jersey, precipitated in part by wage and employee cutbacks and involving dozens of deaths and the calling out of National Guard troops; (2) the Homestead, Pennsylvania, steel strike of the 1890s, growing out of militant management tactics against a fledgling union and leading to several deaths and the utilization of thousands of detectives and National Guard troops; (3) the 1894 Pullman strike of railroad workers, growing out of wage disputes and leading to an estimated 34 deaths, millions of dollars of damage, and the use of federal troops; (4) the 1913–1914 Colorado coal war over union-

---

[23] See Skolnick, *The Politics of Protest,* pp. 14–15.

ization, resulting in 74 deaths and the calling in of National Guard and federal troops; (5) the steel, coal, and railroad strikes in the 1920s, again over unionization, resulting in several dozen persons killed and the use of state and federal troops; (6) in the 1930s, the coal, teamsters, and textile strikes over unionization and wage issues, again involving numerous deaths, extensive property damage, and the use of National Guardsmen.[24]

By 1937 the nation had seen the last large-scale labor war with armed conflict and hundreds of casualties; yet numerous lesser clashes have occurred since that time. Although the intensity of labor violence subsided with the labor victories of the thirties and forties, on occasion workingmen still resorted to collective violence, or their strike actions were met with violence, in their struggle with management. Indeed, deaths for the years since World War II numbered nearly three dozen.[25] In most cases, recent disputes have also eventuated out of the labor-management struggle for power; specific grievances still included the right to unionize, the failure of employers to recognize unions, the termination of union leaders, the use of strikebreakers by employers, and wage and employee cutbacks.

Collective Violence Among White Ethnic Groups

That the collective memory of most white Americans is relatively short is reflected in the still commonly expressed view that if white ethnic groups were able to make it into the American mainstream without disruptive violence so can nonwhite Americans. Yet in reality numerous white ethnic groups, of diverse national and cultural origins, have engaged in collective violence at some time to secure their own vested interests and political goals. Accordingly, much of America's history of violence has a distinctive ethnic character.

---

[24] Almond Lindsey, *The Pullman Strike* (Chicago: University of Chicago Press, 1942); Taft and Ross, "American Labor Violence," pp. 288–360.

[25] Taft and Ross, "American Labor Violence," p. 367.

The Background and Context of Recent Ghetto Violence

In reviewing vigilante violence we saw that in some frontier communities alignments were along ethnic lines, perhaps the most conspicuous example being the attacks of the Protestant San Francisco Vigilance Committee on lower-class Irish Catholics. Class and ethnic lines often coincided in the struggle for control over the government institutions. Moreover, although historical treatments do not seem to stress this aspect, much labor violence might be viewed as a power conflict between diverse ethnic groups. In the late nineteenth century one famous confrontation involved the Molly Maguires, a terrorist group comprised of Irish miners directing their vengeance against Anglo-Saxon mineowners after losing a coal strike, ultimately resulting in the leaders being hanged.[26] After 1900 some disputes in mining states such as Pennsylvania were no longer clashes between north European laborers and owners, for masses of east and south European immigrants had congregated in these mining areas. Thus many twentieth-century disputes increasingly reflected ethnic conflict between the descendants of earlier north European immigrants, in the form of owners and managers, and first-generation immigrants from other areas of Europe, in the form of laborers and workingmen.

Historically, perhaps the most serious riot in the United States —the 1863 antidraft riot—was carried out mainly by members of a white ethnic group, the enraged residents of New York's Irish ghettos. In a very real sense, these first- and second-generation immigrants were at the threshold of the door leading to a significant place in the political structure, particularly in the large cities; yet they were hamstrung by the rigidity of established Anglo-Saxon and other Protestant groups. Lower-class Irish Catholic immigrants often found themselves the victims of the better-off descendants of earlier Protestant immigrants—now businessmen and merchants—who utilized strikebreakers, including black freedmen, in dealing with worker organization and

[26] Richard E. Rubenstein, *Rebels in Eden* (Boston: Little, Brown, 1970), p. 29.

73

strikes.[27] Enraged at the promulgation of a new federal draft policy (the precipitating event) seen as discriminatory action against poor immigrants who could not buy their way out of the draft, Irish immigrants led the riot formations that swept the streets of New York attacking Yankees, the police, and black freedmen. At the head of the rioters were Irish longshoremen, whose recent strikes had been broken by the use of black strike-breakers brought in by well-off New Yorkers under the protection of the local police.[28] In the 1863 riot it was whites who were attacked, sometimes brutally, by the police; the state militia was brought in and fought pitched battles with rioters. The response of established powerholders was swift and violent.[29] Again political violence involved mutual and collective destruction of lives and property. The admittedly imprecise estimates of authorities and observers suggest that this four-day upheaval in the heat of the summer was of gigantic proportions—approximately 400 rioters were killed during the street fighting, with perhaps hundreds more dying later of wounds incurred, and the dead were accompanied by an uncounted number of injured rioters. In addition, at least 18 civilians were killed by the rioters, including 11 freedmen. Numerous policemen and soldiers were also killed. And a conservative estimate placed property destruction at several million dollars.[30] Accepting these rough figures on casualties, it is clear that no American riot, before or since, was of greater seriousness.

Yet the 1863 riot was neither the first nor the last historical example of collective violence along ethnic lines. With the arrival of large numbers of Anglo-Saxon settlers in the seventeenth and eighteenth centuries, settlers who, together with their de-

[27] James McCague, *The Second Rebellion* (New York: Dial Press, 1968), pp. 13ff.

[28] Emerson D. Fite, *Social and Industrial Conditions in the North During the Civil War* (New York: Ungar, 1962), pp. 189–191.

[29] Joel T. Headley, *The Great Riots of New York: 1712–1873* (Indianapolis: Bobbs-Merrill Paperback, 1970), pp. 136–288.

[30] McCague, *The Second Rebellion*, pp. 177–179.

scendants, eventually secured extensive social, economic, and governmental power, the stage was set for generations of ethnic conflict. The strength and resources of English-speaking settlers were reflected in their early domination of the American scene. By 1820 the dominant culture was English and Protestant, with some input from the Scotch, French, and Germans.[31] However, immigrants from these latter groups found themselves, in the earliest stages, pitted against growing English domination.

On occasion, this power struggle, particularly at local and state levels, was reflected in collective violence. Sometimes the Anglo-Saxons inaugurated the violence, if only through governmental agents under their control. Relatively early in American history, "Anglo-Saxon mobs attacked Huguenots in Frenchtown, Rhode Island, and destroyed a Scotch-Irish frontier settlement in Worcester, Massachusetts."[32] At other times, the immigrant minority, finding its way up into the political system blocked, resorted to collective violence.

Unquestionably, from the first decades of the nineteenth century fear of foreign immigrants traumatized the descendants of earlier settlers. Opposition, violent and otherwise, to immigrant groups in America frequently had economic overtones. Indeed, anti-immigrant nativist organizations tended to peak in activity during years of economic tribulation for the descendants of older immigrant groups.[33] In addition, fears were openly expressed in regard to alien influence on government, through increasing voting power, and in regard to their competitive threat in the area of economic resources and power. Attempts were made to limit voting and officeholding rights. Between 1830 and 1850 violence flared in the North, particularly in New York, between

[31] Charles F. Marden and Gladys Meyer, *Minorities in American Society* (3rd ed.; New York: American Book, 1968), pp. 98–99.

[32] Leonard Dinnerstein and Frederic C. Jaher, eds., *The Aliens: A History of Ethnic Minorities in America* (New York: Appleton-Century-Crofts, 1970), p. 4.

[33] George E. Simpson and J. Milton Yinger, *Racial and Cultural Minorities* (3rd ed.; New York: Harper & Row, 1965), p. 90.

CHAPTER 2

Anglo-Saxon groups and immigrant protective groups. Nativist and Know-Nothing groups participated in numerous riots. To the horror of European observers such as Michael Chevalier, who was appalled at the indifference of local residents, a Catholic Convent in Charlestown, Massachusetts, was burned by nativists in the early nineteenth century.[34] Riots against the Irish occurred in Philadelphia and New York, spurred by nativist groups;[35] and the millions of new German immigrants were also confronted by collective violence. In the decade prior to 1860 Germans were attacked by nativist groups in numerous American cities, including Cincinnati, Baltimore, and Covington, Kentucky. Sometimes the Germans reciprocated, attacking the attackers. On occasion, in these early clashes along ethnic lines police played a role on behalf of established powerholding groups, as they would for many subsequent decades.[36] Nor were the millions of new Italian Americans entering in the years around the turn of the twentieth century free from violence; they also found themselves the victims of violent attacks by nativists. Italian Americans were victims of lynching in New Orleans and were "murdered in Colorado, beaten in Mississippi, and shot by mobs in Illinois."[37]

Moreover, from time to time in the nineteenth century, immigrants from white ethnic groups were very active in rioting against established powerholding groups; witness the Flour Riot of 1837 and the Astor Place Riot of 1849 in New York, similar in many ways to riots by the poor in Europe.[38] In the case of the Flour Riot, the hoarding of flour on the part of powerful merchants to keep prices up was seen by the immigrant rioters as

[34] Chevalier, *Society, Manners, and Politics in the United States* p. 390.

[35] Frances Trollope, *Domestic Manners of the Americans* (New York: Knopf, 1949), pp. 285–287.

[36] Dinnerstein and Jaher, *The Aliens*, p. 125.

[37] Ibid., p. 216.

[38] Headley, *The Great Riots of New York, 1712–1873*, pp. 97–135.

cause for collective violence. Moreover, the Astor Place Riot in New York—and numerous others of this type—had roots in similar grievances.

White Violence Against Nonwhite Americans

Yet even this detailed enumeration of collective violence among ethnic groups of European background by no means exhausts the catalog of ethnic and racial violence in American history. Perhaps the most extensive use of organized violence to advance the goals of one ethnic group at the expense of another was on the part of various white European groups against numerous Indian tribes, the indigenous inhabitants whose land was stripped from them; against Chinese and Japanese Americans, who comprised a cheap and sometimes threatening labor pool on the western frontier; and against black Africans who were forcibly torn from their native soil and enslaved, whose propensity for revolt was openly feared in the American South, and whose descendants migrating to the cities were perceived as an ominous political threat.

In the case of the true "native Americans," the Indians, there were violent confrontations with white Europeans from virtually the first decades of colonization. While Europeans and their descendants had the mightier violence—and ultimately won out—the struggle against Indians cost Europeans many casualties. For conspicuous economic reasons Indian tribes were forced to move to other areas or eventually exterminated. Before and after incorporation of the western areas, settlers and businessmen, hungry for land and economic success, drove Indians from their native soil—with the aid of government troops—ignored or violated treaty agreements, and eventually forced the remaining Indians onto white-controlled reservations. Meanwhile, in California there was much collective violence directed not only toward the indigenous peoples, such as the peaceful "Digger" Indians who were driven from their homes and exterminated by white settlers, but also against Chinese and Japanese Americans in the burgeoning new settlements.[39]

Even more relevant to an analysis of collective violence on the part of black Americans is an examination of the use of collective violence by whites to enslave black Americans, and later to keep them in their place or to reduce their competitive threat; in point of fact, such violence dates back to the earliest days of slavery in America. And that most serious of American riots, the 1863 draft riot, involved, in addition to attacks on Yankees and police, one-sided attacks by Irish rioters on free blacks in New York City—what Waskow has termed a "pogrom" and Myrdal a "massacre."[40] Fears of the growing competitive threat of black freedmen apparently motivated many of these Irish rioters.

Moreover, after emancipation, one of the most common types of collective violence directed toward maintaining or re-establishing white power vis-à-vis black challenges to that power can be seen in the omnipresent southern lynch mob. Bent on keeping the freed black southerners in their social, economic, and political place, groups of lynchers were often considered quasi-legal by the majority of white southerners; seldom did governmental authorities interfere. According to Tuskegee Institute records at least 3,400 black Americans were lynched between 1882 and 1959, the ostensible reasons being alleged attacks or insults by the black victims.[41]

Well before the 1960s many serious race riots had occurred in American towns and cities, some taking the form of pogroms, with little or no retaliation by blacks against their white attackers, and others taking the form of a more or less two-way battle, with some retaliation on the part of the blacks. Thus, in terms of deaths, the East St. Louis riot was the most serious riot

[39] Dinnerstein and Jaher, *The Aliens,* p. 7.

[40] Arthur I. Waskow, *From Race Riot to Sit-In* (Garden City, N.Y.: Doubleday, 1966), p. 9. Gunnar Myrdal is cited by Waskow.

[41] Cited in Marden and Meyer, *Minorities in American Society,* pp. 258–259.

in the twentieth century: 39 blacks and 9 whites lost their lives during the 1917 riot. The riot was directly related to the political emergence of blacks on the St. Louis scene. Serious economic conflict lay behind the violence, with unskilled white workers being upset over replacement by black workers.[42] And resentment among whites at the growing voting power of the "Negro bloc" played a significant part in the buildup to rioting. Although groups of blacks rioted and killed isolated whites in the ghetto of East St. Louis, most of the action was by whites, and the casualties were predominantly black.[43] However, it is significant that not all ghetto residents were passive during this early riot.

Waskow has written perhaps the best analysis of these early riots in a book entitled *From Race Riot to Sit-In*.[44] In the summer of 1919 seven major riots occurred in Charleston, South Carolina; Longview, Texas; Phillips County, Arkansas; Washington, D.C.; Chicago, Illinois; Knoxville, Tennessee; and Omaha, Nebraska. The first two riots, those in Charleston and Longview, mainly involved white attacks on blacks, with black casualties running much higher than those for whites. The essentially white-dominated riots in Washington and Chicago involved significantly more white casualties. But the 1919 Chicago riot probably came the closest to being a clash between blacks and whites on an equal basis, Waskow's ideal type of the true "race riot."[45] Approximately 15 whites and 23 blacks were killed; and the strong commitment of many Chicago blacks to meet white violence with counterviolence was evident. Yet most of these riots, including that in Chicago, were dominated by white violence directed against black migrants to the city and their descendants. Apparently, most were related to racial competition growing out of the changing urban and industrial structure during the war

[42] Elliott M. Rudwick, *Race Riot at East St. Louis* (Carbondale: Southern Illinois University Press, 1964), p. 218.

[43] Ibid., p. 227.

[44] Waskow, *From Race Riot to Sit-in*.

[45] Ibid., p. 10.

period, to the fundamental goals of certain white groups, including the goal of re-establishing a rigid racial structure and maintaining the power of white Americans over the social, economic, and governmental institutions.

In addition, it is important to note that in the rioting the role of governmental authorities and their coercive agents, the police, was seldom neutral. In many situations the police were ultimately subject to the influence of those white groups actually involved in rioting against blacks, or to those sympathetic to the rioting:

> In Longview, Washington, Chicago, and Arkansas the unneutral actions of the police on behalf of the white community had much to do with turning initial incidents into full-scale riots. . . . To whites, unneutral behavior by the police meant that it was "open season" on Negroes, and that the usual protections afforded by the law were temporarily in abeyance.[46]

In summary, then, collective violence directly related to control of resources and patterns of powerholding in regard to critical institutions has been part of the weave of the American fabric for centuries. It would also seem that American society has seldom gone for more than a decade without some type of collective violence involving alignments of one economic group against another or one ethnic group against another. Moreover, governmental agents, particularly coercive agents, have seldom been absent from violent clashes, either in the triggering of violence, in the channeling of violence, or as involved intimately in issues of power and influence lying behind or emerging out of group violence.

[46] Ibid., pp. 209–210.

The Background and Context of Recent Ghetto Violence

The Political Tactics of Black Americans

So far we have seen that the United States is not unique among nations in collective violence, nor is the decade of the 1960s unique in violence in American history, although it was certainly an important period. We have also examined the use of collective violence at the hands of many vested-interest groups, including numerous white ethnic groups. Reviewing this international and national context provides an important backdrop for examining collective behavior among black Americans, including collective violence against established authorities and the influential interest groups lying behind them. Neither the political character of ghetto riots nor the lack of neutrality of governmental authorities in the collective violence seems unique in view of this historical background.

A definitive history of the violent and nonviolent tactics used by black Americans in their attempts to secure full citizenship in American society is yet to be written; indeed, recent attention to collective violence in ghettos may well have obscured the need to examine the broad historical sweep of black political action. While definitiveness is beyond the scope of this chapter, we will here sketch out the broad outlines of black political action, its diversity and complexity, prior to the ghetto violence of the 1960s. In examining this history, it has become clear to us that the collective actions of black Americans represent more than "protest" movements, more than "objection to" something or a gesture of extreme disapproval. Much of this collective behavior has been intentionally, if often unsuccessfully, directed at altering the shape of the power structure of American society.[47] In Chapter 1 we briefly reviewed the history of black political tac-

[47] See Hobsbawm on eighteenth-century riots: "The classical mob did not riot simply as a protest, but because it expected to achieve something by its riot. It assumed that the authorities would be sensitive to its movements, and probably also that they would make some sort of immediate concession; for the 'mob' was not simply a casual collection of people united for some *ad hoc* purpose, but in a recognized sense a permanent entity." Hobsbawm, *Primitive Rebels,* p. 111.

tics, particularly since the urbanization process began in earnest in the World War I period. Yet black conflict with white America did not begin with the legal activities of the NAACP, which emerged early in that period.

The black struggle for control over life and destiny, for self-determination, actually began in the southern states with the conflict between African slaves and slaveowners. Given the character of control mechanisms in a slaveholding system, collective violence was frequently used on the part of slaveholders to maintain their position. Slave attempts to modify their tightly bound existence took a variety of forms, ranging from suicide and religious withdrawal to organized attack on the property or persons of slaveowners. Collective violence, potential and actual, can be seen in the numerous reported conspiracies of slaves to revolt and a few actual revolts. According to one careful estimate, major conspiracies to revolt numbered at least 250 cases in the first 250 years of slavery in the United States.[48]

In the English colonies blacks were not declared depersonalized slaves until the middle part of the seventeenth century; and the first major plot to revolt took place in Virginia about that time.[49] Together with some white indentured servants, African slaves hatched a plot to rebel, which was quite unsuccessful; as a result, several conspirators were decapitated. While most conspiracies involving large numbers of slaves were betrayed or discovered before the violence actually occurred, quite a number of whites were killed in the few that did succeed. Undoubtedly, the most serious rebellion on record was the now famous Nat Turner rebellion in Southampton County, Virginia, resulting in the deaths of at least 57 whites.[50] Perhaps most important, some rebellious slaves were recorded as advocating more than just re-

[48] Herbert Aptheker, *American Negro Slave Revolts* (New York: International Publishers, 1952), pp. 162–163.

[49] Ibid., p. 165.

[50] William Styron, *The Confessions of Nat Turner* (New York: Random House, 1966); John H. Clarke, ed., *William Styron's Nat Turner* (Boston: Beacon, 1968).

moval of slave-owner control over them; they expressed a desire for a fair share of land and property, a redistribution of economic power and resources.

While a few authors may exaggerate the successes of these early instances of slave violence, since most revolts were quickly subdued by armed groups of whites, these major instances of collective behavior by black Americans have been forgotten in many textbook treatments of slavery. It is also important to remember that, though few in number, some black freedmen prior to the Civil War were active in militant abolitionist societies. By 1850 some freedmen were pressing for the violent overthrow of the institution of slavery.[51]

With the advent of Radical Reconstruction after the Civil War, because of the restriction placed on previously powerful white groups, black southerners began to extend their ability to affect significant decisions within economic and governmental institutions. Under federal protection, black efforts were focused on the mechanisms of voter registration, bloc voting, legislative negotiation, and similar nonviolent political activities. Thus at most of the constitutional conventions in the South after the war, ex-slaves made up a substantial proportion of the delegates; yet, contrary to certain persisting southern myths, blacks attained a majority in only one state.[52] In the other states a majority of the delegates were white, predominantly drawn from nongentry white groups. Consequently, the constitutions prepared by these conventions were radical political documents: abolishing such things as slavery, property qualifications for voting, and imprisonment for debt. In large numbers freedmen participated in state elections, sat in legislatures, held executive offices, and generally gained influence over the governmental decisions affecting their lives. Economic gains seemed to come more slowly, but some were made.

[51] Gunnar Myrdal, *An American Dilemma* (New York: McGraw-Hill Paperback, 1964), Vol. II, pp. 737–738.
[52] John H. Franklin, *From Slavery to Freedom* (3rd ed.; New York: Random House Vintage Books, 1969), p. 316.

Nevertheless, these important political gains were temporary, for by the last decade of the nineteenth-century state governments were again generally in the hands of conservative white groups, primarily as a result of northern withdrawal from the region, the breakdown of the legal protection, and the lack of resources of ex-slaves, coupled with collective violence on the part of whites. Even during this remarkable period of political gains, freedmen were confronted by the violence of those whites who saw themselves slipping out of power. A variety of groups developed, the most powerful of which were the Knights of the White Camelia and the Ku Klux Klan. "Armed with guns, swords, or other weapons, their members patrolled some parts of the South day and night."[53] For example, in 1875 in Mississippi bloody clashes erupted between the black-controlled militia and these white organizations; and much killing preceded the election in which white conservatives regained control over state politics. By forceful means, including the omnipresent menace of lynching, black southerners were pressured to refrain from electoral politics. And southern Democrats soon consolidated their position by effectively disenfranchising the black voters.

In our view, the changing character of black strategies in the struggle to increase resources and power in American society is a subject worthy of much greater attention than it has hitherto received. Indeed, it would seem that the structural processes determining the location, resources, and organization of black Americans have played an extremely important part in the history of political action. Thus "the impact of large structural changes such as urbanization, industrialization, and population growth . . . comes through their creation or destruction of groups contending for power and through their shaping of the available means of coercion."[54] In the slave system the attempts of blacks to modify their status were frequent, but were often doomed to failure because of the dispersion of slaves and the totality of con-

[53] Ibid., p. 327.
[54] Tilly, "Collective Violence in European Perspective," p. 11.

trol which the masters had over both economic and coercive resources. With changes in the slave system brought about by external military pressures, and changes in the distribution and resources of ex-slaves, blacks gained a foothold in southern politics. Tactics in this period were generally nonviolent attempts to use electoral politics. However, the movement upward of blacks was met by increased resistance on the part of whites losing ground, including extensive collective violence. With the withdrawal of northern protection and certain other structural changes, the basis for full membership in southern politics was lacking, and blacks soon dropped to the point of not being a serious political contender.

The next structural change of great importance was the large-scale urbanization and industrialization of blacks, in the North and in the South. These basic structural processes again laid the basis for new black political strategies. Urbanization and industrialization not only grouped blacks in larger homogeneous blocs in the ghettos of southern and northern cities, and expanded their available resources, it also grouped people posing a great political threat near established interest groups of whites and stimulated these groups, and governmental authorities, to adopt new approaches to controlling potential challengers. The cityward movement saw a rise in black consciousness and group pride, coupled with new organizations, such as civil rights groups and the black press, and an increase in other resources, including educational attainment. Coupled with increasing urbanization and industrialization came a new type of black militancy, developing in the face of white attempts to rigidify racism and segregation in that period.

Indeed, it is more than fortuitous that early legal challenges spurred by militant rights organizations such as the NAACP had an urban flavor. Black political mobilization in the first few decades in the form of organizations such as the so-called "civil rights" groups (so-called because most were interested in much more than civil or legal rights) was frequently aided by the leadership and other resources emerging in black ghettos in the growing towns and cities; from the beginning of large-scale urbanization, the first stirrings of mobilization occurred in the North as well as in the South.

Moreover, as we will see in examining most post-urbanization actions among black Americans, the shape of black strategies was typically related to the actions of powerholding groups, whose organization and resources were also affected by the structural processes of urbanization and industrialization. The most obvious reason for this interaction was that established groups viewed blacks as an important new challenger to the structure of decision-making, particularly on the urban scene. While the particular control mechanisms used by established authorities in situations of collective action by dissidents can have a significant effect on the "extent, location, and timing" of these collective actions, including violence, over the long run, "however, the kinds of challenges they face . . . depend rather little on the tactics of crowd control and a great deal on the way the entire political system apportions power and responds to grievances."[55]

The rise of black action in the twentieth century may well have begun at an important meeting of urban black leadership in the North. Reacting against the philosophy of accommodation of Booker T. Washington, cosmopolitan black leader, W. E. B. DuBois, joined by other black leaders and, supported by some influential whites, created the Niagara movement in 1905. Meeting in several northern cities, they pressed for aggressive militancy among black Americans, particularly with regard to legal and voting rights. Economic issues were also stressed.[56] A few years later, some of these Niagara radicals participated in the formation of the NAACP, an organization designed to press for the removal of forced segregation, for equal education, and for the black enfranchisement. DuBois, the new NAACP director of publicity and research, soon began a campaign in the magazine *Crisis* against lynching. In addition to publicity and propa-

[55] Ibid., p. 42.
[56] Franklin, *From Slavery to Freedom*, pp. 444–451.

ganda, the thrust of NAACP efforts over the next several decades was mainly a legal and educational one, with some efforts at improving economic opportunities. During the decades of the twenties and thirties the NAACP won important cases involving legal rights. Moreover, in the early World War I period several other organizations were formed, as diverse as the Urban League and the Committee for Improving Industrial Conditions. Thus, the emphasis in these early decades of the twentieth century was on working through legal channels: publicity, persuasion of employers to employ more Negroes, eliciting philanthropy, the founding of settlement houses.

As we have noted earlier, the growing numbers of migrants to city ghettos faced new obstacles to mobilization, including neo-colonial invasions, collective violence, and even attempts at exclusion. Franklin notes that the South was by no means the only inhospitable region:

> Crowds of white hoodlums frequently attacked Negroes in large Northern cities such as Philadelphia and New York. . . . As the migration of Negroes to the North increased hostility toward them grew. Some towns tolerated them; others did not. Syracuse, Ohio, forbade any Negroes to settle there, while several towns in Indiana . . . did not permit any Negro residents within their limits.[57]

Well before the 1917 East St. Louis riot, numerous riots against black urbanites had occurred in the North, including Springfield, Ohio, and Springfield, Illinois. Moreover, the increasingly significant presence of blacks in northern cities was dramatized by the 1917–1920 riots. Behind these riots lay realistic white fears of black competition, fears that blacks wanted into the decision-making structure of the cities. It is important, too, to realize that in these violent struggles the first signs of the black will to retaliate with violence were glimpsed.

[57] Ibid., p. 443.

In the years after World War I black migrants continued to flood the cities, North and South, such that the majority of ghetto residents at any one time were doubtless relatively recent arrivals in the city, pressed heavily with the immediate problems of food, housing, and employment. The evolution of black political strategies in the twenties, thirties, and forties appeared to take two directions, affected to some extent by all-encompassing events such as the Depression and World War II. Not that efforts slowed, for on the one hand groups like the NAACP pressed ahead with legal and philanthropic tactics. New cases were won, and the areas in which they were won were increasingly more important. Educational resources, too, were slowly increasing.

On the other hand, even among the relatively recent arrivals to cities there were significant stirrings of black pride and group consciousness, developments critical to further mobilization in the direction of new political strategies. The movements emphasizing black history and culture, literature and music, in the twenties and thirties were basically protest movements; the manifest aim was to "enhance self-respect and race-respect among Negroes by substituting a belief in race achievements for the traditional belief in race inferiority."[58] In an era dominated, nationally and internationally, by perhaps the most extensive propaganda on behalf of racism in the history of the Western world this was no easy accomplishment.

Organizational developments were also linked to this burgeoning group consciousness, including Marcus Garvey's Universal Negro Improvement Association (UNIA), business and professional organizations, and the National Negro Congress. Reflecting antidiscrimination sentiment, such represented the groundwork "for attempts at broader organizations."[59] Several mass movements with a self-help and black-capitalism flavor emerged in this period, with a definite appeal to the lower socioeconomic groups. Particularly important was Garvey's UNIA, which gen-

[58] Myrdal, *An American Dilemma,* II, p. 752.
[59] Ibid., p. 817.

erated and reinforced group pride among blacks, increasingly victims of neocolonial incursions.[60] On the practical side, Garvey moved in the direction of consolidating black assets into several black enterprises, the most important being a shipping organization aimed at helping blacks return to Africa. On the ideological side, Garvey may well be seen as a precursor contributing to the emergence of black power and black self-determination strategies in later decades.

In the Depression and World War II periods yet other black tactics were emerging, if only briefly, while legal and educational tactics continued to be predominant. As we have noted in Chapter 1, early electoral and party politics strategies on the part of blacks were generally ineffective in the cities because of a rigidified power structure unwilling to reapportion power and respond to black grievances. Indeed, perhaps the first major examples of collective violence on the part of black urbanites in the twentieth century, which were more than defensive reactions to attacks by groups of whites, occurred in America's first large urban ghetto, New York's Harlem.

A harbinger of things to come, and overshadowed by collective violence *against* blacks in this period, the 1935 Harlem riot was quite different from the riots (1917–1920) that had preceded it. There was little conflict between black and white civilians; rather, the focus of the violence was generally on white-owned businesses and policemen.[61] Underlying conditions included only token governmental representation and impotency in regard to other urban institutions, while the precipitating incident in-

[60] Amy J. Garvey, *Garvey and Garveyism* (New York: Collier Books, 1970); Edmund D. Cronon, *Black Moses* (Madison: University of Wisconsin Press, 1968).

[61] "Excerpts from the Complete Harlem Riot Report, March 19, 1935," *Racial Violence in the United States,* ed. Allen D. Grimshaw (Chicago: Aldine, 1969), pp. 119–128. See also Allen D. Grimshaw, "The Harlem Disturbances of 1935 and 1943: Deviant Cases," *Racial Violence in the United States,* ed. Allen D. Grimshaw (Chicago: Aldine, 1969), pp. 117–119.

volved the alleged mistreatment of a Negro boy by a white policeman, and the subsequent actions of the police. In many respects—the police incidents, the looting, the attacks on white-owned stores—this first major ghetto riot was a precursor of the ghetto riots of the sixties. Even prominent explanations of the riot were similar: Mayor La Guardia stressed that the riot was the result of the acts of hoodlums and other irresponsible blacks, described as a tiny minority of the residents of Harlem's ghetto.[62] In addition, thousands of blacks rioted again in 1943, precipitated by the shooting of a black soldier by a white policeman; this riot was similar to the earlier one in 1935. In terms of the character of the collective violence, the 1935 and 1943 ghetto riots were early signs that violent strategies to alter the powerless situation of black America were no longer foreign to at least a small segment of the ghetto population.[63] At least one ghetto now had the resources to sustain offensive violence on a large scale.

Another major riot occurred during the war. However, the 1943 Detroit riot was more similar to earlier riots dominated by white civilians than to the 1935 or 1943 Harlem riots. As in riots such as that in Chicago in 1919, there were pitched battles between black and white civilians. Groups of whites injured and killed blacks on the city streets, burned numerous cars, and attempted to invade black areas. Black rioters, on the other hand, most commonly stoned streetcars, looted stores, and destroyed white property, particularly focusing on exploitative white-owned stores.[64] As would be the case in many later riots, no black-owned stores were hit by the looters. Consequently, again many more blacks than whites were killed (25 to 9). One analysis concludes that "the Negroes probably held their own in the ston-

[62] Robert B. Fogelson, "Violence as Protest," *Urban Riots,* ed. Robert H. Connery (New York: Random House Vintage Books, 1969), p. 40.

[63] Alfred M. Lee and Norman D. Humphrey, *Race Riot* (New York: Dryden, 1943), p. 99.

[64] Ibid., pp. 2–81.

ing and destroyed and looted more property than did the whites, but they did not do so well in the shooting."[65] Given the economic overtones of the events leading up to and reflected in the riot, white fears of black social and economic competition, the relationship of this riot to jockeying for power in Detroit seems evident.

The Fifties and Early Sixties

The most recent period of the black struggle has seen a continuation of the basic structural changes of urbanization and industrialization, especially stimulated in the war and postwar periods. In the forties, fifties, and sixties black Americans continued to swell the ghettos of the cities, in the North and the South; the numbers of outmigrants from the South reached an all-time high in the forties and fifties. No longer was there only a handful of large ghettos. By 1960 there were many large black ghettos, and dramatically growing numbers of black Americans were native to those ghettos. As we suggested in Chapter 1, this growth meant increased organization along formal and informal lines and the development of the population and resource prerequisites for large-scale political movements. More and more in the fifties and sixties, large numbers of black Americans became involved in actions designed not only to protest existing conditions but also to restructure those conditions in line with black goals and aspirations.

Looking at this period, several observers have suggested that there was an evolutionary development in the tactics of the black struggle for power, from court and legal action to increasingly militant types of nonviolent action:

But in a very short time court action lost its preeminence as the method for applying the power of the Negro minority. Through experience in bus boycotts, selective buying cam-

[65] Ibid., p. 84.

paigns, and nonviolent resistance, Negroes discovered other sanctions which they might apply.[66]

Waskow sees the evolution in terms of a move to the politics of "creative disorder": first the wave of sit-ins, then the freedom rides, then demonstrations centered on voter registration and many other race-related issues, then even more disruptive rent strikes and job blockades.[67] Foreshadowed by the projected March-on-Washington threatened in early 1941, which resulted in an executive order designed to desegregate jobs in the defense industries, the new wave of nonviolent confrontation activity began in earnest shortly after the 1954 Supreme Court decision; in the city of Montgomery, Alabama, a massive bus boycott by black urbanites catapulted Martin Luther King, Jr., into prominence in the movement for equality. Boycott tactics were supplemented on a large scale by the sit-in confrontations, beginning in 1960 with the student sit-ins in Greensboro, North Carolina. Eventually, thousands of blacks, together with sympathetic whites, participated in more than 800 sit-ins in more than 100 cities in the North as well as the South.[68] With the development of this militancy came into prominence several important rights organizations, including the Congress of Racial Equality (CORE), Student Nonviolent Coordinating Committee (SNCC), and the Southern Christian Leadership Conference (SCLC). Not that the new political tactics ever completely supplanted older tactics. Court action continued to be pushed by civil rights organizations, and voter registration was militantly pursued.

While most discussions of black political tactics in the late fifties and sixties focus on the South, it would be a serious mis-

[66] Lewis M. Killian and Charles Grigg, *Racial Crisis in America* (Englewood Cliffs, N.J.: Prentice-Hall, 1964), p. 20.

[67] Waskow, *From Race Riot to Sit-In,* pp. 225–246.

[68] Bryan T. Downes and Stephen W. Burks, "The Historical Development of the Black Protest Movement," *Blacks in the United States,* ed. Norval D. Glenn and Charles M. Bonjean (San Francisco: Chandler, 1969), pp. 322–344.

take to overlook the increasingly militant actions of large numbers of black northerners. Not only was there growing activity in nationalist movements such as the Black Muslims, which continued to mobilize black pride and group consciousness, but in this period there was also an escalation of nonviolent activities in the North. "During the years 1961–1964, CORE chapters in the North escalated their campaigns against discrimination in employment, housing, and schools."[69] Northern blacks, consequently, contributed to the development of militant strategies in the struggle to penetrate urban decision-making systems. Northern cities saw numerous school boycotts, rent strikes, and mass picketing at construction sites. Indeed, in the year or two prior to the major ghetto riots, nonviolent tactics seemed to take an increasingly more militant direction. Widespread job blockades were developed by CORE chapters in an attempt to force economic restructuring. And one of the most famous attempts at even more radical social disruption occurred in connection with the World's Fair. In the spring of 1964 an attempt was made by New York blacks to halt traffic by a sit-down on a major bridge, followed by a threatened stall-in which cut opening-day attendance at the World's Fair. Both events not only communicated to a wide audience some of the grievances of New York's ghetto dwellers, but they also generated broader proposals for radical social disruption, including an ill-fated proposal to disrupt the workaday proceedings of Congress.

Moreover, the apparent tardiness in the participation of northern blacks in civil disobedience actions is more than a matter of historical neglect; it may well reflect the effects of migration on northern ghetto dwellers. In the peak periods of migration in the forties and fifties northern ghetto residents were probably preoccupied with the fundamental problem of migrant survival in, and integration into, the urban sphere. However, by the early

[69] Inge P. Bell, *CORE and the Strategy of Nonviolence* (New York: Random House Paperback, 1968), p. 13. See also Waskow, *From Race Riot to Sit-In,* pp. 239–246.

sixties, increasingly large numbers of ghetto dwellers were native-born or long-term residents. By this time thousands had been in the cities long enough to experience on many fronts and in many situations their lack of control over the important decisions that affected their lives. The essentially political goal of seizing control of the decision-making machinery was apparently becoming widespread.

Conclusion: Collective Violence Before Harlem and Watts

Most discussions of recent ghetto violence begin with the Harlem and Bedford-Stuyvesant (New York City) riots in the summer of 1964. Yet even if one focuses only on the decade of the sixties, it would be erroneous to conclude that collective violence at the hands of black Americans suddenly emerged in that summer. Indeed, it appears that collective violence, of an "offensive" type, erupted in the years 1962–1963.

Our intention in this section was to trace out the year-by-year development of collective violence on the part of black Americans for the first few years of the sixties, prior to the much-discussed events of later years. However, examining the available data made it clear that a substantial number of the instances of collective violence in these years involved white attacks on blacks demonstrating nonviolently. The following discussion, therefore, is more than a continuation of our argument that there has been an evolution in the tactics of black Americans in challenging the established power structure: from legal tactics, to the tactics of creative disorder, to the tactics of social disruption and rioting. Indeed, the tactics of nonviolence and of rioting particularly overlap in the early sixties. The materials analyzed here also indicate the continuation of violence on the part of groups of Americans in power—in this case white southerners and northerners—attempting to maintain established positions.

Apparently only one source has detailed the collective violence of the early sixties. According to a Library of Congress report on

The Background and Context of Recent Ghetto Violence

the years 1961–1964 there were more than two dozen important events involving collective engagement in racially oriented violence.[70] Significantly, in 1961 all six reported instances primarily involved *white* attacks on black demonstrators. In five of these instances whites threatened by the mobility of blacks attempted to prevent them from securing equality in the sphere of public accommodations. In the other instance, the only one outside the South, fearful whites in Chicago threatened to attack a church housing black refugees from a fire. In most of these encounters blacks did not retaliate with violence, although in a 1961 Monroe, North Carolina, incident some blacks did eventually use arms in self-defense.[71] The events of 1961 clearly show the continuation of collective violence on the part of whites concerned with maintaining the social and political status quo; it is also significant that most violent attacks by white civilians in the decade of the sixties generally grew out of nonviolent political tactics engaged in by blacks.

By 1962 black willingness to engage in collective violence, beyond defensive retaliation, could be glimpsed in a number of incidents.[72] Of the five events of racially related collective violence reported for that year, only one in Mississippi involved an attacking group of white citizens, in combat primarily with federal forces. In the other four localities, two southern, one western, and one in a border area, there were clashes between black groups and the police and/or attacks by black groups on property. Although existing data provide few details on the context or development of the violence, it appears that in three instances the precipitating incident involved a police-ghetto resident en-

[70] Reported in "Urban Problems and Civil Disorder," *Congressional Quarterly Weekly Report,* September 8, 1967, p. 3.

[71] Robert F. Williams, *Negroes with Guns,* ed. Marc Schleifer (New York: Marzani and Munsell, 1962); Truman Nelson, *The Right of Revolution* (Boston: Beacon, 1968).

[72] "Urban Problems and Civil Disorder," *Congressional Quarterly Weekly Report,* p. 3.

counter. Yet the relatively small scale of the violence in 1961–1962 can be seen in the fact that the collective actions generally lasted for one day or less.

The year 1963 and the first half of 1964 saw a continuation of several types of collective violence. Typically they consisted of black reactions to coercive police acts with regard to nonviolent demonstrations or white violence in attempts to prevent demonstrations forcibly. By 1963 the number of reported violent events had grown to twelve, three quarters involving collective violence on the part of black Americans and most again taking place in southern or border states.[73] In Birmingham, Alabama, weeks of nonviolent demonstrations by black southerners had produced important negotiations between black and white leaders; then the killing of several black children in a church in May precipitated two days of protest and conflict. And a few months later, after the bombings of the homes of black leaders in Birmingham, hundred of local blacks made national news with a riot, openly attacking the white police. Consequently, the riot resulted in numerous casualties to the rioters because the suppression of the rioting by the police was particularly brutal.[74]

Again the Library of Congress report provides us with few details on the development of rioting. Nevertheless, in Lexington, North Carolina, black and white civilians clashed. In Savannah, Georgia, two riots occurred, growing out of police actions with regard to prior peaceful demonstrations; it appears that these riots grew out of an interaction with civic authorities and the police, being precipitated by the arrest of nonviolent demonstrators. Similar postdemonstration riots reportedly occurred in Charleston, South Carolina, and also in Chicago, Illinois. However, collective violence on the part of whites again accounted for one quarter of the cases. In Cambridge, Maryland, and in the northern cities of Foxcroft, Pennsylvania, and Chicago, Illinois, groups of whites were involved in attacking black demonstra-

[73] Ibid.
[74] Downes and Burks, "The Historical Development of the Black Protest Movement," p. 337.

tions and black attempts at residential desegregation. Yet the last-recorded event involving collective violence for the year 1963 was different from those preceding it. Since it did not grow out of a nonviolent demonstration, it was rather similar to many of the major riots that followed. Blacks in a northern ghetto—that of Philadelphia, Pennsylvania—rioted against police and property after a policeman killed a ghetto resident.

Even in the first months of 1964 several instances of collective violence were tabulated prior to the more widely reported Harlem and Bedford-Stuyvesant riots later that year. The oscillating and diverse character of these events, the defensive militancy of blacks, the connection of collective violence with civil rights demonstrations in the 1961–1964 period, and the southern location of some of these events, can be illustrated by quoting the following terse and intriguing section from the Library of Congress record:

Jacksonville, Florida, May 24 [1964] and days following—After conviction of Negro sit-ins and shooting to death of a Negro woman by a sniper, Negro gangs fought police, attacked white persons, damaged property; riot marked first major use of Molotov cocktails in race riots.

Cleveland, Ohio, April 7—Negroes attacked police with stones and other missiles after a white minister, demonstrating at a school construction site, was run over and killed by a bulldozer.

Cambridge, Maryland, May 26—Negroes attacked National Guardsmen with missiles when the soldiers prevented them from fighting with a group of white persons.

St. Augustine, Florida, June 25—Segregationists broke through police line and attacked integrationist demonstrators.

Henderson, N.C., July 12—Negroes and white persons fought when Negroes sought service at a truck-stop restaurant.[75]

[75] "Urban Problems and Civil Disorder," *Congressional Quarterly Weekly Report,* p. 3.

CHAPTER 2

Within a few months of these diverse and violent events, rioting by very large numbers of blacks broke out in numerous northern ghettos, including such areas as Harlem, Bedford-Stuyvesant, Rochester, Chicago, Jersey City, and Philadelphia. By the end of the decade of the 1960s hundreds of American cities had seen large-scale rioting on the part of rank-and-file black Americans.

Ghetto Rioting in the Sixties: Some Basic Questions

Beginning in the summer of 1964 with the widely heralded rioting in two of America's largest urban ghettos, the twin New York ghettos of Harlem and Bedford-Stuyvesant, many long summers of collective violence were to pass before the eyes of black and white Americans before the end of the decade. By the end of the sixties more than three hundred American cities had seen group violence on the part of black Americans. To many Americans the escalation of collective violence in urban ghettos during the sixties probably seemed totally unexpected and inexplicable, for during that same decade black citizens had achieved perceptible economic improvement, national legislation protecting civil rights, and entrance into social and occupational positions from which they had formerly been barred. The willingness of black Americans to resort to activities that sharply disrupted social order and stability left most white persons and political leaders bewildered and hostile. In comparison with the restrictions that had been previously imposed upon black people, certain events in the decade seemed to denote a new era of racial progress that made the eruption of violence even more difficult to comprehend.

Yet, as we have seen in Chapter 2, the development of ghetto uprisings in the sixties can be viewed as an extension of the centuries of struggle that have marked the efforts by black citizens to gain equal rights. The attempt by various racial and ethnic groups in the nation's history to attain political equality has often involved collective violence on the part of both dissidents and established authorities, commonly preceded by less violent tactics such as verbal persuasion, the exercise of voting strength, and various types of nonviolent action on the part of dissidents. In the period following the famous 1954 Supreme Court decision on school desegregation (*Brown* v. *Board of Education of Topeka*), and especially as the fifties gave way to the sixties, some important black victories in social and legal areas were won through sit-ins, freedom marches, and other nonviolent demonstrations. Understandably, the perception that a minority group was making visible progress toward the achievement of its objectives was confused by many whites with the view that members of this group were (or should be) satisfied with the rate of that progress. Although black Americans have made important gains in moving slowly from the status of slaves to the level of second-class citizens, to the point where they have a toehold on the rough incline leading to realistic equality, they still have not reached the point where they can enjoy the privileges and power exercised by most groups of white Americans. In many respects, the contrasting interpretations of ghetto revolts which have surfaced in recent years seem to reflect crucial discrepancies in the basic perceptions of white and black Americans. While most white observers were apparently impressed by the speed and extent of racial progress during the 1960s, black Americans have emphasized their failure to achieve fundamental objectives and the continuing chasm that remained between their present political impotence and the goals of self-determination and community control they had long sought.

In this chapter we will focus on a series of important questions about collective black actions in this riotous decade of the 1960s, including the number and definition of collectively violent events, the conditions underlying rioting, and certain relevant hypotheses generated from the explanatory theories considered previously. The final section will examine the issue of black attitudes seen as an important aspect of "underlying conditions."

How Many Riots?

Just how many ghetto riots were there in the decade of the 1960s? How many of the riots were massive or serious? How many casualties were there? In spite of the dramatic growth of research on ghetto violence during recent years, it is surprisingly difficult to answer questions such as these with precision. In the first place, social accounting on the part of governmental and private agencies is a relatively new phenomenon. Published enumerations of events considered to be ghetto riots are rare, even for selected periods during this decade. Even a cursory review of the social science research which has examined the social and economic correlates of rioting illustrates this point: in their research social science analysts have been forced to provide their own enumerations, relying heavily on newspapers, almost always including *The New York Times.* In addition, as we have noted in the preceding chapter, it is difficult to pinpoint exactly the beginning of ghetto rioting, and it is equally difficult to determine the end of ghetto rioting. Attempts at answers to these enumeration questions reveal yet other crucial questions: What is a "riot"? What are the essential characteristics which lead one to define a particular collective event as a "riot"? That the definition of a "riot" is inextricably intertwined with the question of the actual number of riots becomes clear when one examines the few attempts that have been made to enumerate and classify ghetto riots.

In this section we will examine collective violence on the part of black Americans in the period beginning with 1964 and ending with 1970–1971—admittedly an arbitrary delimitation of ghetto rioting, but necessitated by limitations of the data available. Drawing on several sources including *The New York Times,* one careful investigation by Downes estimated that there were

329 important riots, termed "hostile outbursts," in the five years between 1964 and the end of 1968, involving thousands of black rioters in 257 cities scattered around the country.[1] Reportedly, the most violent year was 1967, during which 71 important riots were recorded in 82 cities. Turning to yet other dimensions of the rioting in that five-year period, this same report provided estimates of the rather large number of persons arrested for riot-related offenses (52,629) and of the number injured (8,371). Perhaps the most important index of the seriousness of the ghetto riots in these years can be seen in the estimate of the number killed—220 persons, mostly black civilians. While these estimates of the extent and consequences of ghetto rioting are the most detailed as yet available for an extended period, they probably underestimate to a significant degree the actual extent of collective violence on the part of black Americans even in this limited five-year period. Indeed, this might well be expected, given the fact that this particular investigation provided an inadequate definition of the terminology used. Neither "riot" nor "hostile outburst" was defined in terms of scale or level of violence, and it appears that the implicit definition used resulted in the exclusion of numerous collective events tabulated by other observers as riotous.

To illustrate this contention, we can turn to the careful account of race riots prepared by the Civil Disorder Clearinghouse at Brandeis University. (Actually, they prefer the term "civil disorders.") For one year in this 1964–1968 period, the year 1967, they tabulated 233 disorders, occurring in 168 cities distributed around the country.[2] According to this careful accounting, in

[1] Bryan T. Downes, "A Critical Reexamination of the Social and Political Characteristics of Riot Cities," *Social Science Quarterly,* **51** (September 1970), 349–360.

[2] Lemberg Center for the Study of Violence, Brandeis University, "April Aftermath of the King Assassination," *Riot Data Review,* No. 2 (August 1968), 60. (Mimeographed.) These figures do not include 16 "equivocal" disorders in an additional eight cities.

that year 18,800 persons were arrested, 3,400 were injured, and 82 persons were killed in these disorders. Except for the number killed, these figures are larger than the estimates for the same period provided by the Downes investigation discussed in the previous paragraph. While these Clearinghouse statistics do include some disorders that were dominated by white (civilian) violence directed against blacks—in point of fact a small minority of the disorders in that year—the major difference between these two accounts seems to lie both in the more exhaustive accounting and in the inclusion of smaller-scale events in the Clearinghouse figures. Indeed, the Clearinghouse utilized the following operational definition of a "race-related civil disorder," one of the few explicit definitions attempted:

> Civil disorder refers to incidents involving crowd behavior, characterized by either damage to persons or property, or defiance of civil authority, or aggressive disruptions which violate civil law (such as building seizures). More specifically, crowd behavior refers to the activities of 4 or more people acting in concert. . . . Our review of civil disorders is confined to these episodes arising from racial tension.[3]

With this definition as the basis for the tabulation procedure, it is clear that somewhat less serious collective events involving civil disruption were included in the tally of 233 disorders, including a number that were school-centered.

Perhaps one of the most thorough—and certainly the most influential—analysis of the 1967 riots was provided by the final report of the National Advisory Commission on Civil Disorders. The Commission also reported differences in the definitions and enumerations of civil disorders in their own sources, with their analysis being limited to the first nine months of 1967:

[3] Lemberg Center for the Study of Violence, Brandeis University, "U.S. Race-Related Civil Disorders, July–December 1969" (Waltham, Mass., n.d.), p. 1. (Mimeographed.)

103

CHAPTER 3

Because definitions of "civil disorder" vary widely, between 51 and 217 disorders were recorded by various agencies as having occurred during the first nine months of 1967. From these sources we have developed a list of 164 disorders which occurred during that period.[4]

This Commission's estimate of 164 disorders included what they termed "major," "serious," and "minor" riots and seems in line with that of the Civil Disorder Clearinghouse, whose estimate was for the entire year of 1967. Although no comprehensive definition was provided for "riots" or "civil disorders," the Commission report did rank the enumerated disorders into three categories—major, serious, and minor—on the basis of specific operational criteria focusing on behavior and actions, including degree of violence, number of rioters, and the scale of government response to the riot.[5] By their calculations 75 percent (123 disorders) were evaluated as minor, involving only a few fires and broken windows, small numbers of people, local police, and lasting only one day. Events involving less in the way of violence, or participants, were apparently not considered riots. Twenty percent (33 disorders) were rated as serious, involving escalation in all of these categories, and 5 percent (8 disorders) were regarded as major. The operational criteria for major riots were (1) many fires, intensive looting, and reports of sniping, (2) violence for more than two days, (3) large crowds, and (4) use of the National Guard and outside police forces. Using these useful but still rather imprecise criteria, the Commission ascertained that the cities seeing major riots in 1967 included seven northern areas—Buffalo, New York; Cincinnati, Ohio (June); Detroit, Michigan; Milwaukee, Wisconsin; Minneapolis, Minnesota; Newark, New Jersey; Plainfield, New Jersey—and one southern area —Tampa, Florida (June).[6]

[4] *Report of the National Advisory Commission on Civil Disorders* (New York: Bantam, 1968), pp. 112–113.
[5] Ibid., p. 113.
[6] Ibid., pp. 158–159.

Ghetto Rioting in the Sixties: Some Basic Questions

To what extent are estimates of the number of ghetto riots available for the violent years after the much-discussed year of 1967? After the 1967–1968 period, the apparent mass-media withdrawal from concern over ghetto rioting was also reflected in the relative lack of attention devoted to later riot years both by the media and by scholars. In fact, we have been able to locate only a few sources publishing detailed enumerations of the later Negro riots. For the year 1968 the aforementioned investigation by Downes does provide an estimate of 155 outbursts in 106 cities, resulting ultimately in 75 deaths. Again relatively small-scale events were excluded from this particular count.[7] Viewing civil disorders in terms of their clearcut definition, which includes a wide range of violent events, the Civil Disorder Clearinghouse has provided estimates of the number of disorders for the one-month period just after the Martin Luther King assassination in 1968. In that period more cities saw ghetto violence than during all of the year 1967, reflecting a major escalation in the number of cities experiencing collective violence.[8] In that month no fewer than 172 American cities experienced 202 racially motivated civil disorders, in which 27,000 arrests were made for riot-related offenses, 3,500 persons were injured, and 43 persons were killed. Moreover, during the first four months of that same year, an estimated 295 civil disorders took place.[9]

Furthermore, one mimeographed report of the Clearinghouse reported a significant increase in the number of racially motivated violent events for the year 1969, a riot year that has so far received little attention in the research literature. That year saw what was probably the largest number of tabulated disorders for any year in the decade of the sixties—a final total of more than 500 civil disorders was reported for the twelve-month period. Re-

[7] Downes, "A Critical Reexamination of the Social and Political Characteristics of Riot Cities," 352.

[8] Lemberg Center for the Study of Violence, "April Aftermath of the King Assassination," 60. "Equivocal" disorders have apparently been omitted.

[9] Ibid., p. 73.

portedly more than 9,400 persons were arrested and injuries totaled more than 2,000 persons.[10] By the end of the year at least 23 persons had been killed in these disorders. Another 6 persons were killed in an additional 136 "equivocal" disorders, termed thus by the Clearinghouse because of lack of complete information on the racial aspect of the events. Again only a small minority of these tabulated instances of collective violence was dominated by white civilians. Thus, although 1969 has generally been considered to be a relatively calm year in terms of rioting by black Americans, in point of fact it was not calm by the usual measures. While no massive insurrections such as those in Watts (1965) or Detroit (1967) occurred in 1969, that year probably saw more black-dominated riots, more casualties, and more arrests than some earlier riot years.[11]

Even rough estimates of the number of ghetto riots in the years after 1969 are difficult to secure. Recent figures released by the U.S. Department of Justice include all "civil disturbances," racial and nonracial, in a given year. Thus 195 civil disturbances were reported for 1970, with 18 of these considered to be "major" by the National Advisory Commission criteria cited above. Data for the first eight months of 1971 indicated that there were 176 disturbances, with 11 considered to be "major."[12] That the ma-

[10] These figures were calculated from the data in Lemberg Center for the Study of Violence, Brandeis University, "U.S. Race-Related Civil Disorders, January–June 1969" (Waltham, Mass., n.d., mimeographed); and Lemberg Center for the Study of Violence, "U.S. Race-Related Civil Disorders, July–December 1969." "Equivocal" disorders have again been excluded from these figures.

[11] "Probably" is used here because the figures for earlier years fail to take into account the somewhat smaller-scale events included in the Clearinghouse figures. Even taking that into account, the 1969 figures appear higher than for certain earlier years.

[12] U.S. Department of Commerce, *Pocket Data Book: USA 1971* (Washington, D.C.: U.S. Government Printing Office, 1971), p. 126. The 1971 Department of Justice figures are cited in John Herbers, "Summer's Urban Violence Stirs Fears of Terrorism," *The New York Times,* September 21, 1971, pp. 1 and 34.

jority of these were probably ghetto riots is suggested by a separately released Federal Bureau of Investigation estimate of 249
race-related disturbances in American cities in the 1970–1971
period.[13] Although these sketchy and vaguely defined figures are
the best that are currently available from government sources
and thus do not allow for firm conclusions, they do indicate that
ghetto revolts did continue well into the 1970s.

It is also quite difficult to assess with accuracy the trend in the
seriousness of rioting between the early 1960s and the early
1970s, since few analysts have differentiated ghetto riots into several different categories of varying degrees of seriousness. One
notable exception was the careful analysis supplied by the 1967–
1968 National Advisory Commission. As noted previously, 8 of
the 164 riots the Commission examined were considered "major"
by their explicit criteria; another 33 were viewed as "serious."
So far as we have been able to discover, however, no subsequent
counts of ghetto riots have been attempted using these well-
defined criteria.

One relatively brief analysis of 1967–1971 race-related civil
disorders, recently released by the Civil Disorder Clearinghouse,
provides some evidence on the post-1967 trend, although the
data are limited just to the three summer months.[14] According to
their tabulations the total number of *summer* riots decreased
from 176 in 1967 to 46 in 1971. The proportion of the summer
revolts that involved what the Clearinghouse termed "more serious acts of violence," for example, firebombing and sniping, decreased from 70 percent of the total in 1967 to 53 percent in
1968. Yet the proportion did not decrease significantly between
1968 and 1970; in each of those three summers the proportion of
riots encompassing very serious acts of violence hovered around
50 percent. By the summer of 1971 the proportion did decrease

[13] The FBI release is discussed in a brief news report in *Justice
Magazine,* February, 1972, p. 21.
[14] Jane A. Baskin et al., "The Long, Hot Summer?" *Justice Magazine,* February, 1972, pp. 18–21.

again, this time to 27 percent of the total number. However, by other measures of seriousness than those primarily involving the actions of ghetto rioters—such as deaths and injuries among rioters—this stair-step decrease in the level of seriousness over the 1967–1971 period was not confirmed. Although much of the Clearinghouse data supports the conclusion drawn that there was a trend in the direction of a "cooling" of collective violence between 1967 and 1971, the evidence presented is perhaps more suggestive than conclusive. In particular, one must be careful in generalizing from data on summer riots, since summer riots apparently accounted for less than *one fifth* of all race-related civil disorders in the 1968–1971 period.

Caution should also be observed lest we jump to the hasty conclusion that serious ghetto rioting virtually disappeared from the American scene by the year 1969—a conclusion that many leaders and rank-and-file Americans presumably drew from the relatively meager information available to them in the mass media. Even the limited research data available indicate that this conclusion is unwarranted, since serious ghetto rioting continued well into the 1970s. Indeed, the Clearinghouse report just discussed notes that there were more instances of race-related collective violence in the "cool" summer of 1971 than in the summer of 1966, considered by many at the time as a "long hot summer." And numerous ghetto riots during the years (not just summers) of 1970 and 1971 attained the level that by National Advisory Commission criteria would be considered "serious" or "major." Thus, even this brief review of the available evidence on ghetto riots during the last decade indicates to us the need for much additional research on the questions of number and seriousness that we have raised here. Moreover, while it is not within the scope of this book to grapple with certain other related questions, we might conclude this section by at least listing them: Why has the ghetto rioting of the 1969–1971 period received so little attention in the mass media? Why are no figures available from government agencies for the ghetto riots in this period? Why have no government reports focused on the rioting in this period?

Ghetto Rioting in the Sixties: Some Basic Questions

Underlying Conditions

Given that hundreds of thousands of black Americans did in fact participate in hundreds of riots in numerous American cities during the sixties, and that thousands suffered injury and death as a result, several other crucial questions arise: Why did riots occur in that period? Why did they occur in some localities but not in others? These are just two of the hard questions one encounters in thinking seriously about the emergence and causation of recent riots by black Americans. Indeed, most of the theories discussed in Chapter 1 involve an attempt at explaining the causes and development of rioting. Yet surprisingly little empirical research has been directed at sorting out in a descriptive or systematic way the range of possible answers to these basic questions.

Not that this is a unique problem confronted only by those concerned with recent violent events in black ghettos, for systematic research on the white-dominated riots both during and prior to the 1960s is also lacking in the collective behavior literature. Apparently, only one independent attempt has been made to examine the development of the numerous race riots in earlier decades of American history. In a pioneering analysis of the many earlier riots between 1913 and 1963, Lieberson and Silverman conveniently distinguished between the "immediate precipitants" and "underlying conditions" of 76 events of collective violence with racial overtones—distinctions commonly used in subsequent analyses of rioting.[15] Surveying these early twentieth-century riots with regard to immediate precipitants, they found all but a few had recorded precipitating events just prior to the collective violence, most of which involved "inter-racial violations of intense social norms."[16] Regarding precipitating events as necessary but not sufficient causes of these events, these investi-

[15] Stanley Lieberson and Arnold R. Silverman, "The Precipitants and Underlying Conditions of Race Riots," *American Sociological Review,* **30** (December 1965), 887–898. Only a small percentage of the riots they examined were in the sixties.

[16] Ibid., p. 891.

gators then examined those underlying conditions which in their view restrained one major segment of the urban population from accepting "the normal institutional response" to the precipitating event.[17] It is important to note that this reasoning about the character of underlying conditions is in line with the social science theorizing about riots, remote and recent, which emphasizes structural conduciveness and strain and the breakdown of social control as crucial to the emergence of collective violence.

Rejecting the argument that riots were random occurrences, Silverman and Lieberson argued that certain socioeconomic conditions increase the likelihood that the immediate precipitating event will be a prologue to a riot. Certain conditions increase the riot proneness of a city. When compared with nonriot cities, cities having riots in the years 1913–1963 tended to have not only *smaller* proportions of blacks unemployed and in unskilled occupations, similar black median incomes and housing conditions, and lower ratios of black policemen, but also similar white unemployment rates, lower white incomes, smaller black-white differences in median incomes, and higher ratios of population to city councilman (or elections at large).[18] Several of these factors suggested to Lieberson and Silverman that the encroachment of blacks on the white occupational world, viewed as an economic threat, might well lead to white-dominated riots. Moreover, an important negative finding was in regard to the common migration explanation for rioting. Surprisingly, neither black nor white population increase was found to be associated with the probability of riots. In the light of these somewhat unexpected socioeconomic patterns the reasons for the occurrence of riots proposed by Lieberson and Silverman stressed both the deprivation of the racial groups involved, the buildup of unresolved grievances, and institutional malfunctioning:

[17] Ibid., p. 892.
[18] Ibid., pp. 893–897.

Ghetto Rioting in the Sixties: Some Basic Questions

. . . we suggest that riots are more likely to occur when social institutions function inadequately, or when grievances are not resolved, or cannot be resolved under the existing institutional arrangements. Populations are predisposed or prone to riot; they are not simply neutral aggregates transformed into a violent mob by the agitation or charisma of individuals. Indeed, the immediate precipitant simply ignites prior community tensions revolving around basic institutional difficulties.[19]

It should be noted that in a subsequent reanalysis of these same materials, Bloombaum found these riot cities to be differentiated with respect to time and place, with the institutional breakdown theory having less utility in explaining southern riots after World War II than in accounting for northern riots prior to 1945.[20] Nevertheless several of these themes directed at explaining variations in riot proneness, including the institutional breakdown theory, have been utilized in analyses of race riots in the postwar period.

Research studies on ghetto riots in the sixties have not only used the Lieberson-Silverman dichotomy of immediate precipitating events and underlying conditions but also explanations for riots similar to the deprivation buildup and institutional malfunctioning theories. Perhaps most prominently, a variety of deprivation explanations have been developed, some proposing that riots are most likely to occur where the *absolute* deprivation of blacks is the greatest, some proposing that riots occur where black deprivation *relative* to whites is greatest, and still others proposing that riots occur where black deprivation *relative* to

[19] Ibid., p. 897.
[20] Milton Bloombaum, "The Conditions Underlying Race Riots as Portrayed by Multidimensional Scalogram Analysis: A Reanalysis of Lieberson and Silverman's Data," *American Sociological Review,* **33** (February 1968), 76–91.

whites is the least if rapid black gains have resulted in a narrowing of the gap.

One of the first systematic attempts to relate empirical data, in this case census data on city characteristics, to the occurrence of riots made use of several of these ideas in developing explanations for ghetto riots, although for the most part the explanations are left relatively undeveloped.[21] Studying over 200 riots in the turbulent period betwen 1964 and 1968, Downes analyzed the relationship between riot occurrence and the socioeconomic characteristics of American cities, including cities which had not experienced riots. In contrast to the Lieberson-Silverman study of the earlier 1913–1963 riots, Downes found population shifts to be directly related to occurrence of ghetto rioting. Riot cities were more likely than nonriot cities to be large cities, declining in population, and densely populated. Support for an anomie, or normlessness, explanation for rioting, left undeveloped, was suggested by the finding that riot cities were more likely than nonriot cities to have seen a significant increase in nonwhite population and to have a relatively larger proportion of non-whites, such factors being seen as disruptive of the "ongoing social order" and accentuating "existing problems in the black community."[22] Moreover, in an examination of riots in larger cities, those over 100,000 in population, White found similar relationships between total population, density, percent nonwhite, and a measure of riot occurrence.[23]

An absolute deprivation explanation, again relatively undeveloped, was suggested by Downes' findings on education, income, and unemployment. Although black and white figures

[21] Bryan T. Downes, "Social and Political Characteristics of Riot Cities: A Comparative Study," *Blacks in the United States,* ed. Norval D. Glenn and Charles M. Bonjean (San Francisco: Chandler, 1969), pp. 427–443.

[22] Ibid., p. 436.

[23] John G. White, "Riots and Theory Building," *Riots and Rebellion,* ed. Louis H. Masotti and Don R. Bowen (Beverly Hills: Sage Publications, 1968), pp. 157–166.

were not reported separately, riot cities were found to have relatively higher unemployment rates, higher proportions of poor-quality housing, and lower levels of educational attainment. In addition to likelihood of riot occurrence, the intensity level of the riots (whether they were minor or major) was found to be correlated in a similar way with these measures of socioeconomic deprivation. Surprisingly, examination of crude measures of political representation and governmental effectiveness revealed that riot cities were more likely than nonriot cities to have municipal governmental structures potentially more responsive to interest groups within the electorate, lending no support to the institutional malfunctioning explanation previously offered by Silverman and Lieberson to explain variations in riot proneness.[24]

Touching on several explanations for riots in his analysis and drawing on his limited and uncontrolled correlational data, Downes concludes with a special emphasis on variations in cities, particularly on absolute deprivation. As social and economic conditions worsen, a city's riot potential increases:

> Indeed, one might hypothesize that collective racial violence is likely to occur in a municipality when a certain *threshold* in some of these conditions is reached—that is, when environmental conditions within a particular city reach a particularly "explosive" point. This implies that hostile outbursts occur largely because a set of contextual conditions become such that strains arise which further the spread of hostile beliefs among individuals in the black community.[25]

In point of fact, a number of examinations of rioting in the sixties, including a number of governmental reports, have stressed the deprived conditions of black Americans as the basic conditions underlying the development of recent rioting, although

[24] Downes, "Social and Political Characteristics of Riot Cities: A Comparative Study," pp. 436–442.
[25] Ibid., pp. 442–443.

some such analyses (in contrast to the researcher just noted) neglect the possibility that conditions in nonriot cities might have been as bad as those in cities with riots. For example, in looking at pre-riot conditions, the *Report of the National Advisory Commission on Civil Disorders* primarily stressed socioeconomic characteristics, working with a fairly explicit disadvantage or absolute deprivation explanation of riot occurrence. Examining background conditions in 20 cities where riots had occurred during the first nine months of 1967, Commission researchers found that black urbanites residing in ghettos were deprived across the board, when compared with whites in the surrounding area.[26] In each city surveyed median educational attainment and income figures were lower for blacks than for whites; blacks were more likely to be unemployed and in unskilled jobs than whites; and blacks found themselves paying relatively more for housing and receiving less in terms of housing quality. The numerous grievances of ghetto residents in riot areas were systematically cataloged in detail.

In addition to the stress on the relatively disadvantaged condition of black urbanites in riot areas, yet another explanatory theme in the Commission report emphasized certain pre-riot governmental conditions generally comparable to those described in the Lieberson-Silverman study of early twentieth-century riots and the Downes examination of later riots: the malfunctioning of existing mechanisms, especially local government structures, in resolving the grievances of ghetto residents. Although all forms of municipal government were found in the 20 riot cities closely examined in the Commission report (limited to those with ghetto violence in 1967), serious problems were observed in local government structure and functioning:

> In a substantial minority of instances, a combination of at-large election of legislators and a "weak-mayor" system

[26] *Report of the National Advisory Commission on Civil Disorders,* pp. 136–137.

resulted in fragmentation of political responsibility and accountability. The proportion of Negroes in government was substantially smaller than the Negro proportion of the population. Almost all the cities had a formal grievance machinery, but typically it was regarded by most Negroes interviewed as ineffective, and generally ignored.[27]

These findings led to a conclusion similar to that of Lieberson and Silverman: that across-the-board political impotence on the part of black urbanites was a significant underlying condition in cities torn by riots. Reflected in the weakness of formal grievance machinery, such a factor was seen as a critical riot-fostering condition.

Although the emphasis on variations in underlying socioeconomic conditions has characterized much research on riot occurrence, and makes sense both in conceptual and common-sense terms, we have long felt an uneasiness about explanatory approaches giving exclusive emphasis to such factors. In fact, research studies emphasizing variation in deprivation among urban localities sometimes present data that point toward a conclusion, usually not emphasized in the results, that ghetto conditions relative to whites were rather bad, that serious deprivation existed, in virtually every American ghetto, including ghettos that saw little in the way of interracial violence. Variations in that deprivation seemed less important than the extent of deprivation everywhere. The questions then are: Were not ghetto conditions so bad nationwide, prior to the beginning of the riots in the early sixties, that a deprivation threshold ("explosive conditions") had been reached in virtually all urban ghettos? Why then did rioting occur in some cities and not in others? And why did some cities have minor riots and some more serious riots?

Thus examination of census data for many American ghettos, small and large, revealed that black Americans were consistently

[27] Ibid., p. 137.

deprived in socioeconomic terms, relative to whites in surrounding areas. Specific evidence on the malfunctioning of formal grievance resolution mechanisms, including governmental mechanisms, was not as accessible, but what was available suggested that black Americans in only a small number of ghettos had governmental representation approaching adequacy. Furthermore, only a small minority were being aided in the early sixties by War-on-Poverty or related governmental programs, even in model cities such as Detroit with well-publicized aid programs. In addition, opinion data collected by pollsters in the early sixties pointed up the pervasiveness of a sense of deprivation among black Americans in all parts of the country.[28]

Our hunch about the universality and endemic character of deprivation and grievances in America's ghettos can be related to the arguments made by recent exponents of the riot ideology approach, an explanation developed by researchers working with materials collected after the 1965 Watts riot in Los Angeles. Working mainly with postriot attitudinal data for this one major ghetto, coupled with impressions of other riot areas, Tomlinson made the following relatively speculative argument:

> Riots have occurred in cities with every type of administrative structure. They have occurred in model cities . . . in cities receiving relatively large sums of poverty money, and ones receiving relatively small amounts . . . in cities with relatively high Negro employment and wage rates (Detroit) and in cities with relatively low rates (Watts). . . . Clearly what produces riots is not related to the political or economic differences between cities. What produces riots is the shared agreement by most Negro Americans that their lot in life is unacceptable, coupled with the view by a significant

[28] See the data in William Brink and Louis Harris, *The Negro Revolution in America* (New York: Simon and Schuster, 1964), especially pp. 48–73, 190–201.

minority that riots are a legitimate and productive mode of protest.[29]

The Watts researchers were impressed by the lack of variation between riot and nonriot cities in terms of important economic and governmental conditions. Indeed, it was this very argument that Downes was explicitly attempting to refute in the previously discussed article examining the social, economic, and governmental correlates of ghetto rioting in the period between 1964 and 1968. Although the riot ideology explanation is not developed by Tomlinson beyond these brief suggestions, it does give emphasis to a neglected but apparently critical characteristic of riot cities—the existence and size of the minority of ghetto blacks who felt violence to be a legitimate and productive mode of political or protest action. We find this argument persuasive, although we would suggest that the apparently spreading riot ideology often viewed rioting not only as a method of protest but also as a tactic that might bring actual structural and political change to the cities.

Empirical support for questioning the alleged relationship between riot occurrence and variations in socioeconomic conditions has recently emerged in social science journal papers re-examining the socioeconomic correlates of rioting. Ford and Moore, for example, went a step beyond earlier analyses to examine urban demographic data specifically for *nonwhites* in relation to riot occurrence. On the whole, their findings did not support a variation-in-deprivation approach to explaining riot development.[30] Measures of nonwhite deprivation did not consistently relate to riot occurrence. Indeed, some of their findings pointed toward

[29] T. M. Tomlinson, "The Development of a Riot Ideology among Urban Negroes," *Racial Violence in the United States,* ed. Allen D. Grimshaw (Chicago: Aldine, 1969), pp. 230–231.

[30] William F. Ford and John H. Moore, "Additional Evidence on the Social Characteristics of Riot Cities," *Social Science Quarterly,* 51 (September 1970), 339–348.

an interpretation quite different from that stressing absolute deprivation. Nonwhite income was found to correlate positively with both the occurrence and intensity of rioting; the better off that nonwhites were in terms of income, the more likely their city was to have had a riot.

Furthermore, in perhaps the most exhaustive examination yet of underlying pre-riot conditions, Seymour Spilerman has taken us several steps beyond earlier assessments of the demography or ecology of rioting. Examining cities over 25,000 in population, including those that had "spontaneous" disorders between 1961 and 1968 and those that had no disorders, Spilerman first rejected the random hypothesis of an equal probability of violence in all cities.[31] Riot proneness varied greatly from city to city. "Disorders" were here defined as instances of collective black aggression involving 30 or more individuals.

On the basis of available riot data for the sixties, positive and negative reinforcement hypotheses and the geographic contagion hypothesis were also rejected or seriously questioned. With regard to the negative reinforcement thesis—that cities having had one riot would be unlikely to have another—the findings indicated that the 15 cities with riots in the 1961–1964 period were more likely than other cities to have also had a riot in the 1965–1968 period. Nor was one version of the positive reinforcement explanation—that over time increases in disorder proneness would occur primarily in those cities that had had riots in the early sixties—substantiated, for each new riot year saw a tremendous increase in the number of new riot cities, those with no prior record of rioting. Also rejected was the argument that geographic contagion uniquely explains the clustering of riot cities in certain areas, such as Michigan or New Jersey, a phenomenon noted in the report of the National Advisory Commission on Civil Disorders. Examination of clustered riots in Michigan and

[31] Seymour Spilerman, "The Causes of Racial Disturbances: A Comparison of Alternative Explanations," *American Sociological Review,* 35 (August 1970), 627–649.

Ghetto Rioting in the Sixties: Some Basic Questions

New Jersey indicated that the *size* alone of the ghettos involved in the city clusters adequately explained the contiguous grouping, without the addition of a contagion assumption.[32] The all-encompassing importance of ghetto size was here suggested; its significance will soon become evident.

Other major hypotheses about riot development, particularly those derived from explanatory theories emphasizing variation in community socioeconomic characteristics, were also systematically analyzed. We have previously discussed these explanatory frameworks in Chapter 1. Anomie (normlessness) and social disorganization approaches suggested the hypothesis that 1961–1968 riots would be more frequent in urban localities with high levels of population turnover, social disorganization, or deviance. Deprivation explanations proposed that rioting tends to occur where either absolute or relative (to whites) deprivation in material terms is high for black ghetto residents. Another variation on the deprivation approach emphasizes nearness to the objective, the narrowing gap between expectations based on attainments of the white reference group and actual reality for black urbanites; rioting would be more likely in areas where the gap is narrowing but still manifest. Yet another view of collective violence is the governmental malfunctioning perspective, which asserts that rioting is more likely to occur in localities where institutionalized channels for redress have broken down, or where representation in the government is the weakest for the dissident minority.

Spilerman reported significant correlations between indexes of relevant socioeconomic variables linked to each of these specific theories and the dependent variable, an index indicating the number of disorders in a city (ranging from 0 to 11 disorders per city). Using census materials on matters such as white and nonwhite income, education, and so forth, and figures on governmental structure, Spilerman examined basic hypotheses linked

[32] Ibid., pp. 634–639.

to the anomie, deprivation, and government malfunction explanations, using a comprehensive multivariate analysis. His correlational results, however, do not correspond with the one earlier comprehensive analysis, that of Downes, perhaps in part because Spilerman used data specifically for nonwhites. Before applying controls for such factors as black population size and region, the correlational results were similar to those of Ford and Moore, pointing to the following conclusions:

> . . . it is evident that racial disorders are more likely to occur where the level of life for the Negro is least oppressive according to objective measures. There are more disturbances where Negro disadvantage, relative to white residents, is small and where Negro attainment surpasses that of Negroes living elsewhere. Moreover, disorder-prone communities tend to have stable populations and better quality housing.[33]

However, the most striking results were yet to come. When controls for black population size and region were applied to these basic relationships between each socioeconomic indicator and the index of riot occurrence, *the relationships were reduced to little or no significance.*

With the effect of absolute black population size and region removed, all the other variables had little effect on the dependent variable, the number of riots. That is, for large ghettos taken as a group, and small ghettos taken as a group, there was *no* significant relationship between, to take one example, the nonwhite-white income ratio and riot occurrence. The critical relationship was between the size of the black population in a city and riot occurrence.[34] At least one subsequent study using

[33] Ibid., pp. 642–643.

[34] Ibid., pp. 643–645. See also Seymour Spilerman, "The Causes of Racial Disturbances: Tests of an Explanation," *American Sociological Review,* **36** (June 1971), 427–442.

controls confirmed these extraordinarily important findings; Jibou also concluded that size and region were the critical riot-determining variables.[35]

Nor was this pattern limited to riot location or frequency. Measures of riot intensity, in a subsequent analysis, also were not significantly related to the various socioeconomic variables relevant to predictions from the perspective of anomie, deprivation, and government structure theories, when controls for black population size and region were applied. Variations in living conditions for black urbanites, from one city to another, did not relate to riot intensity.[36] Black population size and region were the best predictors not only of the location of riots but also of the severity level of the riots. The larger the size of the black population the more severe the riot was likely to be, and for the period examined, riots in southern cities tended to be somewhat less destructive than in the North.

Arguing with the conclusions of researchers who did not look at the possibility of confounding variables, Spilerman comes to a very important and thought-provoking conclusion: that many of the socioeconomic characteristics found to be associated with riot-prone cities "have little to do with a community being prone to racial disorder, and are instead the incidental characteristics of cities with large Negro populations."[37] These findings are in line with the argument we outlined in Chapter 1—to the effect that universal ghetto problems are closely related to the emergence of rioting, everywhere reflected in great differentials

[35] Robert M. Jibou, "City Characteristics, Differential Stratification, and the Occurrence of Interracial Violence," *Social Science Quarterly*, 52 (December 1971), 508–520.

[36] Seymour Spilerman, "Structural Characteristics of Cities and the Severity of Racial Disorders" (Paper presented at the American Sociological Association meeting, Denver, Colorado, August 30–September 2, 1971).

[37] Spilerman, "The Causes of Racial Disturbances: A Comparison of Alternative Explanations," 645.

in social, economic, and governmental power in urban areas. One can thus argue provocatively that it is not the *unique* deprivation characteristics of certain ghettos, or the cities surrounding them, that primarily determine the seriousness of rioting, but the deprivation characteristics *common* to all black ghettos, coupled with factors like the actual number of blacks in areas where riots occur. The grievance or deprivation threshold has apparently been exceeded in every city. Moreover, there is no longer such a thing as a purely local grievance, given the omnipresence of newspapers, television, and radio in ghetto areas. The widespread existence of the mass media has often meant the rapid diffusion of what once would have been local political problems to the full view of a national black audience. In a very real sense, what happens to blacks in one ghetto, such as Harlem in New York City, happens to blacks everywhere; and successes in one area may affect the views of black Americans elsewhere.

In addition, there would seem to be a critical minimum ghetto size necessary for generating and sustaining a riot. The 261 cities with a black population of less than 1,000 reported no riots at all for the 1961–1968 period, while there were 0.12 riots per city for those cities with a black population in the neighborhood of 1,000–2,500, and so forth, up to a high of 4.9 per city for cities with a black population greater than 100,000 persons.[38] Thus the number of riots per city rises more or less systematically with increases in the numerical size of the black population.

Why is ghetto population size such a critical factor? Why does it seem to be a most important "underlying condition"? Population size relates to the origin and seriousness of riots in that larger ghettos seem likely to have (1) a greater number of violence-oriented residents, those viewing violence as a legitimate political tactic, (2) a greater resource potential for mobilizing

[38] Spilerman, "The Causes of Racial Disturbances: Tests of an Explanation," 431. Riots involving fewer than 30 participants are excluded. Our interpretation, which follows, elaborates on Spilerman's ideas.

and sustaining riots (e.g., more weapons, more potential participants, more ghetto organization of a formal and informal nature), and (3) more numerous frictional encounters between ghetto residents and white police and merchants, events historically likely to precipitate a ghetto riot.

We would argue that critical to the development of rioting has been the spread of a view among ghetto residents which condones or approves collective violence—violence seen as a legitimate and potentially productive form of political action. Nurtured and fostered by disillusionment with the tactics of electoral politics and nonviolence, the growth of such a view of collective violence, coupled with a corresponding rise in black pride and militancy, might also be linked in part to the general influence of the communications media in presenting the arguments of militant advocates and with regard to later riots, to assessments (however correct) of the beneficial political consequences of earlier riots, such as those in Harlem, Bedford-Stuyvesant, and Watts. In addition, larger ghettos can better provide what seem to be the essential resources for mobilizing and sustaining a riot, particularly a serious riot. A certain number of male ghetto residents below the age of forty seems to be crucial to sustaining collective violence; and the extent and density of the organization and networks of ghetto residents, formal and informal, probably varies with ghetto size, also entering into the mobilization and sustaining of a riot. Yet another very important factor related to population size is interracial friction. The larger the ghetto, the greater the number of ghetto residents, police, and merchants. The more police and ghetto residents, the more police-resident encounters, which are potentially riot-precipitating events.

In addition to size, Spilerman found that the regional factor was also predictive of rioting for the period he examined. Given the variation in southern and northern racial traditions, an acute observer would probably have predicted the correlation which Spilerman found between region and riot occurrence: in the 1961–1968 period ghetto revolts were less likely in southern cities than in northern cities.[39] The development of violence orientations would be less likely, or come more slowly, in the South than in the North, given the history of far-reaching slavery, segregation, and repression in that region. But the South may have been changing in the late sixties, for Spilerman reported not only that the "distribution of outbreaks in the South has been converging over time to the pattern which has been characteristic of the non-South" but also that numerical size of the black population in cities was the major variable affecting the distribution of riots in the South, paralleling the results for the North.[40]

Black Perspectives and Underlying Conditions

In the quest for satisfactory explanations of ghetto rioting, the predominant focus of empirical researchers zeroing in on underlying conditions has been on demographic indicators, coupled on occasion with measures of government structure. Yet many general approaches to pre-riot conditions have made certain problematical sociopsychological assumptions. Examples of this can be found particularly in analyses stressing the relationship between deprivation, whether absolute or relative, and riot occurrence. One important and common assumption appears to be that where there is greater "objective" deprivation for blacks relative to whites—for example, as measured by income differentials—there will be a more intensive grievance ideology. Variations in objective conditions across riot and nonriot cities have been assumed to be linked to variations in perception of deprivation across the same cities. While this may seem to some a reasonable assumption, there is as yet little systematic evidence to support it.

[39] Spilerman, "The Causes of Racial Disturbances: A Comparison of Alternative Explanations," 643.
[40] Spilerman, "The Causes of Racial Disturbances: Tests of an Explanation," 439–440.

Ghetto Rioting in the Sixties: Some Basic Questions

Not that the issue of perceptions has been entirely neglected. Some attention to perception of conditions and intensity of grievances in regard to riot areas has been provided in the *Report of the National Advisory Commission on Civil Disorders.* Based on postriot interviews and other field research on 20 cities which had riots in 1967, Commission researchers concluded that there was a widespread consensus among riot-area residents on the following expressed grievances: (1) at the first level of intensity and extensiveness—police malpractice, unemployment and underemployment, inadequate housing conditions; and (2) at the second level of intensity and extensiveness—inadequate educational systems, poor recreational facilities, and ineffective political structures and grievance mechanisms.[41] One might conclude from these materials that many if not most black Americans in riot areas were well aware of and concerned about the objective deprivation delineated in the now common demographic analyses of ghetto conditions. Furthermore, the sociopsychological link between actual conditions of socioeconomic deprivation and intensity of grievance ideology is at least suggested, if not demonstrated, by materials such as these.

Yet the problem remains that these grievances may have been as strongly held in cities that had no riots. The link between objective deprivation and intensity or extensiveness of grievances held is not proven here, since this would require not only surveys in riot and nonriot cities but also a relating of actual conditions to grievance levels. One limited research study commissioned by the National Advisory Commission and published after the final *Report* did shed some light on the question of perceived grievance levels in riot and nonriot cities. Studying 10 riot and 5 nonriot cities in the North, for the years up to and including 1967, the researchers found no systematic differences in levels of grievances between black samples in these two groups of cities. They concluded that their data did not substantiate a local

[41] *Report of the National Advisory Commission on Civil Disorders,* pp. 143–148.

determinism model of riot occurrence, at least not in terms of these particular grievance factors.[42] Although much additional research as yet remains to be done on these sociopsychological questions, including the relationship of perceived grievance levels to objective deprivation conditions, in the light of current research data on both objective socioeconomic conditions and perception of deprivation conditions, one might well reject the local determinism theory, perhaps concluding that the critical grievance perception threshold has been exceeded in virtually every urban ghetto.[43]

The Issue of Shifts in Black Perspectives

The research examined thus far, demographic and attitudinal, is generally bound by the limitation of working with city data for one point in time. With few exceptions demographic analyses have relied on data for the year 1960, the date of the national census prior to recent ghetto rioting. Similarly, survey data on ghetto attitudes have generally been collected for only one point in time. Little analysis beyond the impressionistic level has been devoted to the issue of shifts over time, either in black conditions or in black perspectives on those conditions, whether in regard to such important factors as grievances perceived, legitimacy of existing governmental arrangements, or perspectives on violence.

An emphasis on longitudinal shifts in perspectives within black communities seems to be important to a number of argu-

---

[42] Peter R. Rossi and Richard A. Berk, "Local Political Leadership and Popular Discontent in the Ghetto," *The Annals of the American Academy of Political and Social Science,* **391** (September 1970), 113–115. See also Peter H. Rossi et al., "Between White and Black: The Faces of American Institutions in the Ghetto," *Supplemental Studies for the National Advisory Commission on Civil Disorders* (Washington, D.C.: U.S. Government Printing Office, 1968), pp. 74ff.

[43] See also Thomas F. Pettigrew, *Racially Separate or Together?* (New York: McGraw-Hill, 1971), pp. 148–152.

ments about the emergence of rioting. From one point of view, that emphasizing riot ideology, one might argue that a growing orientation toward violence was an important part of this shift in perspectives—a growth particularly important for the larger ghettos, where even small percentages mean relatively large numbers. Further, such a shift may have been accompanied by increased questioning of the legitimacy of the power exercised by established groups and by increases in racial solidarity and the desire for community self-determination. Factors such as these are not directly tapped in the usual examination of an assortment of community conditions, such as median incomes, unemployment, substandard housing, or methods of electing councilmen. Yet they may be essential to riot development.

Much has been written about the views of black Americans in recent years, so one might initially expect an excursion into longitudinal shifts in black attitudes to be relatively easy. Ideally, one might examine the attitudes of ghetto residents in riot communities at several points in time to see if they had shifted in the direction of a greater emphasis, for example, on the legitimacy of violence. One might also wish to examine shifting black reactions to the operation of local grievance resolution mechanisms. Such longitudinal shifts might then be compared with changes in perspectives in nonriot cities. Unfortunately, as noted previously, published data allowing for comparison of attitudes in riot and nonriot areas are not as yet available.

Some might argue that this lack of specific information is not particularly serious, at least from the vantage point of those emphasizing the emergence of riot or grievance ideologies on a nationwide basis. From this point of view, the critical riot-precipitating factor is a posited nationwide shift in black perspectives over time, coupled with the absolute number of blacks in specific riot ghettos who hold to such views. One might thus examine survey data available on a nationwide basis.

Yet even on this broader issue there are remarkably little data, particularly on black views prior to 1963, whether for the nation taken as a whole or for more limited geographical areas. Prior to 1963 what is available seems to be limited to the World War II period—and that material is not based on national surveys. Predominantly white, social scientists and pollsters have perhaps expressed their own racial biases by ignoring until recently minority views on any issue, including civil rights and related political issues. Such a state of affairs makes systematic examination of the growth of violence or grievance ideologies—or other race-related issues for that matter—virtually impossible, especially with regard to the crucial pre-riot period running from the fifties to the early 1960s.

Nevertheless, it may be of some heuristic value to explore briefly the survey data that are available on black attitudes for the forties and to compare these data in a crude way with more satisfactory survey materials for several points in time during the sixties. We will here confine ourselves to questions impinging directly or indirectly on the issue of the legitimacy of existing political arrangements and on the related issue of violent tactics directed at altering existing arrangements—those with some rough degree of comparability.

To what extent have black Americans over the last few decades been committed to the national government and its actions? On the basis of data collected from soldiers and civilians in the forties, one might propose that less than wholehearted commitment to the American system has long been characteristic of a sizable black minority. Some evidence of this was revealed in an extensive survey of several thousand black soldiers during World War II. At that time one fifth did not feel that the war was as much their affair as anyone else's.[44] When the black responses were contrasted with those of white soldiers, blacks were much less likely to "express a sense of identification with the war or to endorse idealistic views of the war."[45] Explanations of this attitude focused on discrimination. Although there is little evidence

[44] Samuel A. Stouffer et al., *Adjustment During Army Life,* Volume I of *The American Soldier* (New York: Wiley Science Editions, 1965), p. 508.
[45] Ibid., p. 507.

of a transfer of commitment to a new national authority in these answers, indirect questioning of the legitimacy of established political arrangements is reflected. Ghetto residents back home, if one can extrapolate from a limited 1943 Harlem postriot survey, were less enthusiastic about the war than black soldiers; two thirds of those interviewed felt that blacks generally were not "all out for this war."[46]

Looking at the sixties (data on these issues for the fifties are virtually nonexistent[47]), one finds that the questions asked about U.S. military action were much more extreme than those asked in the forties. Yet there appears to have been an increase in negativism, at least after 1966. In a 1963 nationwide survey, before the 1964 riots in Harlem and Bedford-Stuyvesant, just under one tenth of the black respondents took the relatively extreme position that the United States was not worth fighting for even in the event of a major war.[48] By 1966 the proportion had dropped a little, to one seventeenth; by 1969 it had increased again, to one seventh.[49] Surveys in two large urban ghettos found substantially more questioning. In Detroit and Newark postriot surveys (1967), self-reported rioters (39 percent and 53 percent respectively) were much more likely than nonrioters to see this country as not worth fighting for; however, even nonrioters (16

[46] Kenneth B. Clark, "Group Violence: A Preliminary Study of the Attitudinal Pattern of Its Acceptance and Rejection: A Study of the 1943 Harlem Riot," *The Journal of Social Psychology*, **19** (1944), 319–337.

[47] One exception to this comment about the fifties is the series of surveys done under the auspices of Robin Williams and his associates. However, the data are for only a few cities and do not touch on the issues we are concerned with here. See Robin M. Williams, *Strangers Next Door* (Englewood Cliffs, N.J.: Prentice-Hall, 1964), pp. 223–310.

[48] Brink and Harris, *The Negro Revolution*, p. 61. Brink and Harris add that even "among the majority who would fight, their answers sometimes revealed reservations."

[49] William Brink and Louis Harris, *Black and White* (New York: Simon and Schuster, 1967), pp. 274–275; "Report from Black America," *Newsweek*, June 30, 1969, p. 19.

percent in Detroit and 28 percent in Newark) in these large ghettos were more likely to be negative than blacks in general.[50]

Another rough measure of the degree of legitimacy attributed to the existing system can be seen in black support for extreme separatism for the sixties; unfortunately, no surveys were conducted on this issue in earlier decades. In a 1963 nationwide survey 4 percent expressed support for a separate state in the South or in Africa for blacks.[51] Five years later in another nationwide survey, the proportion supporting separate states or a separate country outside the United States as a solution to racial strife was 8 percent.[52] And a 1969 Gallup survey found an even larger proportion of a black sample supporting the idea of a separate black nation in the United States—one fifth.[53] These responses, taken together with replies to questions about support for the United States in a major war, point to the suggestion that an apparently growing minority of blacks had by the late sixties become relatively extreme in their questioning of existing national political authority. Compared to the responses in the forties, these views may reflect a long-term change in such extreme questioning, although the data are such that no firm conclusions can be drawn.

What can we ascertain about black attitudes toward various governmental agencies? Was there a longitudinal change in black attitudes toward the federal government, local government officials, or the police before or during the decade of the sixties? Again we lack data for the decade prior to 1963. For the sixties, with regard to the federal government, there seems to have been a shift. In a 1963 nationwide poll eight in ten black Americans felt the federal government had been more helpful than harmful in the equal rights cause. By 1966 the figure had dropped to

[50] *Report of the National Advisory Commission on Civil Disorders,* p. 135.

[51] Brink and Harris, *The Negro Revolution in America,* p. 119.

[52] Joe R. Feagin, "White Separatists and Black Separatists: A Comparative Analysis," *Social Problems,* **19** (Fall 1971), 167–180.

[53] *Newsweek,* "Report from Black America," p. 20.

seven in ten.[54] By 1969, in part reflecting the advent of a "benign neglect" Republican administration, the figure decreased to one quarter.[55] In 1963 much larger proportions were dissatisfied with the actions of Congress and state governments than with the federal government: barely half saw Congress as more helpful than harmful, while only one third viewed state governments as more helpful than harmful. These figures may well reflect nation-wide increases in black dissatisfaction since the fifties, but we can only speculate on this point. In the later 1966 and 1969 nationwide surveys large proportions still expressed political dissatisfaction. However, in 1966 the proportion favorable increased to 60 percent for the Congress and 42 percent for state governments, with decreases reported in the subsequent 1969 survey (to 52 percent and 36 percent).[56] Thus there was no linear increase in questioning.

Perhaps more important was the apparent growth in questioning of local government agencies and their enforcement arms, the local police, over the decade of the sixties. While we have been unable to find materials on black attitudes toward local government over time, we did find that, of all the branches of local establishments, the police force seems to have drawn the greatest black criticism.[57] Given the general character of riot-precipitating events, this is an extraordinarily important point. By the time of a 1966 nationwide survey, only 26 percent of black Americans felt the police were more helpful than harmful to Negro rights, and 41 percent were uncertain.[58] Continuing negative assessments of the police were also reflected in a 1969 *Newsweek* poll (with only 25 percent seeing the police as more

[54] Brink and Harris, *Black and White,* p. 238.
[55] Peter Goldman, *Report from Black America* (New York: Simon and Schuster, 1970), p. 256.
[56] Ibid., pp. 256–257.
[57] Some limited data are available on this issue. *Report of the National Advisory Commission on Civil Disorders,* p. 135; Nathan Cohen, ed., *The Los Angeles Riots* (New York: Praeger, 1970).
[58] Brink and Harris, *Black and White,* p. 234.

helpful than harmful). By the time of a 1970 Harris poll the following extremely negative view of the police was found:

> Only 20% believe that many local police apply the law equally; 62% feel the cops are against blacks. By a 73%–to–12% margin, blacks believe local police are dishonest; by a similar 67%–to–18%, they feel police are "more interested in cracking black heads than in stopping crime."[59]

By the end of the decade a positive view of the police could be located only among a small minority of black Americans.[60]

Examination of the limited survey data available leads us to the following limited and tentative conclusions about black perspectives and possible shifts in those perspectives: (1) Both in the forties and in the sixties a small but important minority of black Americans were weak in their commitment and loyalty to the American system. (2) During the sixties there was an apparent decrease in loyalty to the American system, manifested in an uneven increase in unwillingness to fight for the United States and in support for relatively extreme separatist solutions to the political dilemma. (3) During the sixties black Americans became increasingly critical of the federal government and the local police, while large proportions remained negative in their assessments of Congress and state governments.

Was support for violence also growing among black Americans —support for fighting or rioting as weapons in the struggle for self-determination? Again, surveys did not deal with this issue for the *critical decade* prior to the sixties. Some recent survey evidence does suggest that there may have been an increase in the proportion of black Americans oriented to violence, at least between 1963 and 1970. In reply to a question about whether

[59] "The Black Mood: More Militant, More Hopeful, More Determined," *Time,* April 6, 1970, p. 28.

[60] For a detailed review of surveys on black views of the police, see Harlan Hahn and Joe R. Feagin, "Riot Precipitating Police Practices: Attitudes in Urban Ghettos," *Phylon* **31** (Summer 1970), 183–193.

equal rights could be won without violence, the proportion of black Americans confident that nonviolence would be sufficient declined in nationwide surveys between 1963 and 1970, while the proportion saying violence would probably be necessary increased from 22 percent to 31 percent over this seven-year period.[61] Interim 1966 and 1969 surveys suggest caution in extrapolating trends, since the proportions in those surveys were 21 percent for violence.[62] However, in a 1970 Harris survey only one in four black respondents was willing to say violence should be avoided at all costs.[63]

Indirect evidence on shifts in violence support comes from several questions asked in the 1943 postriot survey in Harlem. Comparison of these 1943 responses with those to postriot surveys in the sixties lends some support to the argument that there has been a shift among black Americans in the proportion condoning violence over the last few decades. When Harlemites were asked what they thought of the riot there, 30 percent accepted or condoned the riot in some way.[64] Assessing potential riot results, one fifth of the 60 respondents interviewed felt the outcome would be more beneficial than harmful, while another third were either uncertain or expected no change; about four in ten expected the consequences to be more harmful than bene-

[61] Brink and Harris, *The Negro Revolution,* pp. 206–207; "The Black Mood," p. 29.

[62] Goldman, *Report from Black America,* p. 246. It should be noted that the 1969 poll was done by a different pollster. The 1963, 1966, and 1970 polls were all done by Louis Harris.

[63] "The Black Mood," *Time,* p. 29. Further evidence for the possible growth of support for violence in the early sixties can be found in surveys of large urban ghettos. A postriot survey after a major 1964 riot in New York found just under one fifth of those surveyed felt blacks would have to use riots to win equal rights; in a late 1967 survey limited to 15 urban ghettos, just over a third of the sample supported violence as necessary to the achievement of black objectives. Joe R. Feagin, "Social Sources of Support for Violence and Nonviolence in a Negro Ghetto," *Social Problems,* 15 (Fall 1968), 432–441; *Fortune,* January 1968, p. 148.

[64] Clark, "Group Violence," 324–331.

ficial. In the sixties substantially larger proportions of black Americans viewed the riots as having beneficial effects in regard to the black quest for equality. Interviews after the 1965 Watts riot indicated that substantially more than 30 percent accepted or condoned the riot. Specifically, 43 percent of the men and 35 percent of the women there felt the riot would help the black cause, while 23 percent and 19 percent, respectively, felt it would hurt.[65] When asked about its main effects, nearly 60 percent of the sample thought the main effects would be very or somewhat beneficial, with only one quarter saying the main effects would be very or somewhat harmful. In a 1966 nationwide survey of blacks, in the North and South, no less than 34 percent felt the prior riots had helped the black cause, while 20 percent felt they had hurt.[66] And later in the sixties, in a 1969 Gallup poll, 40 percent of those interviewed saw the riots as more helpful than harmful, while 29 percent were of the opposite opinion.[67]

Conclusion

By 1970 hundreds of ghetto riots had taken place in numerous American cities, with participation reaching into the hundreds of thousands of black Americans, arrests into the tens of thousands, and injuries and deaths into the thousands. While the decade of the sixties did not see riots as serious, at least in terms of human casualties, as the 1863 antidraft riot of Irish Americans in New York City or the 1917 East St. Louis riot of white workers, it did encompass a serious era in the history of collective political violence in America. And toward the end of the 1960s there were signs of shifts in collective violence by black Americans toward southern cities and school-centered situations.

In this chapter we have probably raised more questions than

[65] Raymond J. Murphy and James M. Watson, *The Structure of Discontent* (Los Angeles: UCLA Institute of Government and Public Affairs, 1967), p. 35.

[66] Brink and Harris, *Black and White,* p. 264.

[67] "Report from Black America," *Time,* p. 23.

we have answered. Not the least of these problems is the definition of a riot. Many analysts of riots have simply used the term and avoided defining what a "riot" is, whether in regard to historical violence or recent ghetto events. One can search in vain for a good systematic delineation of rioting. Examination of several leading social science textbooks and handbooks revealed to us that, while specific riots are discussed, no explicit definition of what a riot is, or is not, has apparently been attempted. For example, leading textbooks on collective behavior, those by Lang and Lang and by Turner and Killian, neglect to define a riot, and collective behavior articles in important handbooks such as the *Handbook of Modern Sociology* also ignore this definitional issue.[68]

The same seems to be more or less true of the extensive literature that has developed in regard to the "ghetto riots" in the sixties. The most common terms applied to these instances of collective violence have been "riot," "civil disorder," and "hostile outburst," terms usually left undefined or vaguely specified. Only a few have specified, for example, just how many individuals need to be involved in order to define an event as riotous. Even among these there is no agreement. One important data-gathering organization has chosen 4 individuals as the requisite minimum. Others have suggested 30 or 100 persons as the criterion. In addition, some authors apparently view all instances of black group violence as riots; others have indicated that spontaneous events are what they have in mind, with collective violence growing out of demonstrations being excluded. And most analysts implicitly limit ghetto rioting to black violence involving groups of individuals. Yet these are not the only dimensions of riots which need to be addressed. Other important dimensions are

[68] See Ralph H. Turner and Lewis M. Killian, *Collective Behavior* (Englewood Cliffs, N.J.: Prentice-Hall, 1957); Kurt Lang and Gladys E. Lang, *Collective Dynamics* (New York: Thomas Y. Crowell, 1961); Ralph H. Turner, "Collective Behavior," *Handbook of Modern Sociology*, ed. Robert E. L. Faris (Chicago: Rand McNally, 1964), pp. 382–425.

suggested by the following questions: Was the violence racially motivated? Did it challenge civil authority? Did it involve attacks against the property or persons of another group? Were the individuals acting in concert or simply as isolated individuals? Did the violence involve police forces?

Admittedly, some traditional conceptual labels have been applied to ghetto riots, most notably Smelser's term "hostile outburst." To illustrate, Downes views riots in these terms, a riot being seen as "the mobilization of individuals for action under a hostile belief."[69] Yet this brief definition only tells us that we are looking at groups forming in regard to a vaguely conceived hostile belief. It suggests little about the numbers involved, the motivation involved, the direction of the action, or the levels and types of group action.

In our review of the empirical literature on collective violence in urban ghettos, the most systematic and satisfactory definition of riots, actually termed "race-related civil disorders," is that of the Civil Disorder Clearinghouse—a definition cited earlier in this chapter. The working definition of the Civil Disorder Clearinghouse is quite explicit, emphasizing as it does the collective character of disorders, the direction and type of collective action (e.g., damage to persons or property, defiance of civil authority), the number involved (4 or more persons acting in concert), and the character of the collective action (arising from racial tensions). With the addition of the stipulation that instances of "race-related civil disorders" involving black ghettoites are the focus of this particular analysis, this might provide a good working definition of "ghetto riots."

Yet even this framework does not include the important dimension of police violence and the involvement of established authorities, which in our view are essential to defining a ghetto riot. Mutual coercion seems to be a critical feature of ghetto riots. To raise yet another issue, we would note that neither

[69] Downes, "Social and Political Characteristics of Riot Cities: A Comparative Study," p. 427.

Ghetto Rioting in the Sixties: Some Basic Questions

the definition nor the subsequent analysis of riots by the Civil Disorder Clearinghouse delves into the question of levels of rioting. When is a riot to be deemed serious? The *Report of the National Advisory Commission on Civil Disorders* does provide a useful trichotomy with regard to both the involvement of authorities and riot levels. Three levels were depicted there—minor, serious, and major—each being linked to the level of police reaction (local police, state police, National Guard, federal troops), as well as to the level (looting, arson, sniping) and duration of ghetto resident violence.

Taking into consideration these various factors, we would propose for future empirical research the following definition of a "ghetto riot" (or "black riot"):

A racially motivated incident involving mutual and collective coercion within the political context of a local black ghetto area, characterized on the part of black dissidents by violence toward persons or property and the defiance of civil authority, and by the violent reaction of established white authorities seeking to regain exclusive control over the means of coercion. "Collective" refers to the actions of four or more persons acting in concert; "racially motivated" refers both to the identification of participants with salient racial groups and the defining of white property and white persons as the relevant targets by dissidents.

This operational definition of a ghetto riot is one which we have tried to keep in mind throughout this book. A basic problem we have faced again and again is associated with the aforementioned problem of levels of rioting. Most empirical analyses of riots or rioters do not explicitly raise this issue. We have sometimes been faced with using data on riots with the degree of seriousness left completely unspecified. But it is our general impression that most analysts focus on what the National Advisory Commission has called "serious" or "major" riots—those involving substantial looting, arson, numbers of police, and lasting for several days. Thus, much of the analysis of causes, character, and consequences of rioting in this book is based heavily on materials drawn from the more serious instances of ghetto violence.

Turning to the issue of underlying conditions, we have come to the conclusion that *variations* in the socioeconomic conditions of black Americans, in deprivation, were not linked directly either to riot occurrence or to riot intensity. In a careful study, Spilerman found that by far the most significant correlates of ghetto rioting were the absolute size of the black population in cities and regional location. Drawing on this finding and the riot ideology approach of Tomlinson and others, we have suggested that by the time of the riots a grievance threshold had been exceeded in virtually every urban ghetto. The limited survey data on grievances perceived also offer some limited support for this contention.

Indeed, there does seem to be a critical population size necessary to riot development. During the 1961–1968 period Spilerman reported that the 261 cities with a black population of less than 1,000 experienced no riots. Riot intensity or seriousness has also been linked empirically to black population size. The greater likelihood of rioting (and more intense rioting) in larger ghetto areas seems to result from the more numerous potentially precipitating events, the greater resource potential for mobilizing and sustaining a riot, and the greater number of blacks oriented to collective violence as a way of forcing change in the American system.

The final section of this chapter raised in an exploratory way the issue of black perspectives as predisposing riot conditions, contrasted with the socioeconomic conditions usually emphasized. There is a severe lack of evidence, both in regard to cross-sectional comparisons of black perspectives in riot and nonriot cities and especially in regard to critical longitudinal shifts in black views. Examination of black views of the American government did suggest that a significant and perhaps growing minority of blacks were quite weak in their commitment to the American system. We also found some data suggesting a shift in the proportion of blacks condoning or approving violence. However, we are well aware of the problems involved in assessing these attitudinal data. In addition to the more obvious problems of data absence and question comparability, there is the chicken-and-egg problem. It seems likely that black views on these various issues both shaped, and were shaped by, riot developments. What we do wish to emphasize here is the importance of examining shifts in black perspectives in thoroughgoing presentations of underlying conditions.

Although all of these problems relative to the issue of underlying conditions seem important, as we have noted previously perhaps the most crucial of all problems relates to the role and perspectives of established authorities. Relatively little research attention has been given to this aspect of predisposing riot conditions. Some have examined a few rough indicators of governmental structure and responsiveness. But Spilerman's sophisticated analysis found no relationship between these measures of governmental structure and either the occurrence or intensity of rioting when controls were applied for Negro population size and region.

Nevertheless, this problem needs to be pursued beyond these few rough measures. Indeed, some evidence indicates that there is a significant correlation between the intensity of the rioting and the use of the police or the National Guard in the riot years 1967–1968, although the more important question in relation to predisposing conditions concerns the actions of the police *prior* to the emergence of the rioting.[70] To our knowledge, no one has yet looked at the character of police patrolling practices, which often generate frictional encounters, or at a variety of relevant police practices and attitudes and the emergence or intensity of

[70] See the relevant data in the various appendices of the *Report of the National Advisory Commission on Civil Disorders.*

ghetto rioting. Moreover, the extent of merchant discrimination and the character of merchant attitudes might also be important variables for future examinations of riot correlates.

In conclusion, then, we wish to emphasize that we would have preferred a more balanced presentation directly emphasizing the important role of established authorities—their practices and perspectives—in predisposing populations to riot, but we could not because of the limitations in the available data. However, in subsequent chapters we will chart the role that civil authorities, and particularly the police, have played in the immediate events frequently precipitating ghetto riots.

4

The Development of Ghetto Riots: Precipitants and Patterns

The historical overlapping of violent and nonviolent actions by black Americans has led to much confusion and not a few misinterpretations of the character of the recent black thrust for equality. Since ghetto riots followed and sometimes accompanied the development of nonviolent protests within a relatively short span of time, without further reflection many white Americans equated "violence" and "nonviolent demonstrations." Violence was commonly regarded as synonymous with the characteristic black protest style. This misperception probably has had unfortunate consequences for the comprehension of both ghetto revolts and nonviolent protest demonstrations.

On the one hand, the widespread expectation that peaceful demonstrations will inevitably evolve into collective violence has often impelled white citizens and officials to neglect the objectives of such protests, the grievances they represent, and the desire of protest leaders to negotiate for the amelioration of confrontation-spawning circumstances. On the other hand, the instinctive equation of violent upheavals and peaceful protests also has obscured the intentions and the meaning of ghetto rioting. It seems to us that most recent occurrences of ghetto rioting have been grounded in similar types of grievances, but they generally reflected more than attempts to protest or to focus the attention of white leaders on ghetto problems. Ghetto revolts

141

often have seemed to encompass a relatively direct assault upon established authorities and an effort to have a major impact on existing arrangements and processes. The propensity to attribute the characteristics of ghetto rioting to nonviolent protest movements and to ascribe certain features of nonviolent demonstrations to violent upheavals, therefore, has probably clouded the understanding of both types of events.

A major difficulty has arisen because of the chronological proximity of ghetto revolts and nonviolent protests. A common and erroneous belief is that serious ghetto outbreaks typically emerged out of, or were closely associated with, organized protest demonstrations. Yet the incidents that precipitated ghetto rioting much more often than not reflected other circumstances, which we will consider in the next section of this chapter.

Final Precipitating Incidents

One of the most salient features of recent ghetto riots is the final precipitating incident, the specific and immediate occurrence that appears to ignite the outbreak of collective violence. Although many analysts have regarded these riots as an instantaneous outpouring of deciduous discontent, few have resorted to the thesis of spontaneous combustion to explain this outpouring. And since the immediate events that have commonly played a triggering role provide readily available material for causative explanations, emphasis has been placed upon precipitating incidents in numerous discussions of the ghetto riots.

In what is probably the first major attempt to grapple with the nature of the immediate precipitants of American race riots, Lieberson and Silverman have emphasized the distinctive character of the events which commonly ignited racial violence:

> The immediate precipitants of race riots almost always involve some confrontation between the groups in which members of one race are deeply "wronged" in fact or in rumor by members of the other. Precipitants tend to be transgres-

sions of strongly held mores by a representative of the other group.[1]

Final precipitating incidents, therefore, are viewed as interactive events of an exceptionally provocative and inflammatory character—events that involve the violation of important racial taboos.

Reviewing and analyzing 76 race riots in the half century between 1913 and 1963, these researchers carefully classified the immediate precipitants of racially motivated collective violence into four major categories:[2]

Interracial fights or shootings	36%
Killings of or interference with Negro men by white policemen	20%
Civil liberties, public facilities	18%
Attacks on white women by Negro men	13%

The remaining riots had a diverse assortment of final precipitants, including conflict over the use of black strikebreakers and other job-related incidents. (Four had no reported immediate precipitating events.) Even a cursory assessment of the character of these critical events reveals that most do fit the classification of transgressions of strongly held racial taboos, particularly important are those incidents involving black men and white policemen or black men and white women. Of course, these diverse precipitants characteristically led to rather different types of race

[1] Stanley Lieberson and Arnold R. Silverman, "The Precipitants and Underlying Conditions of Race Riots," *American Sociological Review,* **30** (December 1965), 888. Only a small percentage of the riots examined fell into the 1960–1963 period.

[2] The percentages have been calculated from the raw numbers presented in ibid., p. 889. It should be noted that much of this analysis relies on newspaper reporting of events; indeed, a fair amount of the data drawn on in the rest of this chapter comes either from newspaper stories on riots or from books on riots by newspaper reporters.

CHAPTER 4

riots in this half century period; in fact, a major weakness in this analysis is the inclusion without differentiation of a minority of black-dominated riots with the majority of white-dominated riots in these important decades of collective violence.

Turning to the decade of the 1960s, we find that the immediate precipitants of the black-dominated riots (in terms of rank-and-file participation, at least) were more likely than those of earlier riots to involve transgressions of the beliefs or taboos of black communities, to be exceptionally provocative from the black point of view:

> The precipitating incident has always been a local event such as an arrest perceived as brutal by people in a black community, or a failure of the city authorities to act on a particular issue which is regarded by the blacks as provocative. . . . An "inflammatory event" is usually an incident which is initiated by white people and which is perceived by black people as an act of injustice or as in [sic] insult to their community. The greater the injustice is perceived to be, the more "inflammatory" is the effect of the incident.[3]

Provocative acts by the police or other city authorities, including actions reflecting an unwillingness to correct what are perceived by local ghetto residents as flagrant instances of injustice, have frequently been the triggering events behind ghetto revolts.

Several examinations of serious ghetto rioting in the sixties have indicated that one category of taboo transgressions is of overriding importance: the killing of, arrest of, or interference with black men and women by policemen, commonly by white policemen. For example, an investigation by Newsom focused

[3] Lemberg Center for the Study of Violence, Brandeis University, "April Aftermath of the King Assassination," *Riot Data Review,* Number 2 (August 1968), 69 (Mimeographed). The last part of the quote in the text is from an earlier report by the Lemberg Center and is quoted on page 69 of the 1968 report.

The Development of Ghetto Riots: Precipitants and Patterns

solely on "major" ghetto riots, using the National Advisory Commission on Civil Disorders criteria to determine the level of rioting. For the 1964–1967 period, 14 major riots were identified and examined in detail, the resulting distribution of final precipitating events being as follows:[4]

Killings of or interference with Negroes by policemen	50%
Civil liberties, public facilities, demonstrations	22%
Miscellaneous altercations (race unspecified)	14%
Interracial fights	7%

The precipitant of one additional riot could not be determined. By far, the most important category here is that of encounters between the police and ghetto residents—incidents perceived by the black community as inflammatory and as acts of injustice or insults to the black community. Moreover, a number of protest demonstrations that seemed to be the immediate events prior to other riots also involved the police, since they were designed to protest prior acts of injustice by police authorities.[5]

Surveying numerous riots in 1967, the National Advisory Commission presented data to the public which generally corroborated these findings, particularly in the case of ghetto outbreaks viewed as serious. In fact, police-resident encounters appeared to be somewhat more common as triggering events of serious rioting in this year. Distinguishing between three levels of rioting, one can classify the Commission data on final precipitating incidents as follows:[6]

[4] R. K. Newsom, "Relative Deprivation and Ghetto Riots" (Paper presented at the annual meeting of the Southwestern Social Science Association, Houston, Texas, April 3–5, 1969), Appendix D.

[5] See evidence on this for the 1967 riots in *Report of the National Advisory Commission on Civil Disorders* (Washington, D.C.: U.S. Government Printing Office, 1968), p. 70.

[6] Ibid., pp. 68–71, 323–327. It should be obvious from this tabulation that the special Commission study of 24 riots is biased in the direction of relatively more serious instances.

	ALL RIOTS (N = 24)	MAJOR RIOTS (N = 6)	SERIOUS RIOTS (N = 10)	MINOR RIOTS (N = 8)
Police actions	50%	67%	60%	25%
Negro protest activities	21%	33%	20%	13%
Previous disorders in other cities	21%	0%	10%	50%
Other	8%	0%	10%	13%

As can be clearly seen, police actions perceived by the residents of black communities as abusive or discriminatory loom large among final precipitants at all levels of ghetto rioting. But they were particularly important in regard to those riots analyzed as serious or major.

During the first nine months of 1967, the period from which the Commission drew riot accounts for intensive analysis, at least two thirds of the major outbreaks of violence were sparked by encounters between the police and ghetto residents. In the case of those classified as serious, the proportion was similar. However, even these figures probably underestimate the extent to which the local police establishment has been involved in final precipitating incidents, for in one additional major riot and two additional serious riots a prior event involving alleged police brutality was the central issue at the protest meetings which have been counted as final incidents prior to the outbreak of rioting. Taking these as cases of police-related incidents would raise the proportions to 80 percent of both major and serious riots. Indeed, these serious instances of rioting seem to be what the Commissioners had in mind when they wrote in a more general vein that "almost invariably the incident that ignites disorder arises from police action."[7]

Apparently, half of the minor riots examined by the Commission either had no local precipitating events or else the reports

[7] Ibid., p. 93.

The Development of Ghetto Riots: Precipitants and Patterns

on these outbreaks were inadequate or incomplete. As a result, previous disorders in nearby cities were considered to be the only incidents that could be identified as final precipitants in four of the eight minor outbreaks analyzed. Yet the Commission notes that the police may have played a part in riot development even in these minor instances, since riots in contiguous cities triggered "substantial mobilization of police and extensive patrolling of the ghetto area in anticipation of violence."[8]

From our examination of the literature, we would conclude that very little research on or enumeration of riot precipitants has been undertaken for riots that occurred after the 1964–1967 period. Apparently there was something of a shift in the character of immediate precipitants after this period, at least for those ghetto revolts which took place shortly after the King assassination in the spring of 1968. The King murder came as a severe blow to blacks in ghettos across the country, and was seen not only as an act of injustice but also as another example of the impotence of nonviolent resistance. This extraordinarily provocative event, apparently the work of a white assassin, certainly falls into the general category of a transgression of strongly held taboos of black Americans. Nonetheless, the reaction of black communities was neither uniform nor automatic. A complete explanation for this variation would doubtless include factors we have mentioned previously, including the size of the ghetto population, the number of violence-oriented ghetto residents, and the resources for riot escalation.

Moreover, local developments and frictional events seem to have played an important role in determining the timing and character of the black response to the King assassination.[9] The Lemberg Center for the Study of Violence has prepared the only careful investigation of the immediate precipitants of the 1968 outbreaks of ghetto violence, classifying the riots into four dif-

[8] Ibid., p. 70.
[9] Lemberg Center for the Study of Violence, "April Aftermath of the King Assassination," 69.

ferent categories depending on the nature of the precipitants: (1) riots which were direct, spontaneous reactions to the King assassination, with no apparent local incident intervening; (2) riots triggered by local precipitating incidents concluding a chain of events set ultimately in motion by the King assassination; (3) riots triggered by local incidents with no apparent relationship to the King assassination; (4) riots for which the precipitants could not be determined—those for which the records are inadequate or unclear on the character or existence of a local precipitating event. Looking at the 233 outbreaks in April 1968, the Lemberg Center found that two thirds of the riots fell under the indeterminate catchall rubric, while 4 percent appeared to be directly linked to the assassination. Seventeen percent were indirectly linked by means of a local precipitant. The rest (15 percent) had precipitants that were not related to the King assassination.[10] Since this indeterminate category is by far the largest, it is not possible to typify the general character of the final precipitants of the postassassination riots. Either many precipitating events were not adequately reported by observers of the riots in the indeterminate category or the assassination alone was a sufficient trigger for these particular outbreaks; perhaps a number of these riots were stimulated by crowds forming at intersections to bemoan the King murder. Nevertheless, if one focuses solely on the riots where there is a clear report on the events which took place, then he must conclude that local events played a critical role in precipitating the April 1968 riots. In numerous cases these events also involved police encounters with local ghetto residents, although no one has as yet detailed the precise character of these final precipitating events.[11]

[10] Ibid., pp. 70–73.

[11] The one other analysis of precipitants of which we are aware briefly treats the 1968 riots, analyzed together with earlier riots. Thirty-six percent of the 1964–1968 riots were found to be spontaneous (no reported precipitant), most being set off by the King death. Twenty-seven percent were found to be precipitated by police incidents; 14 percent involved interracial conflict; 10 percent involved civil liberties

The Development of Ghetto Riots: Precipitants and Patterns

A Chain of Events?

While most serious outbreaks of ghetto violence, particularly those prior to 1968, in one way or another have been attributed to a final precipitating incident, the immediate event that ignited a ghetto riot normally did not represent an isolated or even an unusual happening. In most instances for which we have information there seems to have been a chain or series of prior incidents, perhaps focusing and cumulating grievances into what has been termed a ghetto "grievance bank."[12] For example, the investigation conducted by the National Advisory Commission of violent disruptions in 23 riot cities found that these communities had experienced at least three—and in some cases as many as ten—events somewhat similar to the final precipitant in the months preceding. Drawing on materials such as these, the Commission concluded that "violence was generated by an increasingly disturbed social atmosphere, in which typically not one, but a series of incidents occurred over a period of weeks or months prior to the outbreak of disorder."[13] These findings call attention to two important characteristics of recent ghetto revolts. First, they demonstrate the fallacy of regarding such riots as phenomena "caused" by one unique precipitating event. Second, even though a single precipitating event often was followed by the outbreak of violence within a short period of time and in the

---

or demonstrations; the rest had miscellaneous or unknown precipitants. Thus, in these figures police events do not loom as large as they do in the 1967 figures of the National Advisory Commission or in the 1964–1967 figures on major riots developed by Newsom. This, it should be noted, included 239 riots of varying degrees of intensity in the 1964–1968 period. It seems likely that the discrepancy exists because of the inclusion of a large number of relatively less severe riots. See Bryan T. Downes, "Social and Political Characteristics of Riot Cities: A Comparative Study," *Blacks in the United States,* ed. Norval D. Glenn and Charles M. Bonjean (San Francisco: Chandler, 1969), p. 435.

[12] Hans W. Mattick, "The Form and Content of Recent Riots," *Midway,* **9** (Summer 1968), 9.

[13] *Report of the National Advisory Commission on Civil Disorders,* p. 68.

same location, in many cases that incident was simply the final link in a long chain of circumstances that actually were the true precipitants of the riot. The specific precipitating incident that sparked the ghetto violence was directly linked to mounting ghetto discontent.

Perhaps most important, the National Advisory Commission also concluded that the final precipitating incident usually was similar in type or character to one or more of the prior incidents. Thus the provocative encounter that immediately precipitated the violence did not usually appear to be a random or atypical occurrence; the conflictual contacts between ghetto residents and policemen that ignited many of the most serious riots can be directly related to a history of friction between the community and representatives of political authorities, most notably the police. More specifically, the Commission listing of the incidents prior to the final precipitating events in 23 cities that had riots in 1967 revealed that no less than 40 percent directly involved police-civilian encounters. Other significant categories of these prior events leading up to the final precipitant were black protest activities and demonstrations in regard to police and other official actions, activities by whites to intimidate ghetto residents, official actions or inaction in regard to black grievances, and prior riots in the same cities, particularly where the handling of these riots had become a major issue.[14] Thus descriptions and analyses of recent ghetto violence that focus exclusively on the final precipitant and subsequent riot events, and that characterize the riots as purposeless or apolitical, have neglected the evidence that ghetto violence was preceded not only by one unique event seen as sparking the violence but also by an extended series of incidents that reflected both the focusing of local political discontent and the same general type of fundamental ghetto grievances that were manifested in the final incident. Much in these findings, therefore, lends critical support to the argument that most serious ghetto riots both reflected an accu-

14 Ibid., pp. 69–71.

mulation of politically relevant local grievances and were purposively directed at relevant local targets.

The Critical Role of the Local Police

Despite the variable nature of riot precipitants, a very large proportion of the serious outbreaks did finally stem from a common source. As we have just shown, in many serious occurrences of recent collective violence on the part of black Americans, the immediate incident involved an encounter between law enforcement officers and ghetto residents. The repetition with which serious ghetto uprisings were stimulated by heated interactions with police officers has focused increasing interest on the activities of the police and ascribed more than ordinary importance to the role of these agents of social control in ghetto neighborhoods.

However, the intervention of police personnel in a ghetto situation probably should not be considered a universal or sufficient impetus to rioting. Policemen are highly involved in ghetto life; not all, or even an appreciable proportion of, encounters with neighborhood residents become riot precipitating incidents. And as we have noted, a large number of smaller and less destructive manifestations of violence apparently were not triggered directly by police behavior. The meaning of this, nevertheless, appears difficult to discern. On the one hand, some might argue that relatively less serious riots may not have been provoked by the police because police involvement actually is neither essential nor closely related to the occurrence of ghetto violence. On the other hand, others might assert that the failure of many relatively limited violent incidents to escalate into serious or major conflagrations might have been related to the fact that most of those events were *not* sparked by provocative encounters with the police. While emphasis solely on precipitants might not yield an adequate characterization of riots, the triggering events could have a pronounced impact in shaping subsequent riot development.

One of the most persistent features of urban ghettos has been the intense negativism black Americans direct against local police officers. Very large proportions have expressed strong criticism of the police that patrol ghetto areas. Policemen are often viewed as abusive or unjust, as the oppressors rather than the protectors of ghetto life and property. As a result, the image and role of police officers in urban ghettos are not unlike that of an occupying army in a colonial territory, primarily serving the alien and dominant white authorities rather than the indigenous residents who must depend as much as, if not more than, other citizens on police for the maintenance of local order.

The involvement of police officers in riot-precipitating incidents, therefore, is more than accidental. In many of the nation's most serious ghetto revolts, the specific encounter that ignited the violence reflected what might seem to the outside observer to be routine police practices, such as the arrest of black youths for a traffic violation in Watts, the arrest of a black cab driver in Newark, and a large-scale police raid on an after-hours liquor joint in Detroit. In each case, however, the actions of the police sparked a smoldering residue of mutual suspicion and animosity between residents and policemen. Animosity toward law enforcement officers apparently was so prevalent and so intense that the mere presence of a white policeman performing routine duties in a large ghetto, when coupled with other conducive conditions, was sufficient to ignite a riot.

The intense antagonism that has developed between law enforcement officers and ghetto residents stands in sharp contrast to the relationship that exists between policemen and whites. Local and national surveys reveal that most white Americans express favorable opinions of police performance and support the law enforcement actions.[15] Policemen frequently state that they regard whites as more respectful of police authority than black

[15] See the Task Force on the Police, President's Commission on Law Enforcement and the Administration of Justice, *The Police* (Washington, D.C.: U.S. Government Printing Office, 1967), pp. 144–146.

citizens. Furthermore, most police officers display little sympathy with the plight of black Americans. Even among patrolmen assigned to ghetto neighborhoods, the majority seem to feel that black citizens enjoy advantages rather than disadvantages, when compared with whites.[16]

However, the actions of policemen have often been perceived by black citizens as discriminatory.[17] Although historically the relationship between law enforcement officers and residents of low-income neighborhoods, regardless of racial characteristics, has been one of friction, some evidence indicates that blacks who have experienced major riots regard police practices as expressions of racial rather than socioeconomic inequality. In a random sample survey which we conducted in the Twelfth Street area of Detroit shortly after the 1967 riot there, nearly three hundred black respondents were asked to evaluate the police protection *normally* received by white and black urbanites at comparable socioeconomic levels. The majority of the respondents felt that whites were granted more protection by the police than black persons of similar status.[18]

Yet negative appraisals of police behavior have been based not only on perceived inequalities in performance but also on actual experience with police mistreatment and malpractice. One sur-

[16] See the material in ibid., pp. 164–165; David H. Bayley and Harold Mendelsohn, *Minorities and the Police* (New York: Free Press of Glencoe, 1969), pp. 143ff.

[17] For a detailed review of surveys on black resident views of police brutality and malpractice, see Harlan Hahn and Joe R. Feagin, "Riot Precipitating Police Practices: Attitudes in Urban Ghettos," *Phylon,* 31 (Summer 1970), 183–193.

[18] In this and subsequent chapters we will frequently refer to the Twelfth Street data. These data were collected in the Twelfth Street area of Detroit shortly after the 1967 riot there, from a modified probability sample of 270 ghetto residents interviewed by trained black interviewers. A variety of riot-related questions were asked. For further details on the methodology and the survey, see Harlan Hahn and Joe R. Feagin, "Rank-and-File Versus Congressional Perceptions of Ghetto Riots," *Social Science Quarterly,* 51 (September 1970), 361–373.

vey conducted after the 1965 Watts riot, for example, asked blacks living in that ghetto about six forms of questionable police actions: insulting language and lack of respect, unnecessary rousting and frisking, unnecessary car searches, use of excessive force in making arrests, beating up suspects in custody, and unnecessary home searches. Large percentages expressed the view that such practices had occurred in their ghetto area, ranging from a low of two fifths for unnecessary searching of homes to three quarters for unnecessary rousting and frisking. Furthermore, from one seventh (on searching homes) to two fifths (on unnecessary rousting and frisking) had seen it happen. From 4 percent (on being beaten up in custody) to one fifth (on the use of insulting language and unnecessary rousting) reported that *it had happened to them*.[19] Other studies conducted in Harlem, Bedford-Stuyvesant, and numerous other ghettos have consistently disclosed that large proportions, ranging from 40 to 50 percent, among ghetto residents specifically believe that police brutality and malpractice exist in their areas.[20] Thus, evidence yielded by studies of urban ghettos, as well as observational investigations of police behavior, has clearly indicated that the negativism blacks direct toward the police is based on specific police actions.

The animosity between ghetto residents and local policemen reflects more than a conflict between mutually suspicious racial groups. In urban black neighborhoods, police officers often are ubiquitous, constantly intervening in the daily lives of the residents in a provocative way. Since urban ghettos—like other low-income areas—frequently have high rates of crime, law enforcement agencies commonly assign relatively large numbers of officers to those areas—officers who may act more aggressively

[19] Walter J. Raine, "The Perception of Police Brutality in South Central Los Angeles," *The Los Angeles Riots,* ed. Nathan Cohen (New York: Praeger, 1970), p. 386.

[20] See the discussion in Hahn and Feagin, "Riot Precipitating Police Practices," 188–189; *Report of the National Advisory Commission on Civil Disorders,* pp. 158–159.

to prevent actual or potential crimes than they would in other sectors of the city. As the police are the only government agents that circulate through the black community on an around-the-clock basis, blacks must often summon the police to perform many emergency personal services such as resolving marital or youth problems, securing medical assistance, and adjusting personal disputes that normally might be referred to other professionals in higher-status areas. Yet surveys of ghetto areas have revealed not only intense local hostility toward police brutality but also great dissatisfaction with the services or protection provided by the police. In many black communities, including those that have experienced major riots, popular criticism of the police for their failure to offer police services and adequate safeguards against crime often has approximated, even exceeded, the volume of objections to police harassment or brutality.[21] Moreover, concrete documentation of this discrimination in protection has been provided by outside observers of police department practices.[22]

To many, the two major black complaints about policing may seem contradictory. While the disapproval of police brutality and mistreatment appears to reflect a demand for less interference, complaints about the inadequacy of police protection suggest a desire for even more interference in ghetto life by police. Presumably, law enforcement agencies would be criticized both for relaxing their control of a ghetto area and for expanding their intervention in a community. Perhaps as a result of this seeming paradox, black attitudes toward police activities have often been viewed by law enforcement officials as relatively unimportant, even irrelevant.

Ironically, however, these sentiments of black citizens actually may have been produced by specific policies that have been adopted by an increasing number of urban police departments.

[21] Hahn and Feagin, "Riot Precipitating Police Practices," 188–192.
[22] For example, see *Report of the National Advisory Commission on Civil Disorders,* pp. 162ff.

In recent years the leaders of such law enforcement agencies have tried to cope with crime in city areas by focusing on high crime rate areas, particularly by adopting a procedure sometimes termed "aggressive preventive patrolling." This practice usually entails stopping and questioning, often indiscriminately, a large number of persons in certain high crime districts to discover whether or not they have been involved in serious crimes reported in that area or in other areas of the city. This program can be seen as part of the natural movement toward police professionalization, a movement toward adopting crime prevention measures. Since persons who live in areas with high crime rates, alleged or real, are more likely to have participated in crimes than those residing in other areas, the practice of preventive patrolling might appear to represent an efficient method of locating many persons likely to be involved in illegal operations. Despite the apparent logic, however, few systematic efforts have been made to evaluate the overall effectiveness of preventive patrolling.

Moreover, the practice of preventive patrolling appears to have yielded two serious disadvantages, linked to the intensification of ghetto discontent. Preventive patrolling undoubtedly has produced an increasing number of abrasive contacts between police officers and ghetto residents, many of whom would be recognized by a beat patrolman as respected residents of a neighborhood.[23] The general adoption of the policy of preventive patrolling by major urban police departments has promoted the growth of ghetto resentment of police insensitivity and mistreatment. There is, however, another important but less widely recognized consequence of preventive patrolling operations. The practice of stopping large numbers of suspicious persons frequently has been focused on the prevention of relatively serious crimes such as robbery, burglary, and physical assaults and of vice activities that may have important ramifications for the entire city. Yet

[23] Ibid., p. 159

156

the crimes that more often plague the ghetto residents include seemingly minor infractions such as vandalism, noisy fights, muggings, and petty larceny. Thus the practice of preventive patrolling reflects an emphasis on crimes of major concern to white urbanites and a relative neglect of illegal actions that have a serious impact on blacks. The practice of questioning many persons on the street has deflected law enforcement officers from adequately servicing calls for police assistance from ghetto residents. Studies have indicated that urban police officers take from two to four times longer to respond to calls from black victims in ghetto districts than from other sections of the city.[24] Since the volume of crime in cities, especially in ghetto areas, usually exceeds police resources, law enforcement agencies have devoted relatively minimal attention to incidents imposing a major burden on black urbanites.

Perhaps most important, police officers represent accessible agents of government that directly link the black public to the highest levels of governmental decision-making. Policemen are the extended arm of the government, and blacks probably have more contact with law enforcement officers than with any other political representatives. For many, therefore, abstract concepts of governance are personified more by the cop in the police car or on the street than by elected leaders. The argument that ghetto riots have reflected a basic assault on white-dominated political institutions derives support from the fact that the police are one of very few accessible embodiments of political authority available for attack. In addition, policemen not only have signified the primary agents of white political authority but they also have represented the major enforcers of social control. In the view of many residents of black urban ghettos, the white public and political leaders not only have neglected the grievances of black neighborhoods but also have been reluctant to relinquish

[24] Ibid., pp. 159–163; Hahn and Feagin, "Riot Precipitating Police Practices."

domination of those communities; the only interest that most white urbanites have exhibited concerning ghetto areas has been an interest in control.

Moreover, although the urban judicial system has been charged with dispensing justice impartially, blacks often have been the victims rather than the beneficiaries—institutions of criminal justice traditionally have perpetuated the influence of the white majority. Since black Americans generally have even been excluded from participation in framing the critical laws under which they live, discontent has developed regarding the legal system.[25] To illustrate, results from our Twelfth Street opinion survey in Detroit indicate that a basic lack of confidence in the administration of justice had enveloped the entire neighborhood where the violence erupted. A staggering nine in ten of the ghetto residents interviewed rejected the view that "most of the laws on the books are fair to all people"; no less than 95 percent denied the belief that "laws are enforced equally." Ghetto animosity toward law enforcement officers may have been directed not only at the police qua police but also indirectly at the entire legal process. Attacks on police preceding and during ghetto revolts, therefore, reflected a significance that extended far beyond the simple expression of antagonism between local policemen and black ghetto residents.

In a fundamental sense, rioting has represented the deliberate repudiation of the external social controls manifest in police coercion and a defiance of establishment efforts to re-exert coercive control. Perhaps this characteristic has been the major feature of riots that has prompted some to describe them as disruptive or disorderly; rioting meant a violent disruption of the certain established urban patterns and routines. However, the characterization of urban violence solely as a form of disorder not only

---

[25] See *Report of the National Advisory Commission on Civil Disorders*, p. 183; Task Force on Administration of Justice, The President's Commission on Law Enforcement and Administration of Justice, *The Courts* (Washington, D.C.: U.S. Government Printing Office, 1967).

The Development of Ghetto Riots: Precipitants and Patterns

diverts attention from the purposive aspects of riots but also implies that there exist relatively agreed-upon standards for public order. While all might agree that the outbreak of violence represents a radical departure from not-so-violent modes of behavior, few have attempted a precise definition of "order." As we have noted previously, the resort to violence has been a historically common method by which groups possessing little or no political power have sought to improve their position.

The Developmental Trajectory of Ghetto Riots

Although the outbreak of ghetto revolts was often triggered by a provocative event, such as a volatile confrontation between ghetto residents and law enforcement officers, subsequent riot development usually was not random or chaotic. In fact, the escalation of ghetto riots has often followed a relatively common and recurrent pattern. In the following section, an effort will be made to depict some of the recurrent stages through which riot activities have passed in emerging as episodes of ghetto violence.[26]

[26] In our abstraction of riot development patterns we have been significantly influenced by the following works: (1) Ralph W. Conant, "Rioting, Insurrection and Civil Disobedience," *The American Scholar,* **37** (Summer 1968), 420–433; (2) James R. Hundley, Jr., "The Dynamics of Recent Ghetto Riots," *Journal of Urban Law,* **45** (1968) 627–639; (3) John Spiegel, "Hostility, Aggression and Violence," *Racial Violence in the United States,* ed. Allen D. Grimshaw (Chicago: Aldine, 1969), pp. 331–339; (4) *Report of the National Advisory Commission on Civil Disorders,* pp. 63–73, 325–329. This last reference has been a particularly important source of systematic data on riot development issues for us, but has resulted in overemphasis on 1967 riots, and serious and major riots, in this analysis. Because of the scarcity of systematic analysis of riot development for other years, we have been unable to correct this overemphasis. Where possible, however, we have drawn on descriptive overviews such as the following: (1) Fred C. Shapiro, *Race Riots: New York 1964* (New York: Thomas Y. Crowell, 1964); (2) Jerry Cohen and William S. Murphy, *Burn, Baby, Burn!* (Dutton, 1966); (3) Bert W. Gilbert et al., *Ten Blocks from the White House: Anatomy of the Washington Riots of 1968* (New York: Praeger, 1968); Lemberg Center

However, the reader should note that we are here abstracting a pattern of riot development from available materials, limited as they are, and that a given riot did not necessarily possess all of the characteristics or stages delineated here. In addition, only serious or major riots reached the higher levels of riot intensity described in the following section; and only the most severe riots ordinarily incorporated all of the stages in their developmental trajectory.

The recurrent stages we have abstracted can be briefly outlined as follows: (1) the initial phase of crowd formation and keynoting centering on the final precipitant; (2) a stage in which the initial crowd and the police diverge, followed by new formations of rioters and police in various other places; this phase is characterized by widespread excitement and relatively minor violence on the part of rioters, including rock throwing at police, firemen, and stores and window breaking; (3) a stage of extensive looting, selective attacks on stores, and attacks on control agents who attempt to intervene; (4) a state of siege, characterized by increasing arson, fire bombing, and reports of sniping; a collapse of negotiations and a massive law enforcement response are characteristic of this phase.

Although the final event that precipitates a ghetto riot can often be related to a legacy of provocative incidents, a series of preparatory incidents which may have raised local concern to a critical threshold point, one characteristic that distinguishes the final precipitant from the preceding events seems to be its ability to attract and focus the attention of a relatively large crowd of ghetto residents on a continuing basis.[27] An occurrence of rioting requires the assemblage of a large number of persons who can

---

for the Study of Violence, "April Aftermath of the King Assassination, passim; *Report of the Chicago Riot Study Committee* (Chicago, August 1968).

[27] See Conant, "Rioting, Insurrection and Civil Disobedience," 424; Herbert J. Gans, "The Ghetto Rebellions and Urban Class Conflict," *Urban Riots,* ed. Robert H. Connery (New York: Random House Vintage Books, 1969), p. 46.

be mobilized for collective action. In many cases this assemblage may partially result from the specific character and range of police actions in connection with a given precipitating incident. While firm evidence is difficult to provide because of the sketchiness of existing research on riot development, one might also posit that, if a precipitating incident personified a particularly salient concern within a given ghetto community, there would be an increased probability that a large number of persons will gather at the site of the incident. In addition, most ghetto riots have erupted during the warmer months, when a large proportion of persons in densely populated ghetto neighborhoods go outside to escape the stifling heat, and during evening hours, when pedestrian traffic on the streets is high. Occurrence of precipitants near major intersections and heavy foot traffic often seems to be a contributing factor.

Even the Detroit riot of 1967, which began with a police raid on a "blind pig" early on a Sunday morning, originated in an area of the city in which vice and night life long had been centered. Within a short time after the police raid an estimated two hundred persons had gathered on the street to watch the police. In addition, numerous 1968 riots after the King assassination apparently developed out of the large crowds which had formed on the streets to discuss and protest the assassination, while the final precipitant often may have been a local incident involving official actions or inaction linked indirectly to the assassination. (As we have previously noted, the specific character of the final precipitants of most of these riots remains as yet indeterminate.) The critical point is that the result was the same as for riots before and after 1968—the assemblage of large crowds and the excitement of crowd feelings on a sustained basis. In the serious 1968 riots in Chicago and Washington the assemblage of crowds was particularly common at key intersections and was stimulated by large-scale school walkouts related to the assassination.[28]

[28] Lemberg Center for the Study of Violence, "April Aftermath of the King Assassination," 69–72; Gilbert et al., *Ten Blocks from the*

CHAPTER 4

The development of crowds, therefore, seems a primary requisite for the start of urban violence. The commonly observed meteorological relationship between the outbreak of riots and summer temperatures thus may simply reflect the fact that large numbers of persons have emerged from their private domains to provide the necessary congregation of large groups of people. Moreover, the larger the ghetto the more likely these congregations of people are to form and the larger they are likely to be.

Yet those congregating near the scene of a final precipitating incident probably do not constitute a representative sample of all ghetto residents. The process of crowd formation and subsequent development may in part be a product of selective perception. For example, those especially concerned about the misbehavior of the police may be the most likely to join a congregation of bystanders observing police actions, while many of those not particularly sensitive to the malpractice issue may be inclined to disregard the incident. In addition, the effect of the final precipitant may well depend on the number or proportion of crowd members who share relatively militant convictions and the belief that violence is a necessary means of securing progress for black Americans.

As a heuristic proposition, it could be assumed that the gathering of a large number of people of this persuasion will substantially increase the likelihood of collective violence. Many incidents might not have resulted in extensive violence if a large number of persons had not been generated as a result of the precipitant, or if the predominant mood of the crowd that formed had been moderate rather than militant. The composition of the crowd may also be affected by general trends in the attitudes of black residents in the surrounding community, although the predominant consensus of those in the gathering crowds could conceivably be unrepresentative of community opinions. Indeed,

---

White House, pp. 13ff.; *Report of the Chicago Riot Study Committee,* pp. 33ff.

these factors may partially account for the fact that many provocative incidents do not lead to riots. In sum, then, the start of
a ghetto riot probably results from the conjunction of several
circumstances not always conjoined.

Whatever the bias in initial crowd selection, among those
present at the location of a precipitating incident a diversity of
viewpoints usually are represented. As the crowd forms and increases in number, a process of interpersonal discussion that has
been termed "keynoting" often takes place. In an important
textbook on collective behavior Turner and Killian have argued
that keynoting is critical in the development of crowd action
because of the ambivalent frame of reference of many crowd
members:

> For some people the uncertainty and ambivalence in the in-
> ternal portion of their frame of reference is resolved by the
> keynote statement. One position is reinforced for them and
> they now find it easier to express themselves, agreeing with
> a proposal that someone else has already enunciated.[29]

They view this process as accelerating until it grows to the point
of majority consensus. Yet this view seems to overlook the complexity of crowd interaction. Members of the crowd start to
comment upon the events that are transpiring and to suggest
alternative forms of responsive action. The proposals advanced
by various spokesmen in the crowd often do not suggest a single
course of action, nor is there a unanimous outpouring of vindic-
tiveness against the representatives of outside authority involved.
Several reactions are likely to be advocated, and the crowd may
begin to split and to follow divergent paths of conduct. Those
spokesmen who support a passive orientation, sometimes including respected ghetto leaders, may withdraw from the crowd and

[29] Ralph Turner and Lewis M. Killian, *Collective Behavior* (Englewood Cliffs, N.J.: Prentice-Hall, 1957), p. 117.

carry with them followers who endorse their position. Unless these spokesmen are capable of persuading a substantial segment of the crowd, however, the impact of their point of view is nullified by their departure, although they sometimes reappear at a later stage of the rioting in the form of "counter-rioters," again urging ghetto residents to refrain from participating in violence.[30]

Of those who remain at the scene, however, a substantial share of those assembled probably regard the incident as deserving a violent retaliatory response. As the process of keynoting continues, the individuals remaining in the crowd begin to vie with one another in denouncing the activities of police officers and other authorities. At a critical moment in this stage, a few persons in the crowd may make dramatic and violent gestures, moving the crowd from rhetoric to action. In the Detroit riot of 1967, for example, the intense discussions and keynoting among the crowd that was watching the police raid on a "blind pig" suddenly were interrupted by shouts of rioters and by the crash of bottles on the ground and on a police vehicle.[31] The riot process had entered a new stage. Thus the shift in the mood of a crowd of onlookers from a passive to an active response to the final precipitant marks the end of the first phase of riot development. The growing intensity of the verbal expressions of the assembled crowd has begun to find an active outlet.

Subsequent to this initial phase of crowd formation, keynoting, and the first acts of violence by rioters and police, a diverging of the original formations of police and rioters frequently occurs, soon to be followed by regrouping. Important in this phase is the spread of information and rumors about what has occurred, both in the ghetto community and among public officials and

[30] Conant, "Rioting, Insurrection and Civil Disobedience," 425; *Report of the National Advisory Commission on Civil Disorders,* pp. 68–74; Gilbert et al., *Ten Blocks from the White House,* pp. 16–44.

[31] *Report of the National Advisory Commission on Civil Disorders,* pp. 47–48; Hubert G. Locke, *The Detroit Riot of 1967* (Detroit: Wayne State University Press, 1969), p. 27.

The Development of Ghetto Riots: Precipitants and Patterns

the police. If these processes reach a sufficient crescendo, a "quantum jump in the riot process occurs."[32] As new crowds develop, sometimes regrouping at the scene of the precipitant, sometimes congregating at locations symbolizing the white establishment, the conflict process accelerates. Crowds of rioters gather in both size and momentum, often moving in directions suggested by the more articulate members, while law enforcement agents regroup and begin new tactical strategies. An important new phase emerges, frequently if inaccurately termed the "Roman Holiday" phase. This term has been prompted by the widespread excitement which has characterized this riot stage.

Young adults and teenagers often swell the ranks of the groups already on the streets.[33] Freed from the conventional restrictions of control agencies, the members of the expanding throngs begin to assert their newly discovered independence and demonstrate satisfaction with the new arrangements. Extensive rock and bottle throwing and window breaking often commences again, in various locations, eliciting enthusiastic cheers from the crowds each time a missile reaches the intended target.

Although the uninhibited mood of the participants during this stage of rioting has conveyed an impression of chaos or purposelessness to some observers, the available evidence suggests that many of these activities were structured and purposive. Observation of the main locations of the Detroit riot, for example, revealed that the plateglass windows of the abandoned store fronts that lined the area, which have been common objects of youthful vandalism, remained intact. Moreover, the movement of the crowds through the streets often appears to have been directed by leaders to the site of particular agencies or institutions that have previously aroused rank-and-file criticism. Yet as several

[32] Conant, "Rioting, Insurrection and Civil Disobedience," 425–426.
[33] Ibid.; additional evidence for the young being more active in early riot stages, with older residents coming to play a dominant role later can be found in *Report of the Chicago Riot Study Committee,* p. 3.

observers have noted, widespread looting does not ordinarily occur in these early stages of rioting. "Instead, destructive attacks are most frequently directed against symbols of authority in the community."[34] The most typical symbols which receive the rocks and bottles of rioters are the police, firemen, police and fire department property, and selected local stores. And the damage resulting from such attacks, both in this stage and subsequently, can be staggering. For example, one report on the Watts riot estimated that 170 police cars had been damaged, together with about 100 pieces of fire equipment.[35] Although these acts of rioting may seem to some purposeless, and may have represented for some rioters a pathological outburst, in most riot situations a meaningful pattern was revealed in that the rioters' objects of attack were related to prior community grievances.

Yet another distinguishing feature of this second phase of rioting is the appearance of counterrioters, those ghetto residents opposed to violence, who attempt to persuade rioters to refrain from destructive activities or at least to leave the riot area. In some communities such efforts were more or less authorized by public officials, such as the mayor or the human relations council. In other cities they merely were condoned by local authorities or granted no official recognition.[36] Although no method has been developed for measuring the effectiveness of these counterrioters, some authorities contacted by the National Advisory Commission believed the issuance of armbands or helmets to local youths with instructions to assist police in "cooling" situations was

[34] Russell Dynes and E. L. Quarantelli, "What Looting in Civil Disturbances Really Means," *Violence and Riots in Urban America,* ed. Rodney F. Allen and Charles H. Adair (Worthington, Ohio: Charles A. Jones Publishing Co., 1969), p. 123.

[35] Ibid., pp. 123–124; E. L. Quarantelli and Russell Dynes, "Looting in Civil Disorders: An Index of Social Change," *Riots and Rebellion,* ed. Louis H. Masotti and Don R. Bowen (Beverly Hills, Calif.: Sage Publications, 1968), p. 131.

[36] *Report of the National Advisory Commission on Civil Disorders,* p. 73; Gilbert et al., *Ten Blocks from the White House,* pp. 15ff.; Locke, *The Detroit Riot of 1967,* p. 87.

valuable in lessening the intensity of the rioting.[37] In part, this strategy reflected successful co-optation; but it also may have been successful because it represented to some ghetto residents a formal grant of power for community policing.

Information Transmission and Riot Development

Since riot development has frequently been spurred or channeled by the spread of riot information and messages during the early stages of ghetto riots, we will digress briefly from the delineation of riot stages to consider some important questions about the character and impact of information transmission. The transition from a final precipitating event, through crowd formation and keynoting, to the various later stages of collective action and violence has often been facilitated by the spread of riot information, both accurate riot news and rumors with no basis in fact.

In assessing this important process of news and rumor transmission during the early stages of ghetto rioting, a number of observers have given rather heavy emphasis to the alleged provocative and sensationalizing actions of representatives of the mass media, such as television and the newspapers, especially the effect of these actions in intensifying or determining riot development. A common argument is to the effect that local media broadcast coverage of the various riots in the sixties concentrated on sensationalizing the actions of rioters, on playing to the galleries with frequent emotional accounts of inflammatory riot events, on intentionally spreading numerous unfounded rumors, and on disseminating widely the provocative views of allegedly violence-oriented black militants. Not unexpectedly, these diversified news activities have been seen by many as fostering or contributing in a significant way to the development and escalation of ghetto rioting subsequent to precipitating events; one

[37] *Report of the National Advisory Commission on Civil Disorders,* p. 73.

such observer has even coined a term for this type of activity, "media crowdsmanship."[38] This perspective was apparently so widespread at the time the National Advisory Commission on Civil Disorders began its careful examination of the 1967 riots that even the Commissioners reported that "we first believed that the media had sensationalized the disturbances, consistently overplaying violence and giving disproportionate amounts of time to emotional events and militant leaders."[39]

Surprisingly, however, the systematic research conducted under the auspices of the Commission into the riot-related news on television and in the newspapers generally revealed little support for this general view of the mass media. For example, according to this research, during riot periods most of the sequences broadcast on television were not wildly emotional in tone; the dominant mood of the broadcasts was described as either "normal" or "calm." Even more important, these researchers found a surprisingly heavy emphasis in the broadcasts on riot control activities, on law enforcement actions, and on the riot aftermath, "rather than on scenes of actual mob action, or people looting, sniping, or setting fires, or being injured or killed."[40] In fact, these latter scenes comprised less than 5 percent of all riot scenes broadcast. Little in the way of specific scenes of rioter activity was ordinarily available for would-be rioters to imitate. Nor did systematic investigation reveal that sensationalized television reportage increased with the riot, suggesting that the media probably did not play the continuing, interactive, and accelerative role in riot development that some have posited. The Commission's broad-

[38] Eugene H. Methvin, *The Riot Makers* (New Rochelle, N.Y.: Arlington House, 1970), pp. 501–502.

[39] *Report of the National Advisory Commission on Civil Disorders,* p. 202. Criticism of the mass media can also be found in Morris Janowitz, "Social Control of Escalated Riots," *Racial Violence in the United States,* ed. Allen D. Grimshaw (Chicago: Aldine, 1969), p. 513.

[40] *Report of the National Advisory Commission on Civil Disorders,* p. 204. For a mixed, but more favorable than unfavorable assessment of Detroit riot coverage, see Locke, *The Detroit Riot of 1967,* pp. 80–81ff.

cast analysis revealed that in all but one riot situation media time devoted to riots actually declined very sharply after the first day of the riot, a finding particularly significant in regard to the numerous serious riots lasting for more than one or two days and nights.[41]

Yet another important image of media coverage of rioting has placed great stress on the extensive and disproportionate amount of television time devoted to the views of black militants and violence-oriented agitators, presumably to the serious detriment of the perspectives of the more moderate residents, black and white, of riot-torn cities. Such extensive coverage of militants has been assumed by some to accelerate ghetto rioting. Again, judging from available research, this image too seems a serious distortion of what actually occurred. In the first place, television newscasts on rioting tended to overemphasize the actions of law enforcement agents in the area of social control, including frequent interviews with white police officials and other public authorities. Of even greater importance is the fact that interviews with black militants did not constitute the majority of news interviews with city leaders, even with black leaders. Although black leaders were interviewed relatively infrequently, moderate black leaders were far more likely to be shown or interviewed on television news broadcasts than were leaders who identified with militant or revolutionary organizations and platforms.

It should also be noted that the National Advisory Commission found that the same pattern of calm, factual, and restrained reporting also characterized the dominant tone of newspaper reporting during the 1967 riot period. Thus while the National Advisory Commission was critical of some specific instances of mistakes of fact, rumor circulation, and staging of riot events by the mass media, their general conclusion was that the media on the whole made a successful effort to give calm, balanced accounts of the 1967 riots. Indeed, their greatest criticism was

[41] *Report of the National Advisory Commission on Civil Disorders,* p. 205.

reserved for factors not ordinarily singled out by critics of media riot coverage: the undue reliance of the media on public officials for their sometimes erroneous data, the tendency of the media to portray the events as white-black civilian confrontations, and the failure of the media to report on the background grievances of black Americans adequately.[42] In addition to this national report, the reports of local riot commissions have generally exonerated local mass media.[43] It would seem that the primary bias in media reporting was not sensationalism on behalf of black rioters which might stimulate the participation of more rioters and escalate riot development, but the failure of the media to examine pre-riot conditions such as the excessive use of force and false arrests by law enforcement agents in ghettos. Consequently, post-riot comments by ghetto residents have indicted the mass media for a significant antighetto bias.[44]

If sensationalism, emotionalism, and bias in favor of the activities, grievances, or views of rioters, or violence supporters, have probably not played the dominant role in media coverage of ghetto rioting that some have suggested, how then does one explain the doubtless extensive transmission of information and rumor during the critical stages of crowd formation in ghetto rioting?

Only those partial to the negative image of ghettos as places where transitory and anomic urbanites are virtually isolated from one another could fail to suggest the important role that ordinary social networks in ghetto areas are likely to have played in riot information and rumor transmission. Word of mouth exchanges between relatives and friends, on the streets and in stores and bars, provided numerous important information and rumor linkages other than those provided by the white-dominated media such as television and newspapers. It would

[42] Ibid., pp. 201–205.
[43] See *Report of the Chicago Riot Study Committee,* pp. 82–84.
[44] *Report of the National Advisory Commission on Civil Disorders,* pp. 201–203.

probably be difficult to overemphasize the importance of word-of-mouth communication networks in riot development. A few post-riot studies have suggested that the overwhelming majority of ghetto residents who were not firsthand observers probably heard of the outbreak of a ghetto uprising by way of interpersonal communication networks, doubtless composed of acquaintances, friends, and relatives.[45]

Thus, as new persons joined the original crowd which had formed on the street in conjunction with the final precipitant, and as others began to drift away from the edge of the gathering, some to regroup in crowds elsewhere, excited and sometimes garbled accounts of the event were related in a seemingly endless chain of communications that quickly moved throughout the social networks of the black community. At each succeeding link in this communications network, the description of the final precipitant and related events can become more exaggerated and virulent.[46] Seldom, however, do the messages lose their credibility. The failure of many Negroes to doubt the riot stories and sometimes exaggerated rumors that spread through a community in the early phases of a riot is perhaps related to the prior experiences of ghetto residents. Since a sizable proportion of black residents take a negative view of police officers, they are unlikely to doubt, to take perhaps the most important example, accurate news and inaccurate rumors about police conduct that have

[45] Ibid., p. 207; Benjamin D. Singer, Richard W. Osborn, James A. Geschwender, *Black Rioters* (Lexington, Mass.: Heath, 1970), p. 44. Singer and his associates do suggest that media news of the riot may have initiated the messages which then spread through interpersonal communication networks.

[46] "Rumors significantly aggravated tension and disorder in more than 65 percent of the disorders studied by the Commission." *Report of the National Advisory Commission on Civil Disorders,* p. 173. The role rumors play in the emergence of collectively sanctioned versions of an event has been given much attention in the collective behavior literature. Turner and Killian, *Collective Behavior,* pp. 64ff. See also Gordon W. Allport and Leo Postman, *The Psychology of Rumor* (New York: Holt, 1947).

circulated in the wake of many a final precipitating incident. In addition, the willingness of many persons to act upon the rumors they hear and to join crowds that form in response to the incident may reflect the high degree of salience that a particular type of precipitating incident has in a community. If the precipitating incident represents a problem that has been a long-standing or increasing source of discontent, local residents may be more likely to respond actively to the rumor and to affiliate themselves with street crowds. Thus the recruitment of additional riot participants on the basis of information received about the precipitating incident is greatly facilitated by pre-existing sentiments and experiences.

The Later Stages of Rioting

Although the early stages of rioting characterized by extensive rank-and-file participation commonly have not involved widespread looting, they have set the stage for such activities.[47] Demonstrating that acts of physical destruction usually receive commendation rather than disapproval of people on the street, the initial participants provide definite evidence that the limitations imposed at other times by social control agencies no longer are applied to personal conduct. In many cases, the relatively youthful character of participants has been displaced by an older and more diverse population of rioters. In the middle phase of riot development, looting commonly seems to increase.[48]

During the 1960s much of the ultimate cost of ghetto rioting was borne by ghetto merchants during the looting periods of

[47] Quarantelli and Dynes, "Looting in Civil Disorders: An Index of Social Change," pp. 134–137.

[48] For discussions of looting patterns see Conant, "Rioting, Insurrection and Civil Disobedience," 426; Gilbert et al., *Ten Blocks from the White House*, pp. 31–119; Shapiro and Sullivan, *Race Riots: New York 1964*, pp. 142–159, *passim;* Cohen and Murphy, *Burn, Baby, Burn!*, pp. 42–200.

serious riots, supplemented by losses as a result of window breaking and by arson. In the 1964 Harlem riot, reportedly, at least 112 stores were plundered; during the 1965 Watts riot approximately 600 stores were looted or burned. In the 1967 Newark riot 1,029 stores were looted or damaged, while according to unofficial estimates no fewer than 2,700 establishments were plundered in the 1967 Detroit revolt. In regard to the 1968 Washington riot an estimate of 900 predominantly white-owned businesses damaged has been recorded.[49] The targets of looting included grocery stores, liquor stores, clothing shops, and other businesses that offered gratification of consumer desires. Some may have engaged in looting, at least in part, because the collapse of police control offered an opportunity for the acquisition of goods they would not otherwise have had a chance to acquire.

As the rioting continues to escalate, with destructive activities relatively unchecked, looting seems to become highly selective and to reflect pre-existing sentiments of community residents. Stores are attacked and plundered not simply because they contain goods available for redistribution, goods that promise escape from dreary conditions, but are besieged for other reasons. Businesses representing hated white domination or owned by persons who had developed an especially antagonistic relationship with local ghetto residents are selected. In their systematic study Dynes and Quarantelli have given particular emphasis to the distinctive character of this looting phase, stressing that in contrast to natural disasters such as hurricanes or floods, in riot situations looting by rioters has been common, selective, and condoned by a large segment of the local community.[50] While looters were not always selective and restrained, much evidence indicates that most ghetto

[49] Quarantelli and Dynes, "Looting in Civil Disorders: An Index of Social Change," 131; *Report of the National Advisory Commission on Civil Disorders,* p. 67; Gilbert et al., *Ten Blocks from the White House,* p. 178.

[50] Dynes and Quarantelli, "What Looting in Civil Disturbances Really Means," 122ff.

rioters were conspicuously discriminating in their activities: "Indeed, restraint and selectivity were among the most crucial features of the riots."[51]

As looting progressed, members of the crowds of rioters even began to formulate new patterns of conduct. Congregations of people in the streets have in fact created their own forms of social control, at variance with the pre-existing regulation imposed by outside authorities. In spite of the common perception that riots reflect totally anarchical or undisciplined activities, there is evidence that relatively well-defined rules of the game emerged during the rioting. Policemen, instead of receiving deference and obedience, became the targets of increased defiance and attack. Destructive and expropriating actions emerged as objects of social praise rather than disapproval. Looting did not receive the same reproach that it might otherwise receive. Moreover, even intervening agencies other than the police, such as firemen and their equipment, whose actions threaten the movement of the crowds, were often attacked rather than supported. The normative criteria developed by ghetto rioters were not necessarily in total opposition to the norms applied in less troubled times, since they may well have actualized and extended pre-existing orientations. Perhaps the inability of many observers to recognize the implicit patterns that guided social behavior during ghetto riots resulted from a failure to identify rules of conduct that differed sharply from the formal restrictions usually imposed by white-dominated social control agencies.

In addition to the norms of the crowd that sanctioned assaults upon existing sources of authority, perhaps surprisingly, some rules of conduct developed during riots imposed significant limitations on personal behavior. The sentiments of the crowds on the streets occasionally served not only to condone violent or destructive acts but also to protect certain individuals or institu-

[51] Robert M. Fogelson, *Violence as Protest* (Garden City, N.Y.: Doubleday, 1971), p. 17.

tions from attack. Perhaps the most visible manifestations of this normative structure were the numerous "Soul Brother" signs that were emblazoned on black-owned businesses in riot neighborhoods, signs ordinarily respected by most rioters.[52] In contrast, evidence points to the conclusion that stores with these signs became targets for destruction by the police and the National Guard during or after some riots.[53]

Moreover, riot crowds were sometimes differentiated, in that certain members aided other rioters in the identification of stores and other institutions which should be spared. Attempts to enter businesses with a favorable relationship with the community were often deterred by bystanders. In many instances the emergent norms guiding crowd behavior intervened to protect white persons regarded sympathetically by local residents. In many cases, too, attacks on police and firemen by snipers stopped short of deadly violence.[54] Rioting crowds not only formed definitions of "right" and "wrong" but also sought to impose these views on those joining street groups at later stages of the riots. Evidence of the existence of relatively well-recognized canons of behavior, therefore, was visible in the actions of participants in what have been termed the "commodity riots" of the sixties.[55]

A new normative orientation can also be seen in much of the actual looting behavior of the rioters. As looting expanded, ob-

[52] See *Report of the Chicago Riot Study Committee,* pp. 15, 73; *Report of the National Advisory Commission on Civil Disorders,* p. 67; Gilbert et al., *Ten Blocks from the White House,* pp. 179–180; Anthony Oberschall, "The Los Angeles Riot of August 1965," *Social Problems,* 15 (Winter 1968), 337.

[53] Eyewitness reports of police and National Guard destruction can be found in Governor's Select Commission on Civil Disorder, State of New Jersey, *Report for Action* (New Jersey, February 1968), pp. 119–120.

[54] For example, see *Report of the Chicago Riot Study Committee,* p. 14; Oberschall, "The Los Angeles Riot of August 1965," 337.

[55] This term seems to have been coined in Janowitz, "The Social Control of Escalated Riots," 503.

jects of appropriation included appliances, clothing, television sets, and other consumer items tied to the image of the "good life" in America. Numerous black Americans apparently sought to pursue socially induced goals by obtaining consumer goods during a riot they had previously been unable to acquire because of limited economic means. Rioting, however, represented more than an effort to seize merchandise inaccessible under other conditions. Fundamentally, looting reflected the ongoing power struggle in America's urban centers. In the omnipresent looting can be seen a new normative orientation toward private property, a major redefinition of property rights. Items that were previously distributed on the basis of the prevailing inequitable distribution of financial resources were allocated during the riots according to more egalitarian standards. In the new normative framework of a serious riot, pre-existing principles of ownership and property frequently collapsed, being replaced by more radical criteria.

Nor did looting during serious outbreaks of violence simply reflect isolated or individualistic behavior. Much looting seems to have been performed openly by groups of black ghettoites operating with at least tacit community consent, rather than by individuals fearful of social disapproval and acting in clandestine fashion.[56] Close cooperation among the participants in both the removal and the distribution of stolen goods from local stores was often necessary. In the 1967 Detroit riot, moreover, black residents of riot-torn neighborhoods were sometimes joined by low-income whites in a type of integrated looting that was apparently the first of its kind in the recent history of urban violence.[57] Surprisingly, too, there seems to be little evidence of violent disputes among looters over the division of their booty. In our Twelfth Street survey in Detroit, conducted shortly after

[56] For example, see Quarantelli and Dynes, "Looting in Civil Disorders: An Index of Social Change," 136; other accounts, however, stress the individual character of some looting. See Gilbert et al., *Ten Blocks from the White House,* pp. 140ff.

[57] See Locke, *The Detroit Riot of 1967,* pp. 87–88.

one of the nation's most destructive urban riots, two thirds of a sample of local residents expressed the view that looters primarily took goods for their own use rather than "to sell them to others." As far as we can tell from the limited evidence available, in most cases looting did not reflect an organized plan to resell stolen goods through illegal channels after the collective violence had ended.

Therefore, the activities of both small groups and crowds of rioters often exhibited indications of normative agreement regarding attacks on police officers and local merchants, on the protection of favorably viewed individuals and institutions, and on the redefinition of property or ownership rights. Despite the sharp disparity between pre-existing social restrictions and conventions and the normative standards that emerged during ghetto revolts, the activities of persons who engaged in a serious riot often did seem to be guided by rules of conduct and concepts of "right" and "wrong." Views of proper and improper behavior in the new social order created during a serious riot seemed to be widely shared and respected during the course of the violence in many American cities.

When a particular riot has escalated to higher and higher levels of intensity, with crowds on the street increasing in size, that riot can be viewed as entering a new phase sometimes described as a state of siege:

> The adversary relations between ghetto dwellers and local and City Hall whites reach such a degree of polarization that no direct communications of any kind can be established. Communications, such as they are, consist of symbolic, warlike acts. State and federal military assistance is summoned for even more violent repression.[58]

[58] Conant, "Rioting, Insurrection and Civil Disobedience," 426; see also the discussion of major riots in the *Report of the National Advisory Commission on Civil Disorders,* pp. 30–41, 47–73; Locke, *The Detroit Riot of 1967,* pp. 26–50; Gilbert et al., *Ten Blocks from the White House,* pp. 103–119.

Attacks on available and unpopular local institutions such as the police and ghetto businesses not only expand in scope but also in intensity and destructiveness. Intentional acts of arson, increased fire bombing, and some sniping begin to accompany, even displace, widespread looting. As with the looting, the burning of local stores and other property typically was selective. In our Detroit survey over two thirds of the residents of the riot-torn area argued that "most of the stores that people tried to burn were owned by whites"; six in ten among those interviewed felt that the stores were burned mainly because "the owners deserved it." The spread of arson, the use of fire bombs, and the sniping, therefore, represent a significant escalation of the assault upon white domination of the ghetto.

At this stage of the uprising the activities of both rioters and the police forces attempting to restore establishment control take the form of a pitched battle. Attacks and counterattacks are lauded by participants on both sides; tactical considerations come into play on a large scale. Numerous killings occur in this phase. Curfews frequently are imposed, and the movement of persons in riot areas is sharply curtailed. In addition, reports of sniping may begin to spread through the riot area; reliable, exaggerated, and unfounded accounts of sniper activity manifest a direct and especially frightening threat to the lives of the representatives of external white control—law enforcement personnel. Although law enforcement reports of sniper action, like earlier rumors circulating shortly after precipitating incidents, frequently are exaggerated or unsubstantiated, they seem to play a part in provoking a sharp increase in the character, size, and intensity of police activities.[59]

As a result, unprovoked or senseless deaths and injuries to

[59] The general conclusion in the literature seems to be that sniping reports were made in many serious riots, but law enforcement reports were greatly exaggerated. Almost no blacks were arrested for sniping. See *Report of the National Advisory Commission on Civil Disorders,* p. 180; *Report of the Chicago Riot Study Committee,* p. 15; Fogelson, *Violence as Protest,* pp. 46, 77, 96.

local residents by nervous and fearful law enforcement officers, coupled with accompanying rumors communicating these incidents throughout the riot areas, in turn have spread and fanned the flames of ghetto animosity and actions directed toward the agents of social control. Collective violence continues to escalate, spurred by the mutual assaults and responses of two clearly defined, increasingly antagonistic racial formations in a riotous struggle.

The development of a riot into the siege stage has usually been marked by the calling in of National Guard or federal troops to assist local law enforcement officers. For example, at least seven of the eight 1967 riots regarded as major by the National Advisory Commission saw the mobilization and use of National Guardsmen, ranging from a low of 200 men in Plainfield, New Jersey, to the high of 8,200 men in Detroit, Michigan. Altogether, over 32,000 National Guard and federal troops were used in more than a dozen serious disorders in 1967. Federal troops (4,880 men) were used only once, in suppressing the Detroit riot. Even more federal troops were used in connection with the major riots in 1968, with 5,000 being used in Chicago, 5,100 in Baltimore, and 14,000 in Washington, D.C. Altogether, nearly 60,000 National Guard and federal troops were used to suppress the numerous April 1968 riots after the King assassination.[60] Ultimately a ghetto riot whatever its scale subsides, partly because of the wounds and exhaustion of the rioters and partly because of the massive crushing force available to the established powerholders seeking to end rioting.

It is also important to note that the development of riots into a state of siege often signaled the collapse of negotiations between representatives of the riot-torn ghetto community and city officials. At this stage of the collective violence, the attention of civil leaders usually was not so much on what caused the riots or how they started but on the more immediate and absorbing prob-

[60] Lemberg Center for the Study of Violence, "April Aftermath of the King Assassination," 65–66.

lem of how they might be stopped. As a result, the preoccupation of public influentials turned completely away from the grievances of black residents of the city to the imperative issue of terminating the rioting.

Even prior to escalation to a level of a state of siege, relatively formal negotiations have frequently occurred in connection with ghetto revolts between spokesmen from the areas affected by violence and local government officials. To illustrate, in nine out of ten of the 1967 ghetto revolts analyzed by the National Advisory Commission some type of negotiation between blacks and whites occurred.[61] Discussions have been convened at various stages of the rioting, ranging from before the outbreak of collective violence, to soon after the precipitating incident, to the end of the rioting. Meetings have often been continued for a considerable time during the riots, but they usually displayed a loss of communication as the conflict between riot participants and white authorities became more combative. The representatives of ghetto areas in those negotiations typically were the older, established leaders of the local black community. Sometimes negotiations also included younger adults, teenagers, and others who had not previously secured the status of publicly recognized spokesmen for the black community. The discussion in these negotiations commonly encompassed problems and issues produced by the violence itself, particularly the treatment of riot participants and local residents by law enforcement agents. In addition, the negotiations often extended to pre-existing black grievances related to the surfacing of the collective violence, including such issues as police misconduct before the riots, unemployment, and inadequate housing.[62] The common meetings and negotiations between civil officials and informal or formal black spokesmen that often accompanied urban rioting, therefore, pro-

[61] *Report of the National Advisory Commission on Civil Disorders,* p. 72.
[62] Ibid., p. 73.

vide strong support for the argument that both parties to the conflict recognized that the collective violence reflected important grievances requiring political solutions.

Indeed, negotiations between ghetto representatives and official leaders over the riots of the sixties may be a recent manifestation of a process that has historically characterized the outbreak of collective violence at the hands of the powerless. Studies of civil disorders in European and American cities during the eighteenth and nineteenth centuries have indicated that a type of collective bargaining by collective violence was not uncommon.[63] Although the message transmitted by collective action seldom was clearly articulated, the outbreak of such rioting provided in effect an important means of overcoming inadequacies in existing systems of power distribution and political representation and of ascertaining the grievances of the lower classes before their grievances spurred large-scale revolution. Thus the formal negotiations between ghetto leaders and civil officials during ghetto revolts constituted an explicit expression of political realities characteristic of many instances of collective violence.

In conclusion, then, although riots have been depicted as chaotic and disorderly events, a careful examination of their development indicates that they typically progress, varying of course with the scale of the riot, through several stages: the chain of preparatory events culminating in a final precipitant, the initial stage of keynoting, crowd formation, and the first taste of violence, the "Roman Holiday" stage of regrouping and violent assaults on symbols of public authority, the emergence of a new normative situation coupled with widespread looting behavior, and the siege stage characterized by extensive fires, sniping, and the involvement of outside control forces on a large scale. This

[63] See H. L. Nieburg, *Political Violence* (New York: St. Martin's, 1969); Richard E. Rubenstein, *Rebels in Eden* (Boston: Little, Brown, 1970); E. J. Hobsbawm, *Primitive Rebels* (New York: Norton Paperback, 1965).

developmental sequence should be viewed as describing general trends in ghetto riots in the 1960s, recurring patterns in riot development.

Thus relatively "minor" riots, to use the terminology of the National Advisory Commission, did not reach the later stages of escalated destruction and violence; ordinarily, a minor riot lasted for one day, involved relatively small numbers of black rioters, and did not reach the stages of extensive looting and siege. Characteristic, too, of these smaller-scale instances of collective violence was the limitation of control forces to the local police. "Serious" riots, in contrast, reached higher levels of violence, on the part of both rioters and control agents. Generally these riots lasted for between one and two days, involved at least one sizable crowd and many small crowds, and reached the stage of excitement and widespread looting, perhaps with some arson. They were also characterized by the use of police from outside the local area, most commonly the state police. "Major" riots typically passed through all of these stages to the levels of intensified violence and siege, usually lasting more than two days and characterized by many fires, widespread looting, and sniping reports. The control response, if not immediate, was massive, commonly involving use of National Guard or federal troops to supplement local control forces.[64]

A further indication of the patterning of ghetto riots in terms of stages of severity can be glimpsed in one empirical study of 75 riots undertaken by Wanderer. In a study of riots during 1967 he discovered that riot characteristics could be grouped into several composite patterns and ranked on a cumulative scale of rioting; that is, the 75 riots could be hierarchically arranged so that, with relatively few errors, the most severe riots contained all of the examined characteristics of the lesser riots and the less severe

[64] *Report of the National Advisory Commission on Civil Disorders,* pp. 63–65; *Report of the Chicago Riot Study Committee,* pp. 9–20; Governor's Select Commission on Civil Disorder, *Report for Action,* pp. 104–124.

riots included only one or two of the attributes of the more destructive ones.[65] The seven items of riot severity employed in devising the severity scale were from most to least serious: the killing of a civilian or policeman, the calling in of the National Guard, the calling in of the state police, sniping reports, looting, interference with firemen, and vandalism. This cumulative scale analysis points to the conclusion that ghetto riots were not "bizarre, non-patterned, or randomly generated."[66] It is also noteworthy that the first three categories generally do not relate to the activities of black rioters, but depend on the perceptions and responses of local officials vested by white powerholding groups with the responsibility for suppressing violent dissent.

Official Actions in Ghetto Riot Situations

Up to this point in this chapter, the discussion of the pattern of escalation and development of urban riots has been sprinkled with only a few references to the critical role of official actions. Yet the reactions of public authorities and law enforcement officers constitute the other side of a pattern of mutual interaction that has determinative impact upon the development of ghetto riots. Mattick has given emphasis to this reciprocal character of riots: the form of a riot "consists of challenges and responses between the official and the private participants to the riot, with the challenge and response originating potentially from either side."[67] The typical stages through which a riot passes could conceivably have a thrust that is basically independent of official actions, but examination of available evidence indicates that the intervention of the police and local officials has often shaped the nature, intensity, and outcome of ghetto revolts.

[65] Jules J. Wanderer, "An Index of Riot Severity and Some Correlates," *American Journal of Sociology,* 74 (March 1969), 503. The data were originally reported by city mayors to a U.S. Senate committee.

[66] Ibid., p. 505. We do not intend to suggest here that minor riots were necessarily aborted major riots.

[67] Mattick, "The Form and Content of Recent Riots," 16.

Perhaps the principal role of external groups in ghetto riots has been played by law enforcement officers, the primary agents of white authority in the black communities where riots have occurred. Just as the conduct of policemen before the riots and during the final precipitating incident has had an important effect on the outbreak of ghetto violence, the behavior of police officers and their superiors during the other stages of riots also has been important. In confronting the outbreak and development of violence on the part of ghetto rioters, law enforcement personnel have faced the critical dilemma of choosing from a repertory of possible control responses, frequently the extremes of "undercontrol" and "overcontrol." However, despite the critical nature of the law enforcement response, no one type of response has emerged as the most efficient or the most widely utilized riot control strategy. Proposals for such strategies have ranged from the total withdrawal of all police agencies to permit local leaders and residents to cool the rioting to the instantaneous display of massive force to coerce the rioters into submission.

Although officials in relatively few cities have attempted total withdrawal of policemen from a riot area soon after the occurrence of a final precipitating incident, taken together with a negotiation approach, in any event this strategy would be difficult to administer in most ghetto situations. For this to be an effective strategy, it would seem that either respected leaders in the ghetto or leading white authorities, and perhaps both, must appear at the scenes of early crowd formation and make significant concessions to the potential rioters. Yet black leaders cannot or will not play a role in riot control without major, and thus unlikely, concessions from white officials and white-dominated agencies. In regard to local white officials, Conant has observed that

The response of civil authorities at this point is also crucial. If representatives of local authority appear, listen to complaints and suggest some responsive method for dealing with them, the agitation tends to subside; a "let's wait and see" attitude takes over.[68]

Since those white leaders with the power and resources to rectify long-standing black grievances have generally not been available for direct consultation with aggrieved rioters during early riot stages—or have been unwilling to make major concessions in relation to these grievances—the complete withdrawal of police personnel would not ordinarily terminate ghetto rioting. In addition, to be effective such a strategy would have required a police willingness to withdraw, also a problematical contingency. Even this brief discussion, when linked with an examination of available riot histories, points up the absence of workable and efficient mechanisms for the formulation of immediate political solutions for ghetto grievances in confrontation situations, as well as in the routine affairs of urban ghetto life.

A much more popular and widely proposed control response, especially among the white authorities and white public, to the initial outbreak of ghetto violence is the immediate concentration of well-equipped police agents in as massive a display of force as possible to disperse the emerging crowds and quell a riot. In fact, many have argued that the only remedy for rioting is the "mobilization of the largest possible police or control force as early as possible."[69] As one might expect, police planning and preparations for ghetto violence have usually been relative to crowd dispersal and containment operations. In preparing for such operations police have given the greatest emphasis to relatively technical issues such as special riot training for law enforcement personnel, the development of rapid communication

[68] Conant, "Rioting, Insurrection, and Civil Disobedience," 425.

[69] *Report of the National Advisory Commission on Civil Disorders,* p. 72; Phillip A. Luce, *Road to Revolution* (San Diego, Calif.: Viewpoint Books, 1967), pp. 132–133. Luce goes so far as to suggest the suspension of civil liberties and the use of I.D. cards and detention centers.

185

systems, and the acquisition of special riot control weapons. In fact, much of the police preparation for riots has taken on a military or paramilitary character. The following quote from a recent police manual which details a great variety of specific riot control techniques and materials illustrates this point:

> Currently, regardless of political or self-imposed restraints, desires of elected officials, or past conceptions of the police role in a democratic society, civil law enforcement agencies must train, organize and operate along modified military lines to meet the challenges presented by large-scale riot control operations so often accompanied by armed violence.[70]

Police departments on the whole have devoted little attention to potential minority responses to these riot control techniques and materials, or for that matter to broader riot prevention programs such as community or minority relations activities. In contrast, several studies by prominent citizens of police systems in the United States have argued that a comprehensive community relations program is in effect the "best method of riot control available to the police."[71]

Whatever the police planning and preparations for ghetto violence, however, local police departments have not always attempted to quell the initial outbreak of riots by adopting a strategy entailing massive force aimed at forcing ghetto residents immediately off the streets. Rather, they have actually engaged in a variety of riot control methods. These methods have included (1) dispersal, clearing the area by arrests and crowd dispersal; (2) reconnaissance, the cautious observation and assessment of continuing riot development; and (3) containment, the

---

[70] Rex Applegate, *Riot Control—Materiel and Techniques* (Harrisburg, Pa.: Stackpole Books, 1969), p. 15.

[71] Task Force on the Police, *The Police*, p. 193. Even the 1965 FBI manual on riot control touches briefly on the need to keep police lines of communication to minority communities open. See the sections of the FBI manual quoted in Luce, *Road to Revolution*, p. 149.

imposition of curfews and barricades to cordon off the riot area. According to the National Advisory Commission's review of 1967 riot cities, the most common response to the initial outbreak was crowd dispersal, utilized in about four out of every ten riot situations studied. Crowd dispersal and containment tactics, however, did account for the majority of the police response patterns, sometimes used in combination.[72]

While dispersal and containment tactics may suggest to the observer the use of relatively large numbers of police in as massive and instantaneous a display of force as possible, this relationship does not necessarily have to be present. In at least a few riot situations that have been analyzed the initial control tactics, while involving dispersal and arrest objectives, did not entail the use of enough law enforcement officers to implement such objectives. Nevertheless, one study of the size of initial control forces indicates that in most of the police control situations the policeman-rioter ratio was relatively high. An examination of 22 of the 1967 riots revealed that "in a majority of cases for which we have such information, in 12 out of 22, the initial control force was either larger than the crowd on the street or no fewer than a ratio of one policeman to every five persons on the street."[73] In the other ten cases where information could be secured, the ratio varied considerably; the median ratio was 1 policeman for every 25 persons on the street. These results suggest that in a large proportion of riot development situations, perhaps the great majority, the response of the local control forces was one of massing a relatively large number of officers in riot areas, ordinarily in conjunction with dispersal—arrest sweeps of the riot area or, less often, in cordoning off and constricting the riot area.

Yet despite the relatively immediate, massive, and aggressive police responses in many riot situations, the further development of ghetto violence often was not curtailed. Looking again at the data on the 1967 riots, the National Advisory Commission con-

[72] *Report of the National Advisory Commission on Civil Disorders,* pp. 72–328.
[73] Ibid., p. 328.

cluded that "in at least half of the 24 cases it can reasonably be said that the approach taken by the police" did not prevent the continuation of violence.[74] Of the 13 riot situations where the initial law enforcement response was deemed a serious failure in the control sense, 10 involved the crowd dispersal or cordoning off approaches. Moreover, if ghetto violence accelerated beyond the initial phases, the second control response by law enforcement authorities was even more likely to take the form of dispersal, followed in terms of frequency by a containment approach. The reconnaissance approach, as one might expect, was abandoned by half of those departments that had used it initially. Even in subsequent riot phases, however, the riot control techniques of massing officers for crowd dispersal or cordoning purposes frequently failed to prevent the continuation of ghetto rioting.[75] Nor were comparable police tactics consistently successful in numerous riots that occurred both before and after the 1967 riot period.[76]

Given these materials, one is not surprised to learn that police tactics have often been rather instrumental in contributing to the escalation of ghetto violence to higher levels of intensity and destruction. Police actions resulting in the increase of violence on the part of rioters have sometimes resulted from errors in the implementation of preplanned riot control measures, sometimes from the inability of police agencies to apply the appropriate measures at the requisite stage of riot development, and sometimes from overcontrol, the use of too much force or the misuse of force for punitive purposes.

Efforts to exert massive strength by assigning very large num-

[74] Ibid., p. 72.
[75] Ibid.
[76] On police tactics in the 1964 Harlem and Bedford-Stuyvesant riots, see Shapiro and Sullivan, *Race Riots: New York 1964,* pp. 7, 49–51, 130ff.; on the varying police tactics in the 1968 Washington riot see Gilbert et al., *Ten Blocks from the White House,* pp. 25–67. On the Watts riot see Oberschall, "The Los Angeles Riot of August 1965," 336; Cohen and Murphy, *Burn, Baby, Burn!,* pp. 64–75.

bers of police officers to a riot area, in both initial and subsequent riot phases, have often exacerbated local animosity toward law enforcement agents and increased the number and intensity of attacks on police.[77] The sudden appearance of a large number of police can advance a riot from the initial phases to a more intensive level. Overcontrol has also been reflected in the riot response of local police departments which entails the calling in of outside police forces, the first usually being the state police, then the National Guard or federal troops.[78] Efforts to augment the local police by securing the assistance of external social control agencies can produce an increase in both the pace and the intensity of violence: "Local and state police are rushed to the scene of the confrontation and begin to manhandle everyone in sight."[79] Numerous accounts of urban riots have indicated that National Guardsmen, frequently untrained and poorly equipped for riot duty, have contributed to the escalation rather than reduction of riot intensity.

Relating directly to the character and motivation of law enforcement overcontrol responses, one analyst has argued forcefully that "one can distinguish, for example, between two- and three-day riots (Bedford-Stuyvesant, Cleveland, Washington, D.C., or Chicago, for example) and week-long riots (Watts, Newark, Detroit) on the ground that, in the latter, police or National Guard responses amounted to punitive counterattacks which helped spread both arson and sniping into residential areas."[80] However, a punitive orientation on the part of police forces was not limited to the week-long riots in Detroit and elsewhere. In

[77] Conant, "Rioting, Insurrection, and Civil Disobedience," 427–428. See also references cited in the preceding footnote.

[78] In 13 cities where supplemental control forces were brought in, violence (presumably that of rioters) of equal or greater intensity occurred after the forces arrived. *Report of the National Advisory Commission on Civil Disorders,* p. 72. See also Gilbert et al., *Ten Blocks from the White House,* pp. 42ff.

[79] Conant, "Rioting, Insurrection and Civil Disobedience," 427.

[80] Rubenstein, *Rebels in Eden,* p. 119.

other riot situations aggressive attempts by well-protected officers to disperse crowds of unarmed civilians, particularly when the force was seen as excessively harsh or brutal by surrounding crowds, escalated the riots and led in turn to intensified attacks on the police by the crowds. In some cities major riots were actually stimulated by the punitive character of police behavior in making arrests in the initial police effort to disperse crowds. In reaction to an overresponse by the police, crowds subsequently stormed police stations to secure the release of those thought to be arrested unfairly. A massive police presence at the location of a precipitating event soon after the occurrence of the incident may sometimes constitute an effective riot control strategy when it is coupled with strict exercise of self-restraint, limitations on control violence, and the maintenance of harmonious relations with ghetto residents. When these characteristics are lacking, however, massive action can easily accelerate collective violence.

However, in the heterogeneous responses of control agencies to riot activities, overcontrol was not the only error committed. Undercontrol sometimes played a significant part in the development of ghetto riots. In riot situations where no massive deployment of control forces was possible the inability of police departments to muster an adequate number of officers had rapidly confronted police executives with the dilemma either of keeping the riot under surveillance from a distance and allowing it to continue unabated or of exerting force to suppress the violence, even though the force was insufficient to disperse crowd formations. The latter strategy of attempting to terminate rioting without adequate strength sometimes resulted in increased attacks on police officers and heightened danger to all concerned, not only because of the isolated and vulnerable status of police officers in riot areas but also because of the tendency of these policemen to express their sense of threat and fear by directing increased punitive violence at rioters. Moreover, the mere observation of riot activities by police officers without any concomitant efforts to make concessions to rioters or to curtail the riot exacerbated the growth of ghetto rioting. Allowing formerly restricted acts to go unpunished encouraged expanded riot participation by demonstrating police acquiescence in the newly emerging property norms of the forming crowds.[81] On occasion, the reticence of policemen to intervene in the events may have accelerated the transition of rioting from the early phases of crowd formation and destructive behavior to the stage of extensive looting.

Conceivably, the dilemma confronting police departments that lack sufficient strength during the early phases of ghetto riots might be partially resolved by empowering local residents, such as adult males in riot areas, to patrol for the purpose of cooling down the riot. Such a policy would represent an acknowledgement by public authorities of the desire for self-determination and community control clearly reflected in the actions of rioters. Nonetheless, in most outbreaks of serious rioting law enforcement and other public officials have generally been reluctant to allow community leaders and other ghetto residents to participate in riot control efforts, to any significant degree, either by the withdrawal of police officers and the initiation of immediate productive negotiations with local residents or by seeking extensive assistance from members of the community who are opposed to violence in controlling the rioting.

Whatever the response in early riot phases, the ultimate response of law enforcement agencies in most serious riot situations has been large-scale intervention in the rioting, even if that meant calling in a number of outside control agencies. Eventually the official violence seen in law enforcement repression activities, by some measures, exceeded the amount of violence originating from the actions of riot participants. The acts of violence that occurred during ghetto riots cannot be divorced from their contexts; the behavior of rioters and law enforcement officers normally formed a series of mutual actions eventually determining the cumulative impact and outcome of a particular riot. Al-

---

[81] Conant, "Rioting, Insurrection and Civil Disobedience," 427. See also Cohen and Murphy, *Burn, Baby, Burn!*, pp. 64ff.

though most white Americans may be more inclined to regard the destructive actions by local black citizens as a form of "violence," active conduct by the representatives of political authority resulting in the destruction of life or property must also be considered "violent behavior." Strictly speaking, violence should be defined by its destructive consequences in regard to persons and property rather than by its sources or origins. Thus in the ghetto rebellions of the 1960s the total amount of personal violence directed at riot participants by a variety of law enforcement officers probably exceeded the amount of violence that the rioters directed at those officers or at other personal targets. Deaths and injuries to black civilians, including innocent bystanders and nonrioters, as the result of police and other official actions were significantly more numerous than the fatalities or wounds suffered by law enforcement officers.[82]

Nor was the role of law enforcement agents negligible in the case of property damage. Although the property destruction by rioters was usually greater than that caused by police agencies, the destruction of property by control agents in suppressing riots on occasion produced considerable damage to important neighborhood organizations and contributed to the problem of rebuilding the ghetto. In a number of ghetto riots police actions, particularly in the later stages of violence, resulted in serious destruction of ghetto buildings and agencies that had previously escaped the vengeance of the rioters.[83] For example, an official state government report on the 1967 Newark riot cited several cases of official damage:

[82] One survey of 75 riots in 1967 found that 89 percent of the deaths and 62 percent of the (reported) injuries were civilians, the overwhelming majority being blacks. *Report of the National Advisory Commission on Civil Disorders,* pp. 67, 326. See also Shapiro and Sullivan, *Race Riots: New York 1964,* pp. 203ff.; Cohen and Murphy, *Burn, Baby, Burn!,* passim.

[83] *Report of the National Advisory Commission on Civil Disorders,* p. 67.

The Development of Ghetto Riots: Precipitants and Patterns

The Reverend Herbert G. Draesel, an Episcopal priest, testified that on Friday evening, July 14, he was standing on a corner when several police cars drove down the street, stopped in front of the Colonnade Bar and began firing into the bar for no apparent reason. Suddenly, Father Draesel said, the policemen changed their firing from the bar to the group standing on the corner.[84]

The Commission received much reliable testimony that the police and the National Guard shot up black-owned businesses, especially those marked as "Soul Brother" stores.[85] In addition, one of the most striking findings unveiled by our survey of the Twelfth Street area in Detroit was that no less than 81 percent of the ghetto residents reported hearing stories that "some policemen were involved in taking things or burning stores" during the riots. Although the existing evidence of illegal police conduct such as theft or the destruction of property during the ghetto riots is rather sketchy and difficult to evaluate, there is at least the suggestion here of significant police violence directed against ghetto property.

As a result, by the end of the 1960s many residents and leaders in a ghetto that had had a riot or riots were probably eager to avert further violence of the type seen in ghetto rioting—violence that might result in excessive casualties and suffering to local black civilians. Efforts by black urbanites, including militants, to avoid additional outbreaks of ghetto rioting probably have been inspired not only by the recognition of the superior force available to police agencies but also by a realization that excessive force on the part of police control agents during previous riots had inflicted devastating and irreplaceable damage on the lives and property of the residents of the black community. In the few years following the peak era of massive riots—1967–1968—

[84] Governor's Select Commission on Civil Disorders, *Report for Action*, p. 119.
[85] Ibid., pp. 120–121.

the occurrence of *major* instances of ghetto violence apparently decreased, although collective violence of serious consequence continued. The eventual or long-term consequences of this decrease, however, are rather difficult to assess. Although the fear of official police violence may be an effective deterrent to the immediate resumption of extremely large-scale riot activity of the type seen in Watts or Detroit, the ultimate consequences of a major segment of the population living under the threat of massive police subjugation and repression could be even more destructive to the structure of American society than the open occurrence of ghetto violence.

The tendency of social control agencies to react to the outbreak of ghetto riots by engaging in more interpersonal violence than has been directed at them is not difficult to explain. Since police officers have often been principal targets for attack in the chain of preparatory incidents that have led to collective violence, their responses have in part been shaped by the impulse to defend oneself or the group to which one belongs, a tendency promoted by the strong bonds of brotherhood developed among city policemen. Even more important, rioting in various stages has constituted a direct threat to the pre-existing codes of behavior that police officers have been commanded to enforce. The rejection of the restrictions on conduct enacted by established and previously legitimate political authorities, therefore, has necessitated active intervention to protect established power-holders from new contenders for power. The aggressive, even punitive, reactions of the police during ghetto riots not only have been promoted by police disapproval of disruption of the established order but also have been based on the official conviction that rioting reflects the emergence of a potential revolutionary force.[86] Unlike the reactions of some other observers of ghetto uprisings, the actions of social control authorities during the

[86] See, for example, the comments in Applegate, *Riot Control—Materiel and Techniques,* pp. 15, 99 and passim.

collective violence reflected a recognition that the rioting represented political motivations and political threat.

Specific tactical arrangements and preventive actions of law enforcement agencies sometimes provided definite evidence of fears of revolution. In the Detroit riot of 1967, for example, large contingents from police and National Guard units were stationed with rifles, submachine guns, and armored vehicles at major government buildings and public utilities installations such as waterworks, telephone centers, major electric transformers, and other locations that they feared would become targets of a major insurrection. These preparations of the civil authorities subsequently proved to be based on unfounded apprehensions; yet they did demonstrate the politically related fears present among public officials as they confronted the problem of restoring order.

Recognition of the importance of a large-scale control response in relation to the power-threatening activities of black rioters can also be seen in the mass media. Television and newspaper coverage not only ignored the grievances and activities of black rioters during the 1967 riots but greatly stressed the views, actions, and purpose of law enforcement agents: "This conclusion is based on the relatively high frequency with which television showed and described law enforcement agents, police, national guardsmen, and army troops performing control functions."[87] Newspaper coverage also focused on enforcement issues, particularly on riot control legislation and on the containment or control of rioters. In some cities such as Detroit newsmen even collaborated with the police in riot control activities, most conspicuously in voluntary news blackouts on rioting. In taking this tack, the mass media reinforced the perspectives of law enforcement and other city officials that the re-establishment of coercive control was the most important issue during a critical period of unrest. Thus collective violence on the part of black

[87] *Report of the National Advisory Commission on Civil Disorders,* p. 204.

urbanites was also recognized as a serious threat to prior political arrangements by media representatives.

In addition, the mass media have appeared to play an important role in resonating a variety of official rumors and interpretations of ghetto rioting. In the emergent riot situation there is great need for official interpretations to eliminate the obvious ambiguity and volatility of the riot situation. Mattick has reminded us that private formations of ghetto residents are not the only ones who "intra-act" by means of information and rumors, building the framework for interpreting events and for participation in further violence; city officials intra-act in the same fashion.[88]

This intra-acting on the part of officials, therefore, may partially explain the common focus on outside militants and organizing agitators and on the image of riots as products of black conspiracies to riot.[89] Explanations such as these can be related to a lengthy tradition of explaining political threat and upheaval in the United States over the last few centuries; one need only reflect for a moment on how such terms as "carpetbaggers," "Communists," "outside agitators," and "Yankees" have historically been used in the ideologies of entrenched power groups in situations viewed as threatening. It is not surprising, then, that ghetto uprisings have sometimes been viewed by city officials in terms of conspiracies or the organized plans of outsiders. Nevertheless, this view has so far received little empirical support. After an investigation of available evidence, including studies by various local commissions and agencies, the National Advisory Commission concluded that "the urban disorders of the summer of 1967 were not caused by, nor were they the consequence of, any organized plan or 'conspiracy.' "[90]

[88] Mattick, "The Form and Content of Recent Riots," 17.
[89] Ibid., p. 30.
[90] *Report of the National Advisory Commission on Civil Disorders,* p. 89. See also Governor's Select Commission on Civil Disorders, *Report for Action,* pp. 138–139; *Report of the Chicago Riot Study Committee,* passim.

Conclusion

Although the urban riots of the 1960s have been characterized by many observers as expressions of blind rage or as displays of youthful rampage and undisciplined destructiveness, a careful assessment of the events indicates that riots often reflected patterned and purposive activity. The outbreaks of ghetto violence did not reflect a sudden eruption of ghetto discontent without warning but were closely related to earlier and continuing nonviolent protest movements, and both in turn were directly related to continuing local grievances.

Moreover, the final precipitating event in serious urban riots often involved a direct encounter with law enforcement officers, important enforcers of external white authority in the ghetto. This final precipitating incident produced the gathering of a crowd that engaged in a form of political discussion regarding appropriate collective responses to the incident. The next stage of the riot process normally was marked by excitement and destructiveness, in which residents of riot areas demonstrated that certain established limitations on conduct would no longer apply. The targets of ghetto violence were not selected at random; most had significance within the context of the unequal distribution of power in urban areas. The excitement phase was followed in the case of serious rioting by the appearance of a representative group of ghetto residents and by extensive looting. As the crowds on the street began to recognize the collapse of pre-existing restraints, they developed their own rules of conduct, some condoning activities previously regarded as criminal, some protecting favored individuals or agencies from attack. In the final stage of the riot process, attained during the most serious riots, a state of siege emerged, in which all communications broke down, citizens could no longer move freely, and rioters battled with the large-scale paramilitary forces directed by authorities at rioters.

The development of serious urban riots, moreover, has reflected distinct political motivations and objectives. Perhaps nowhere has this interpretation been more clearly reflected than in the reactions of public officials and law enforcement personnel. The behavior of social control agencies in ghetto revolts has implied a specific recognition that the organization of crowds during the riots constituted a serious threat to established white authority and to the white-dominated system governing urban life.

Ghetto riots constituted a serious attack on existing political institutions, as well as an effort to secure a meaningful response from public officials, but they did not reflect a prevalent desire to overthrow or to withdraw from the basic framework of the present political order. The riots, therefore, seemed to occupy an intermediate position between nonviolent protest of political grievances and the launching of a major revolutionary movement. Unlike the earlier and sometimes coterminous nonviolent movement for civil rights and equal opportunities, the outbreak of rioting perhaps did not reflect as much faith in the impartiality of existing political processes and in their capacity to ameliorate ghetto problems. The riots reflected an assault on extant political arrangements and a desire to secure immediate concessions from local authorities concerning the grievances of the black community.

CHAPTER

The Aftermath of Rioting: The Establishment Response

The mounting tide of violence that engulfed black communities in many cities was clearly regarded by many Americans as a critical danger to the existing fabric of law and social order. As a deliberate repudiation of certain prior restrictions on conduct, ghetto rioting seemed to require and ultimately resulted in active intervention by local government authorities to restore their supremacy in ghetto communities. Numerous public and private leaders indicated by both their speeches and their actions that they saw the defiance of pre-existing laws during rioting as a very serious threat to established authority. In addition, the riot sentiments of many ghetto residents who experienced the nation's destructive riots in the last decade have signified a desire to restructure existing power arrangements and to gain increased local independence and control. The perceptions of officials and ghetto residents, therefore, appeared to reflect at least one basic point of agreement: that the ghetto uprisings confronted the nation with a crisis threatening the foundation of established arrangements and institutions in America's cities.

Despite the gravity of the issues raised by the collective violence in urban ghettos, however, the white community and its leadership devoted relatively little discussion to the deeper political implications of these traumatic events. While in the aftermath of serious riots several riot commission reports did offer

199

dual sets of recommendations of enhanced government support —on the one hand, for policies designed to augment the repressive capabilities of law enforcement agencies and, on the other, for policies constructed to alleviate problems in ghetto areas— both commissions and government officials alike clearly did not contemplate adopting meaningful structural changes to force existing social, economic, and governmental institutions to come under the significant influence of black communities. Moreover, even the sometimes promising riot commission proposals to expand substantially traditional welfare and remedial aid programs to meet ghetto needs were increasingly subjected to public neglect. With the apparent disappearance from the urban scene of really *massive* riots such as those in Los Angeles, Detroit, and Washington, D.C., and as reports of the serious rioting which continued to occur in numerous cities were apparently played down in the mass media, many white leaders apparently concluded that the outbreak of collective violence in American ghettos was merely an ephemeral and temporary phenomenon. Consequently, after some initial efforts, serious consideration of significant policy innovations along traditional lines (much less consideration of completely restructuring existing institutions) seemed to become the victim of the view that ghetto rioting was to be a meaningless, passing stage of urban history. Nonetheless, perhaps as a hedge against continuing collective violence and the possibility of future massive violence, the evidently growing loss of interest in reform did not curtail law enforcement preparations for the use of force against dissenting groups.

Remedies for Ghetto Violence: Some Broad Perspectives

Early in the life of the National Advisory Commission on Civil Disorders (National Advisory Commission), created by President Lyndon Johnson in the summer of 1967, a consultant from the Institute for Defense Analysis wrote a secret memorandum suggesting that there were three broad approaches to assessing the cures for ghetto violence that the Commission might consider: (1) a conservative approach emphasizing that black conspiracy and criminality were behind the ghetto outbreaks and that the remedy should take the form of an expansion of repressive measures; (2) a liberal approach ("middle position") that emphasized impersonal social phenomena as the causes and that remedies should more or less focus on an expansion of traditional approaches to dealing with urban problems; (3) a radical approach stressing that riots reflected a political rebellion on the part of black Americans and that the remedy should take the form of major restructuring of the existing system and bringing black Americans into full participation.[1] Although this outline of perspectives for the National Advisory Commission to consider may have seemed at the time novel and oriented toward future action, in fact it may well have summarized aspects of three general orientations toward the remedies for collective violence which were in the process of emerging as the Commission began its deliberations.

In his excellent assessment of violence in American history Rubenstein has delineated certain critical aspects of the broad conservative perspective:

> The *conservative* position, summarily stated, held that ghetto riots were produced by a combination of explosive material—the black mob or "underclass" consisting of the unemployed, those with criminal records or tendencies and lawless youth—and a spark, the rhetoric of local gang leaders or outside agitators. Reactionaries like George Wallace of Alabama stressed the role of the agitators, seeking to explain their activities as part of a sinister, conspiratorial design to disrupt American society. More sophisticated conservatives

[1] Andrew Kopkind, "White on Black: The Riot Commission and the Rhetoric of Reform," *The Politics of Riot Commissions 1917–1970,* ed. Anthony Platt (New York: Macmillan, 1971), p. 384.

201

emphasized those characteristics of the mob which made them vulnerable to demagoguery and "acting out."[2]

At the very heart of the conservative viewpoint is the notion that the causes of ghetto rioting are to be sought within the black community, that a (if not the) major responsibility for collective violence lay in the pathological, defective, immoral, or un-American characteristics of individuals in certain segments of the black community.[3] Nor is this emphasis limited to ghetto rioting alone, for the conservative position has sometimes viewed a myriad of other ghetto problems—including crime, juvenile delinquency, and welfare—in roughly similar terms. When those subscribing to the conservative point of view have proposed remedies for ghetto rioting, the stress has often been on solutions aimed at incarcerating deviant individuals or restructuring their character and morals.[4] Thus the immediate emphasis is often on repressive measures, on riot control materials and techniques, on special riot training for policemen, on riot control manuals, on special riot squads, and on police communications and intelligence organization. In the long run, the remedy is frequently expressed in terms of strengthening the moral training and character building of black Americans in the home, in the church, and in the schools.

The liberal perspective, on the other hand, tends to accentuate other causative factors and remedies. This "middle position," as some have termed it, accents not so much the highly personalized and individualized agitators and deviant individuals of the conservative viewpoint but rather relatively impersonal social causes for which no specific person or group is to be blamed, at

[2] Richard E. Rubenstein, *Rebels in Eden* (Boston: Little, Brown, 1970), p. 144.

[3] For example, see Eugene H. Methvin, *The Riot Makers* (New Rochelle, N.Y.: Arlington House, 1970), pp. 54ff.; Phillip Abbott Luce, *Road to Revolution* (San Diego: Viewpoint Books, 1968), pp. 17–89.

[4] For example, see Methvin, *The Riot Makers*, pp. 470ff.; Luce, *Road to Revolution*, pp. 130–134.

The Aftermath of Rioting: The Establishment Response

least not on the present scene.[5] Receiving stress is the historical development of the deprived position of black Americans, with a recurrent underlining of the interconnections between such broad forces as the background of slavery, the northward migration, and black family structure. Moreover, the liberal perspective has sometimes emphasized the role of racial prejudice ("white racism") in contributing to the surfacing of recent urban violence, as well as to the more general problems faced by black Americans.[6] When it comes to cures for rioting the liberal tack often is to couple a strong "law and order" call for repressive police measures with weighty recommendations for socioeconomic reforms, sometimes for relatively far-reaching reforms in areas such as employment and housing.[7] Yet the social and economic cures proposed seldom impinge seriously on the power, authority, or wealth of the dominant groups in the society. While the liberal perspective has been rather specific when it comes to proposing novel control materials and techniques for law enforcement agencies, recommendations for reform ordinarily have a traditional and time-worn character. Reports on ghetto problems and ghetto violence influenced by liberals have been rather ambiguous when it comes to proposals that might significantly augment the political power of black urbanites and other dissident minority groups.

Yet a third basic approach to the interpretation of ghetto problems has been characterized by some as a "radical" approach; this perspective takes a rather different view of the causes and development of ghetto violence and particularly of the remedies required. The radical position accents the idea that ghetto riots were actually political rebellions directed against various levels of white-dominated governmental and economic institutions,

[5] See Kopkind, "White on Black," p. 384.

[6] See *Report of the National Advisory Commission on Civil Disorders* (Washington, D.C.: U.S. Government Printing Office, 1968), pp. 91–131.

[7] Ibid., pp. 147–292; see also *Report of the Chicago Riot Study Committee* (Chicago, August 1968), pp. 115–121.

those which essentially determine the life of black communities.[8] The weakness of black Americans in the struggle among competing groups for power and wealth in urban areas is accentuated, with the power struggle sometimes being paralleled with that of the colonized and colonizers in developing countries.[9] The radical perspective goes beyond accentuating historical developments which have played an important role in the development of the black situation, such as slavery or the allegedly wrenching migration northward, to an emphasis on power relationships on the contemporary scene: the crux of the problem is the "system of interlocking elites operating at the local level through the machinery of urban government to keep blacks in a state of quasi-colonial subjection."[10] Nor does the radical perspective on ghetto rioting emphasize the immoral or irresponsible character of black Americans who rioted. Radical remedies for rioting exclude or play down those solutions encompassing the refurbishing of existing official control forces, but include those which would require restructuring existing economic and governmental institutions.[11] Therefore, one basic radical strategy for dealing with the outbreak of rioting would be to increase significantly the power and resources available to black Americans, to decentralize rather than centralize existing power and authority. In this proposal businesses and industrial corporations in the ghetto would be controlled and run by black ghetto residents; and decentralization would also extend to government agencies in the area, including welfare agencies and police forces.[12] Thus, it seems that

[8] Anthony Platt, "The Politics of Riot Commissions, 1917–1970: An Overview," *The Politics of Riot Commissions, 1917–1970,* ed. Anthony Platt (New York: Macmillan, 1971), p. 46.

[9] Robert Blauner, "Whitewash over Watts," *Trans-Action,* 3 (March/ April 1966), 3ff.

[10] Rubenstein, *Rebels in Eden,* p. 149.

[11] Jerome E. Skolnick, *The Politics of Protest* (New York: Simon and Schuster, 1969), pp. 343–346.

[12] William K. Tabb, *The Political Economy of the Black Ghetto* (New York: Norton, 1970); Alan A. Altshuler, *Community Control*

a major reason for a certain candor and directness in the radical approach is—unlike the liberal and conservative approaches—the absence of a strong attachment to the present structure of power in American society.

Not surprisingly, then, these three perspectives on the causes of and remedies for urban violence have been mirrored, albeit sometimes imperfectly, in many aspects of both governmental and private actions taken in regard to ghetto rioting during the last decade. One or another of these views appears to have guided not only the writings and actions of those men who have been appointed to government riot commissions, but also the actions of federal, state, and local officials who have responded in varying ways to the eruption of ghetto violence. In terms of concrete actions the major response to rioting on the part of the white majority apparently has been that of government officials and agencies, supported on occasion by the activities of closely allied business groups and officials. While it is not always possible to ascertain in a comprehensive way exactly what the government response to riots was, primarily because such data have not been systematically reported, in the sections which follow we have attempted to analyze existing information on riot reactions with regard to the following broad categories: (1) assessments of rioting by federal, state, and municipal government violence commissions; (2) the federal, state, and municipal law enforcement response in the aftermath of rioting; (3) federal, state, and municipal attempts to ameliorate socioeconomic conditions in ghettos in the wake of rioting.

An Age of Riot Commissions

Perhaps the most conspicuous governmental reaction to the ghetto riots in the last decade was the generation of a series of important riot and violence commissions charged with docu-

(New York: Western Publishing Company, Pegasus Edition, 1970); Rubenstein, *Rebels in Eden,* pp. 149ff.

menting the causes and development of rioting and with proposing remedies to prohibit their reoccurrence. While some observers
have intimated that the appointment of a "distinguished" commission to investigate the outbreak of collective violence is a new
societal phenomenon precipitated by the unique events of the
last decade, a careful examination of American history reveals
that numerous commissions have been appointed to investigate
collective violence since the beginning of the twentieth century.
For example, there was the special investigative committee set
up by Congress to investigate the 1917 riot in East St. Louis, the
famous Chicago Commission on Race Relations appointed by
the governor of Illinois to investigate the 1919 race riot, the
Mayor's Commission on Conditions in Harlem appointed by the
New York mayor after the 1935 riot, and the Governor's Committee to Investigate Riot Occurring in Detroit set up by the
governor of Michigan after the serious 1943 riot.

Prior to the sixties, however, apparently no riot commission
had been appointed by the federal executive, most previous commissions being established by state or city executives.[13] Yet in
the sixties the two major commissions dealing with urban violence were appointed at the federal level: the National Advisory
Commission and the National Commission on the Causes and
Prevention of Violence (Violence Commission). The final reports
of these two important commissions have constituted the basis
for many of the more sophisticated discussions of urban racial
violence, supplemented by reports of several state and local commissions, especially the Governor's Select Commission on Civil
Disorder (New Jersey Commission), the Governor's Commission
on the Los Angeles Riots (Los Angeles Commission), and the
Chicago Riot Study Committee (Chicago Committee).[14] The his-

---

[13] Platt, *The Politics of Riot Commissions, 1917–1970;* Arthur I.
Waskow, *From Race Riot to Sit-In* (Garden City, N.Y.: Doubleday,
1966).

[14] *Report of the National Advisory Commission on Civil Disorders;
Report of the Chicago Study Committee;* Governor's Commission on
the Los Angeles Riots, *Violence in the City—An End or a Beginning?*

tories and reports of these five major commissions provide the basis for the discussion which follows.

While commissions have become, for better or for worse, a regular and reoccurring feature of governmental response to societal problems, they are unique governmental appendages— precipitously constructed, short-lived, not part of the settled governmental framework or generated out of the regular electoral process. Since such commissions are without either legislative or executive authority, they can "neither make laws nor assume any day-to-day operating responsibility" for the areas which they investigate.[15] Riot commissions, therefore, have ordinarily been delegated only limited investigative and advisory authority by the chief governmental officers who set up the investigating bodies and appointed their members. In the decade of the sixties this meant the President of the United States, the governor of the state concerned, or less often, the mayor of the city involved.

Given that advisory commissions always conduct their affairs at the behest of and under the close scrutiny of the permanent government, it is not surprising that some have perceived the goals delineated in the charges to commissions as restricted, unattainable, sometimes even contradictory. At the outset, in addition to resource limitations, the instructions given to major riot commissions have seriously restricted the scope of their investigation of violence. Looking at perhaps the most important charges to riot commissioners, those given to the 1967–1968 National Advisory Commission and the 1968–1969 Violence Commission, one can ascertain some of the typical ambiguities and dilemmas. The following critical section is from an executive

---

(Los Angeles, 1965); Governor's Select Commission on Civil Disorder, *Report for Action* (State of New Jersey, 1968); National Commission on the Causes and Prevention of Violence, *To Establish Justice, To Insure Domestic Tranquility* (Washington, D.C.: U.S. Government Printing Office, 1969).

[15] James S. Campbell, "The Usefulness of Commission Studies of Collective Violence," *Annals of the American Academy of Political and Social Science,* **391** (September 1970), 169.

order issued by the President in the summer of 1967 establishing the National Advisory Commission:

SECTION 2. *Functions of the Commission.* (a) The Commission shall investigate and make recommendations with respect to:

(1) The origins of the recent major civil disorders in our cities, including the basic causes and factors leading to such disorders and the influence, if any, of organizations or individuals dedicated to the incitement or encouragement of violence.

(2) The development of methods and techniques for averting or controlling such disorders, including the improvement of communications between local authorities and community groups, the training of state and local law enforcement and National Guard personnel in dealing with potential or actual riot situations, and the coordination of efforts of the various law enforcement and governmental units which may become involved in such situations;

(3) The appropriate role of the local, state, and Federal authorities in dealing with civil disorders; and

(4) Such other matters as the President may place before the Commission.[16]

This particular set of instructions clearly reflected official concerns about the causes and prevention of black rioting. Note the elements of the charge which seem to reflect the underlying conservative-liberal debate over the character of ghetto problems and the remedies for them. In regard to riot causation we find not only a concern for "basic causes and factors," perhaps a reference to those underlying conditions stressed by liberals, but also an explicit reference to the conspiracy and agitator theories preferred by conservative analysts. In regard to riot cures we find

[16] *Report of the National Advisory Commission on Civil Disorders,* p. 295.

a somewhat more specific concern with control, the improvement of law enforcement capabilities, than with reform, except for a reference to the improvement of communication links between authorities and community groups. Initially, the radical perspective is implicitly rejected, for no major restructuring of established institutions is envisaged.

Some knowledgeable observers have suggested that President Lyndon Johnson intended for the Violence Commission, established a year later by another executive order in the summer of 1968, to come up with a statement on ghetto rioting and other collective violence in the decade of the sixties which would be more in line with the views of the Democratic administration. Whether or not this was the case, the charge to the Violence Commission was briefer and seemed to have a somewhat more conservative tone than that given to the earlier commission:

SECTION 2. *Functions of the Commission.* The Commission shall investigate and make recommendations with respect to:

(a) The causes and prevention of lawless acts of violence in our society, including assassination, murder and assault;

(b) The causes and prevention of disrespect for law and order, of disrespect for public officials, and of violent disruptions of public order by individuals and groups; and

(c) Such other matters as the President may place before the Commission.[17]

Causes and prevention are again stressed. The conservative-liberal debate shines through, with the wording this time including such phrases as "lawless acts of violence," "disrespect for law and order," "disruptions of public order," code words suggestive of conservative rhetoric. As with the charge to the National Ad-

[17] National Commission on the Causes and Prevention of Violence, *To Establish Justice, To Insure Domestic Tranquility,* preceding Introduction.

visory Commission the tone stresses the essential goodness of existing political arrangements; the possibility of research into official participation in the generation and development of collective violence is precluded. Moreover, charges given to recent state and municipal riot commissions, at least those we have been able to examine, have had a broadly similar thrust, accentuating both the need to probe the why and how of riots and the necessity for palatable remedies, particularly along law enforcement lines.

Who Serves on Riot Commissions?

The instructions given to riot commissions by chief government officers—clearly seen in the informal remarks of President Lyndon Johnson in conjunction with the establishment of the National Advisory Commission—have sometimes suggested that commissioners should disavow conventional wisdom or should with an open mind pursue the whole truth about the violent events being examined.[18] To the outside observer, such a charge might lead to the expectation that the commissioners investigating the collective violence rending American society would be broadly representative of the various segments of this complex society. However, this has not been the case. One investigator recently discovered that riot commission personnel, including the commissioners themselves, have usually come disproportionately from the dominant powerholding groups. In an analysis of the 86 riot commissioners who served on nine government commissions between 1917 and 1970, Platt found that commissioners have been predominantly white, middle-class, middle-aged, and lawyers, and more often than not have been associated with government either before or at the time of their service as riot commissioners.[19] Inspection of the detailed materials in this

[18] *Report of the National Advisory Commission on Civil Disorders,* pp. 296–297. See Platt, "The Politics of Riot Commissions, 1917–1970: An Overview," p. 10.
[19] Ibid., p. 12.

The Aftermath of Rioting: The Establishment Response

sophisticated analysis leads to the conclusion that there is a very serious bias in selection of riot commissioners in favor of a few established groups, in stark contrast to the typical characteristics of violence participants:

> Rioters are predominantly youthful, commissioners are predominantly middle-aged; rioters are predominantly black, commissioners are predominantly white; rioters are predominantly members of the working and lower classes, commissioners are predominantly middle-class professionals and politicians; rioters include a significant number of women, commissioners are almost exclusively males; rioters typically live in areas affected by rioting, commissioners almost always live outside areas affected by rioting.[20]

Moreover, these conclusions about the predominant characteristics of those serving on nine riot commissions between 1917 and 1970, as one might expect, also apply to the composition of the major commissions which were appointed by various branches of the government during the sixties. With few exceptions riot and violence commissions have been composed of those inclined to the conservative and liberal positions we have discussed previously, ordinarily those reflecting the perspectives and views of the established interest groups of business, government, and the law. Thus it is not surprising that commissioners representing power blocs within the existing political framework of American cities have not been inclined to indict that political framework, or even to attribute to those arrangements a major causal role in the etiology of collective violence.

Nevertheless, perhaps the most striking bias in the composition of recent riot commissions can be glimpsed in the relatively minor part that black Americans have played in the makeup of commissions. This is not to say that riot commissions have not had blacks on them, for indeed both major federal commissions

[20] Ibid., pp. 20–21.

211

—the National Advisory Commission and the Violence Commission—did have two black representatives each. State and municipal commissions have had similar black representation. If this bias were not serious enough, yet another can be seen in the characteristics of the black commissioners. Black representatives on national commissions, as well as on state and municipal commissions both in the sixties and in earlier decades, have been conservative and moderate black leaders. Neither young blacks nor black militants of any type have been included among the members appointed by the chief executives who have ordinarily determined the commission membership.[21] Moreover, in an assessment of the *Report of the National Advisory Commission on Civil Disorders,* Kopkind has noted that many black men serving on the research staff became angry over the internal racism, the institutional racism, of the Commission itself. Viewed from their perspective, thus, the final *Report* was seen

> as a white document written by white writers and aimed at a white audience—*about* black people. It was primarily a response to the white response to the riots. It was supposed to prescribe policy for black people, not for whites.[22]

On the Operation of Commissions

How have recent riot commissions operated? Has there been a significant amount of internal dissent? What was the role of social scientists? What kinds of professionals or experts have been selected to write the final reports of commissions? Given the restrictions imposed on riot commissioners by their political context, the charges given to them, and their own socioeconomic backgrounds, one might well expect their deliberations and actions to have a distinctive character. Certain aspects of this background have loomed as especially important, particularly the

[21] Ibid., pp. 14–17.
[22] Kopkind, "White on Black," pp. 385–386.

link to government and the link to the legal establishment. For example, approximately two thirds of the commissioners serving on the 1967–1968 National Advisory Commission and the 1968–1969 Violence Commission were lawyers. Indeed, the majority of riot commissioners serving on municipal, state, and federal commissions both in recent and earlier decades of the twentieth century have been members of the legal profession.[23] Moreover, in recent years the executive staff running the investigative and report-writing operation for the commissioners has also been dominated by men of legal training and thinking. This has led to the domination in commission deliberations of what has been termed an "advocacy" approach, whereby the conclusion to be drawn or the line of thought to be pursued is more or less determined at the outset and then data are collected to support predetermined arguments. As one of the co-directors of the research staff for the Violence Commission has phrased it: "The tendency of the law is to adopt a position and then seek evidence to support that position, to play the role of the advocate, arguing the rightness or wrongness of a course of action."[24]

While men oriented to this advocacy approach were at the highest levels of staff control in the preparation of reports assessing the causes and prevention of collective violence on the part of black Americans, the actual research fieldwork has frequently been in the hands of those with training in the various social sciences. Recent riot commissions—with the notable exceptions of the Los Angeles Commission and the Chicago Committee appointed by Mayor Richard Daley to investigate the 1968 riot there—have relied heavily on social science investigators to turn up detailed information on many of the diverse questions they have been charged to investigate. However, those with social science backgrounds ordinarily have been added only at the level of the research staff; and staff reports have not always been

[23] Platt, "The Politics of Riot Commissions, 1917–1970: An Overview," p. 14.

[24] Stanley Friedman, "Dialogue with James F. Short," *Issues in Criminology,* **5** (Winter 1970), 30. Platt utilizes this quote.

noted or utilized by commissioners. The final reports of recent riot and violence commissions, therefore, did not mirror to any significant degree the force of several important arguments made by social scientists on the basis of the data generation process, although the research staff perspectives were occasionally allowed in supplementary staff reports. The reason for this seems to be that the executive staff, ordinarily composed of those with the same social and economic interests as both the commissioners and the chief governmental officer who appointed the commissions, has served a screening function.[25] Based on his experience as consultant for the National Advisory Commission, Mattick has cogently argued that the upper level of a riot commission staff is the one that screens for ideological content the reports and memoranda of the lower level, the lower level being composed of social scientists and other researchers; thus, the upper level of the National Advisory Commission staff filtered out the concern of the lower-level researchers for both the Vietnam war and more radical interpretations of ghetto violence.[26]

Coupled with the relatively short time span specified for comprehensive research, this screening process contradicts the basic orientation toward research taken by many social scientists. Among social scientists there is a strong and general feeling that substantial research cannot be quickly conceived and conducted and that the research procedure should consist of more than the speedy compiling of facts to support an advocate's predetermined position. Alternative hypotheses should be constructed and circulated, and carefully collected evidence weighed in terms of various possible alternatives; alternatives should not be sidetracked simply because they do not align with prevailing ideologies.[27] Moreover, the two co-directors of the Violence Commission research staff have argued that social scientists must also "present

[25] Platt, "The Politics of Riot Commissions, 1917–1970: An Overview," pp. 25–27.

[26] Hans W. Mattick, "The Form and Content of Recent Riots," *Midway*, **9** (Summer 1968), 3–5.

[27] Friedman, "Dialogue with James F. Short," 30–31.

such facts *and their meaning* in terms of the accumulated body of knowledge of the sciences, and . . . make this presentation to the broadest possible audience, regardless of political power."[28] Expectably, the staff reports that were not reflected in the final report of the Violence Commission contained materials that were far more critical of the existing institutions and wide-ranging in the alternatives considered than the final report. Thus the debate between the upper level of the Violence Commission staff and the lower level was not really that social scientists avoid tough issues which commissioners cannot avoid, as some have contended, for social scientists in staff reports have in fact tackled very difficult political questions that commissioners have been afraid to air.[29]

Indeed, the conflict between social scientists, lawyers, commissioners, and chief executive officers has resulted in an underground history of recent riot commissions, incidents which have either not been reported at all in commission documents and the mass media or have been de-emphasized. For example, a number of developments in connection with the operation of the National Advisory Commission have never been adequately explained:

> The firing of 120 staff members in late 1967 was never explained; the substantial hostility of black staffers towards the Commission's own "institutional" racism was never mentioned; the "underground" Commission document, "The Harvest of Racism," was never examined; the White House veto on employment of staff and consultants active in anti-war work was never disclosed; the tacit agreement to "forget" the war in Vietnam throughout the Commission's investigations and its Report was overlooked; and the secret plan of

[28] James F. Short and Marvin E. Wolfgang, "On Collective Violence: Introduction and Overview," *Annals of the American Academy of Political and Social Science,* **391** (September 1970), 6.
[29] Ibid., p. 7.

Commissioner Charles ("Tex") Thornton to torpedo the Report just before launching is still an untold story.[30]

Of particular interest to those concerned about the relationship between upper and lower levels of riot commission staffs is the strange history of the staff document entitled "The Harvest of American Racism: The Political Meaning of Violence in the Summer of 1967." Working as members of the research staff, several social scientists had written this document touching on the political implications of American racism and apparently had couched its language in terms indicting fundamental institutions. The executive director and other administrative personnel at the higher levels of the Commission staff were admittedly incensed at the boldness of this document; in effect, the "Harvest" report was suppressed. Subsequently, the relations between the higher and lower staffs appeared to deteriorate, and with the firing of 120 investigators on the National Advisory Commission's research staff the social science input became more limited.[31]

Commission Findings and Recommendations

Given these tentative answers to questions about the character and operation of recent riot and violence commissions, a logical question arises as to the conclusions and recommendations of those charged with the investigation of group violence. Previously, we have emphasized that government excursions into the realm of violence evaluation have been situated in an intricate political context, have been enmeshed in the continuing struggle for power in American society. The interpretations and proposals of riot commissions, therefore, have reflected the business and professional origins, the commitments, and basic perspectives of commissioners.

[30] Kopkind, "White on Black," p. 379.

[31] Ibid., pp. 386–388; for a somewhat differing account see Robert Shellow, "Social Scientists and Social Action from Within the Establishment," *Journal of Social Issues,* 26 (Winter 1970), 211–215.

The Aftermath of Rioting: The Establishment Response

Among other important aspects which might be noted about the findings of recent commissions is the variation in resolution of the ongoing conservative-liberal debate over the causes, character, and particularly the prevention of ghetto rioting. While incorporating some of the dimensions of the conservative perspective, recent governmental commissions have taken a more or less liberal approach to outlining the cures for urban riots. The final reports of the 1965 Los Angeles Commission and the 1968 Chicago Committee were perhaps the most conservative in tone. The Los Angeles Commission took a relatively conservative position on the conceptualization of urban violence, on the role of the police, and on those black urbanites who took part. Emphasized was the point that the Watts riot was a "formless, quite senseless" explosion.[32] Moreover, much of the blame for rioting was placed on the black community itself, particularly black leadership locally and nationally, while the role of the police in riot precipitation is denied. Yet even in this report a number of important educational and economic reform measures were proposed, although of a traditional and rather limited nature. The final report of the 1968 Chicago Committee was also relatively conservative in tone, particularly in its heavy emphasis on police repression and other control recommendations, to the general neglect of social and economic reform.

However, three other final commission reports issued in the sixties—those of the Violence Commission, the National Advisory Commission, and the New Jersey Commission—were somewhat more liberal in their interpretation of riot causes and riot remedies, at the same time incorporating a "law and order" thrust. As with the Chicago Committee report, a dual approach stressing both police repression and socioeconomic reform was adopted by these three commissions, with some variation in emphasis. Perhaps the least liberal of the three was the final report of the 1968–1969 Violence Commission whose solution to riot and vio-

[32] Governor's Commission on the Los Angeles Riots, *Violence in the City—An End or a Beginning?*, pp. 4–5.

lence problems can be seen in the title of the final report: *To Establish Justice, To Insure Domestic Tranquility,* phrases taken from the Preamble to the Constitution of the United States. The causes of violence were briefly traced and were seen as including such factors as low incomes, physical deterioration, broken homes, and overcrowding—those usually accentuated in a liberal assessment of urban violence. Although the wording of this final report indicates that the Violence Commission was sympathetic to a reordering of national priorities and conceded the need for significant reform, the governmental programs envisioned as useful in preventing "violent crime" were more limited than those delineated by either the New Jersey Commission or the National Advisory Commission. Specific recommendations for governmental reform encompassed the improvement of the criminal justice system, experimentation with drug substitutes, expanded police-community relations, expanded housing and employment programs, and improvement of federal policy with regard to pressure for equalizing public services. In effect, there was a rather weak call for reform. Moreover, one of the proposals for dealing with violent crime included the rather frightening suggestion of a government plan for the identification of violence-prone individuals, and the related set of recommendations for dealing with "group violence" included only actions designed to improve law enforcement control of dissident minorities.[33]

In its analysis of the dilemmas of urban unrest the 1967–1968 National Advisory Commission adopted a somewhat more liberal approach. In examining riot causes the Commission explicitly rejected the riffraff approach stressed by many conservative analysts. Through careful research rioters were found not to be primarily riffraff or criminal types but to come from many segments of the black community. The conspiracy theory was also examined and rejected.[34] Broad historical trends such as urban-

[33] National Commission on the Causes and Prevention of Violence, *To Establish Justice, To Insure Domestic Tranquility,* pp. 272–275.
[34] *Report of the National Advisory Commission on Civil Disorders,* pp. 73–89.

ization were given great emphasis in assessing the conditions underlying black protest, together with the plight of the black family. Oppressive ghetto conditions were accented. Even "white racism," attitudinal prejudice toward black Americans, was given some attention in the assessment of causes. While these factors are undoubtedly important in a thoroughgoing assessment of racial violence, there was perhaps an excessive emphasis on collective guilt.[35] Indeed, are all groups equally "racist" or equally guilty of creating oppressive ghetto conditions? Such issues were apparently ignored by the Commission.

When it came to recommendations for preventing future violence, the National Advisory Commission adopted the usual twofold approach, stressing both the need for improved control techniques and the necessity for reform. A variety of social and economic reform measures were proposed, the most extensive list outlined of all the riot commissions in the 1960s. Among the more important proposals were increased federal and local efforts to consolidate existing manpower programs, the creation of one million new jobs in the public sector, government action against discriminatory barriers in employment and education, improvement of schools and programs available to disadvantaged minorities, expansion of low-income housing programs, establishment of neighborhood city halls, and reform of court systems and welfare programs.[36] Thus, the *Report of the National Advisory Commission on Civil Disorders* recognized many of the basic problems of ghetto residents and generally took an integrationist tack in proposing solutions to those problems.

Yet the remedies proposed by the National Advisory Commission were in a number of ways not unlike those outlined by conservative analysts. In addition to recommendations for social and economic reform, the final report of the Commission pro-

[35] Robert M. Fogelson, *Violence as Protest* (Garden City, N.Y.: Doubleday, 1971), p. 163.
[36] *Report of the National Advisory Commission on Civil Disorders,* pp. 147–212, 229–265.

posed specific control solutions, such as improved control training and materials for the police establishment, better planning to prevent future disorders, and better-staffed and -supported police departments. And paralleling all recent reports on ghetto rioting, the final report also accentuated the black community, emphasizing interviews with blacks, as though interviews with whites and an analysis of the white community or the actions of white elites and leaders were irrelevant to an adequate understanding of urban violence. In line with this emphasis, then, was the periodically reaffirmed commitment to the goal of integrating black Americans into white society as the ultimate solution to both black violence and the increasing polarization of the black and white communities.[37] As Rubenstein has noted, the "twin proposals of government centralism and racial integration" favored by liberal analysts dominated the final report of the National Advisory Commission, while the report's exploration of the issue of minority participation was rather ambiguous "in recommending measures to increase the collective power of urban blacks at the expense of existing white economic and political interest groups."[38]

While giving considerable attention to the prevention of ghetto rioting, the various riot commissions appointed in the last decade have not explored to any significant degree the potential or probable impact of their recommendations on the surrounding society. One important consideration in regard to the socioeconomic and police proposals recommended by commissions has been the monetary support for new governmental actions, a consideration overlooked by a number of recent commissions. When it came to the question of monetary expenditures for socioeconomic and other governmental reforms, the 1967–1968 National Advisory Commission seemed to take a more aggressive position than most commissions. The view generally espoused in the final report was that the money for both increased repressive capabili-

[37] Ibid., pp. 229–265.
[38] Rubenstein, *Rebels in Eden,* p. 148.

ties and increased reform could come out of existing revenues, particularly money from the increased productivity of an expanding economy, in spite of the Vietnam war and other budget demands.[39] Indeed, it was apparently this line of argument that precipitated the more negative than positive reaction by the chief executive officer who had appointed the Commission.

Although the National Advisory Commission and numerous others deliberating in the decade of the sixties were not often directly critical of specific actions taken by most public officials and never recommended fundamental structural changes, this did not mean that the proposals they did outline were wholeheartedly accepted by government officials. One of the most important examples of this negative response, or the reluctance of a government official to act, can be seen in President Johnson's reaction to the final report of the Commission—both in his ultimate neglect of most of its relatively far-reaching economic and welfare proposals and in his published comments:

This analysis reflected extremely close agreement between the commission's proposals and the administration's program. The major difference lay in the scale of effort recommended. The commission called for a substantially increased outlay of resources, doubling or tripling each ongoing program. The Bureau of the Budget estimated that the recommendations would cost in the vicinity of $30 billion, in addition to the $30 billion plus already in the budget for the poor. . . . I will never understand how the commission expected me to get this same Congress to turn 180 degrees overnight and appropriate an additional $30 billion for the same programs that it was demanding I cut by $6 billion. This would have required a miracle.[40]

[39] *Report of the National Advisory Commission on Civil Disorders,* pp. 229–230.

[40] Lyndon Baines Johnson, *The Vantage Point* (New York: Holt, Rinehart and Winston, 1971), pp. 172–173.

CHAPTER 5

While Johnson seems to have found the *Report of the National Advisory Commission on Civil Disorders* useful in its impact on public views of riots and to some extent in its liberal rather than conservative tone, he not only was critical of the surprising scope of the recommendations but also of some parts of its analysis. Thus a Johnson aide was quoted in the *Washington Post* as very critical of the *Report* because it was "counter-productive in terms of programs for the society as a whole" and because it "over-dramatized the white racism theme."[41] Apparently Johnson wanted the later Violence Commission headed by Eisenhower to investigate civil disorders and come up with conclusions more acceptable to the President—particularly in the area of funding.[42] This would seem to be what in fact did occur, for the argument to postpone significant remedial reforms until after the Vietnam war was ended was supported in the Violence Commission's final report. One of the least candid conclusions in regard to reforms and government funding is the following comment of the 1968–1969 Violence Commission:

> We recognize that substantial amounts of funds cannot be transferred from sterile war purposes to more productive ones until our participation in the Vietnam War is ended. . . . When our participation in the Vietnam War is concluded, we recommend increasing annual general welfare expenditures by about 20 billion dollars (stated in 1968 dollars), partly by reducing military expenditures and partly by use of increased tax revenues resulting from the growth of the Gross National Product.[43]

[41] Joseph A. Califano, quoted in Anthony Platt, "Introduction," *The Politics of Riot Commissions, 1917–1970,* p. 395.

[42] Michael Lipsky and David J. Olson, "Riot Commission Politics," **6,** *Trans-Action* (July/August 1969), 18.

[43] National Commission on the Causes and Prevention of Violence, *To Establish Justice, To Insure Domestic Tranquility,* pp. xxv–xxvii.

The Aftermath of Rioting: The Establishment Response

Even though the Violence Commission explored not only ghetto rioting but many other kinds of violence in American society, it did not deal frankly with the role of official violence, especially in regard to the highly relevant Vietnam war. In its emphasis on the overriding importance and inevitability of the war, the Violence Commission said "a great deal about the need for social change while justifying indefinite inaction."[44] Generally speaking, therefore, the report of the Violence Commission was more optimistic about the future than that of the other major national commission in the sixties, giving no serious attention to the polarization of American society and accentuating the progress being made as a result of the "peaceful revolution" currently taking place.[45] Moreover, the Violence Commission was perhaps typical; in recent years numerous other state, municipal, and federal violence commissions either slighted the problem of revenue sources for reform and repression or suggested that ameliorative actions would have to wait for their proper turn in the governmental order of priorities.

In examining recent government excursions into commission investigation of current societal problems, therefore, one quickly comes to the perhaps not unexpected conclusion that the broad radical perspective on remedies for urban ghetto problems has been ignored, even suppressed when it "breaks out" at lower levels of a riot commission staff. Generally, a more or less liberal point of view has been conveyed by the final report of most recent riot commissions—perhaps of all twentieth-century government investigations into violence—although some have made more or less significant concessions to the conservative perspective on riot causation and prohibitions. The liberal tack is to

[44] Elliott Currie, "Violence and Ideology: A Critique of the Final Report of the Violence Commission," *The Politics of Riot Commissions, 1917–1970*, ed. Anthony Platt (New York: Macmillan, 1971), p. 460. Currie suggests this point about the Vietnam war.

[45] National Commission on the Causes and Prevention of Violence, *To Establish Justice, To Insure Domestic Tranquility*, pp. xxxi–xxxii.

couple a "law and order" call for repressive remedies with an at least equally weighted plea for social reform, sometimes relatively far-reaching reform. However, the social and economic reforms proposed seldom would impinge significantly on the power or wealth of the dominant powerholding groups on the urban scene.

The Significance of Commissions

What part have recent riot and violence commissions played in American politics? Who benefits from the deliberations and reports of riot commissions? Whose purposes do commissions serve? Some controversy and debate have already arisen over the precise answers to these important questions. A number of functions of commissions have been suggested, some mainly benefiting dominant powerholding groups, others potentially of benefit to a broad range of groups including dissident minorities. Those actions potentially benefiting a variety of groups within the society might include the following: (1) collecting important social facts about urban violence and making them available to the general public, including accurate descriptions of what occurred, (2) investigating the substance of myths and rumors about violence, (3) stimulating public debate over the conditions leading to rioting, and (4) occasionally even precipitating modest reforms directed against the socioeconomic conditions seen as spawning collective violence.

However, as Professor Kenneth Clark pointed out in his now widely quoted testimony before the National Advisory Commission, the often benign and liberal analyses of riot commissions in the twentieth century have been broadly similar in regard to many of their conclusions and recommendations, but have not led to major public or private action directed at significantly ameliorating the powerless condition of minority Americans.[46]

[46] *Report of the National Advisory Commission on Civil Disorders,* p. 265.

The Aftermath of Rioting: The Establishment Response

One reason for this may have been the restricted focus of the causal analysis and subsequent proposals for riot prevention, as well as the assessment of monetary sources, which inevitably flow from commissioners representing those groups already in power. From the vantage point of those trying to move up in the existing power structure in American cities, therefore, the major functions of riot commissions may well be seen as those which benefit dominant groups and entrenched elites: (1) giving government executives the opportunity to "buy time" and enabling them to avoid pressures to act immediately to eliminate oppressive ghetto conditions, (2) assuring the public that some action is being taken to deal with the problem, (3) whitewashing established institutions and agencies which are involved, (4) reaffirming the view of American society which sees existing leaders as men of good will and existing arrangements as the best one can expect, and (5) buttressing the official inclination to stress government repression as a main response to collective violence.[47] While not all recent riot and violence commissions have had all these functions, a general assessment of their operation and resulting impact would not fail to bring most of these to light.

As was indicated in the previous analysis of the views adopted in the final reports of riot and violence commissions, there is "a built-in tendency toward the whitewash, to the extent that riot commissions minimize criticism of the public official to whom they must look for primary implementation of the report."[48] There is also a built-in tendency to ignore, or glide over lightly, indictments of existing institutions, not the least reason being the explicit links between the commissioners and those institutions. Platt has argued that this failure to indict existing institutions in a serious and significant way is the most fundamental flaw of all:

[47] Lipsky and Olson, "Riot Commission Politics," 9–21; and Platt, "The Politics of Riot Commissions, 1917–1970: An Overview," pp. 44–45.

[48] Lipsky and Olson, "Riot Commission Politics," 21.

Riot commissions assume that (a) government is not a party to civil disorders, (b) changes in the conditions of blacks can be achieved by appealing to the good faith and reasonableness of government, and (c) fundamental changes in the conditions of blacks can be achieved without fundamental changes in existing political and economic institutions.[49]

The point here is that perhaps the major function of recent violence commissions has been to give a realistic appearance of being concerned about the problems of oppressed minorities, while at the same time avoiding the fundamental issue—that of a head-on attack on the fundamental inequality in the existing arrangements of power and authority, whether in the social, the economic, or the governmental spheres.

The Government Response to Riots: Law Enforcement and Reform Measures

Up to this point in this chapter we have examined one major governmental response to ghetto rioting: that leading to the appointment, deliberations, and recommendations of a number of recent riot and violence commissions. What effect did the interpretations and proposed solutions of these various commissions have on government? More broadly considered, whether in reaction to commission proposals or recommendations from other sources, just what specific actions have federal, state, and municipal governments taken in response to urban riots? How limited were they? The focus in subsequent sections will be on the actions of government executives and agencies, rather than on their verbal responses in regard to ghetto conditions and ghetto rioting. Concomitant supportive actions by private businesses and industry will also be noted where information is available and relevant. Perhaps a useful way to organize the following discus-

[49] Platt, "The Politics of Riot Commissions, 1917–1970: An Overview," p. 46.

sion of responses by government and private agencies to riots is to divide it into two basic parts following the two-pronged approach favored by several recent riot commissions: the law enforcement or control response and the response that focuses on social and economic conditions. In each part an attempt will be made to describe and analyze actions at federal, state, and local levels, insofar as available materials allow such assessments. Moreover, as will soon become clear, it is often impossible to distinguish completely between reactions at the various levels, since in many cases responses to riots involved mutual or cooperative government activities.

The Law Enforcement Response: The National Level

First, we will examine law enforcement responses at the level of the federal government. In addition to setting up commissions which stressed a law enforcement strategy in regard to rioting, the federal government also became involved in riot prevention and police control activities in a number of other ways. For example, an early impact of the National Advisory Commission can be seen in the federal government reaction to a Commission recommendation to spread the then available expertise in riot suppression and prevention from the cities currently informed on these matters to all American cities. In direct response to this proposal the President and the attorney general, in conjunction with the International Association of Chiefs of Police, held several important conferences in Washington, D.C., during the winter immediately following on the long hot summer of 1967. At those gatherings several hundred police and other municipal officials from 136 of the large urban areas met to discuss riot control and prevention.[50] Backed by support from the attorney general, moreover, the International Association of Chiefs of Police reacted in numerous other ways to rioting, such as by

[50] Urban America, Inc., and the Urban Coalition, *One Year Later* (New York: Praeger, 1969), p. 67.

establishing data-collecting facilities and by distributing technical information and providing "consultant services on nonlethal riot weaponry and allied riot-control measures."[51]

In addition, within the federal government apparatus new organizational units were being established to implement proposals from a variety of sources for better intelligence and planning in regard to riots. So great was this concern that new organizations appeared at the highest levels. The Defense Department established a Directorate of Civil Disturbance and Planning, with headquarters at the Pentagon. This was in addition to the Department of Justice's Civil Disturbance Group, which has become involved not only in collecting intelligence data and computerizing information on civil disturbances but also in programs designed to deter and contain rioting. Thus a number of "civil disturbance teams" headed by an assistant attorney general have been sent to troubled cities.[52] Other existing agencies also took action in response to riot commission proposals and higher level government directives; for example, the Federal Communications Commission made 20 new channels available for assignment for police radio services to improve the capacity of local law enforcement departments to respond in civil emergencies including riot situations.[53] And many agencies conducted studies of their responsibilities in regard to ghetto riot prevention.

Perhaps most important, federal military training schools were conducted in riot control for the National Guard, the Army, and city and state policemen. Specific action taken by the United States Army after the 1967 riots, particularly in response to massive riots such as those in Newark and Detroit, included the development of special training courses for National Guard

---

[51] Rex Applegate, *Riot Control—Materiel and Techniques* (Harrisburg, Pa.: Stackpole, 1969), p. 16.

[52] James S. Campbell, Joseph R. Sahid, David P. Stang, *Law and Order Reconsidered* (New York: Bantam, 1970), p. 319; details on the Civil Disturbance Group were determined from Department of Justice press releases on the operation.

[53] Campbell, Sahid, and Stang, *Law and Order Reconsidered*, p. 334.

units. A major example of such programs was the 32-hour course given to all National Guard units in the late summer of 1967. This special course included training in crowd and mob behavior, in weapons and security control, in riot formations, in riot-control agents and munitions, in antisniping and antilooting measures, in intelligence planning, and in the detention and arrest of rioters.[54] While a minor portion of the 32-hour course (about 2 hours) was devoted to crowd behavior and types of disturbances, 13 hours were devoted to riot control formations and 8 hours to a Unit Field Training Exercise.[55] Subsequently, similar courses continued to be given at the United States Army Police School in Georgia to numerous National Guard, Army, state and municipal policemen from around the country. In addition to these Army training programs, local police departments have also received extensive aid from the Federal Bureau of Investigation. Literally thousands of special training sessions on such topics as "mob and riot control" and "extremist groups and violence" have been provided for local law enforcement agencies in the last few years, together with hundreds of general law enforcement conferences.[56]

Moreover, the inclusion of civil disorder "gaming" into such police training programs has apparently increased. As with other aspects of riot and crowd control, expertise in this area had been developed prior to the emergence of serious urban riots in the mid-sixties in the United States—in Department of State programs to train foreign police personnel in counterinsurgency operations.[57]

As these federal law enforcement actions indicate, pressure for federal intervention in local operations appeared to increase substantially during the decade of the sixties and continued into the seventies. Although the Constitution of the United States grants

[54] Applegate, *Riot Control—Materiel and Techniques*, pp. 16, 307.
[55] Ibid., pp. 307–309.
[56] Reported in a Department of Justice press release of a speech by James T. Devine, Civil Disturbance Group, dated October 13, 1970.
[57] Applegate, *Riot Control—Materiel and Techniques*, p. 307.

the states exclusive jurisdiction over domestic control matters, generally permitting federal enforcement intervention only when requested by a state, some analysts have advocated greater federal intervention in the protection of municipal areas from the threat of internal political violence. Such advocates were doubtless pleased not only with the increased involvement of the federal government in the training of local police but also with another major category of actions precipitated to a significant degree by ghetto rioting—congressional hearings and legislation related to riot prevention and control. On the one hand, an extensive investigation by conservative lawmakers was conducted in the Senate. The McClellan Subcommittee on Investigations of the Senate Committee on Government Operations attempted to refute the findings of more liberal commissions "by centering on Office of Economic Opportunity personnel involved in riots, hearing witnesses who allege that there is a conspiracy behind the riots, and generally giving a hostile reception to other witnesses not sympathetic with the committee's more conservative views."[58] Mirrored in these congressional hearings was the dominant concern of many conservatives for a repression approach to ghetto rioting and opposition to legislation "rewarding" rioters.

On the other hand, major legislative action taken by Congress in regard to riot control included the important antiriot provisions of the 1968 Civil Rights Act, an odd place for such provisions. The section of the new public law, and the debate on the legislation as well, reflected a thoroughgoing belief in the outside-agitator theory of riot occurrence. Relatively brief, the basic section of this important 1968 law is as follows:

SECTION 2101. *Riots.*
(a) (1) Whoever travels in interstate or foreign commerce or uses any facility of interstate or foreign commerce, including, but not limited to, the mail, telegraph, telephone, radio, or television, with intent—

[58] Lipsky and Olson, "Riot Commission Politics," 18.

(A) to incite a riot; or

(B) to organize, promote, encourage, participate in, or carry on a riot; or

(C) to commit any act of violence in furtherance of a riot; or

(D) to aid or abet any person in inciting or participating in or carrying on a riot or committing any act of violence in furtherance of a riot; and who either during the course of any such travel or use or thereafter performs or attempts to perform any other overt act for any purpose specified in subparagraph (A), (B), (C), or (D) of this paragraph—

Shall be fined not more than $10,000, or imprisoned not more than five years, or both.[59]

In addition to this section certain qualifications of these stipulations and a definition of the term "riot" were also added to the United States Code, together with subsequent sections providing federal punishment for teaching the use of firearms and explosives or transporting the same across state lines for the purpose of sustaining civil disorders.

Yet another important act of Congress partially in response to ghetto rioting was the enactment in June 1968 of the Omnibus Crime Control and Safe Streets Act (Omnibus Crime Act), which provided for such enforcement activities as a national police training center and programs for fiscal aid to local police agencies to increase their riot control capabilities. While the Omnibus Crime Act envisioned a program of aid to courts, prisons, and the police, it specified that the Law Enforcement Assistance Administration (LEAA) in the Department of Justice should give particular attention to those local law enforcement projects relating to the "organization, education, and training of regular law enforcement officers, special law enforcement units, and law enforcement reserve units for the prevention, detection, and con-

[59] Quoted in M. Cherif Bassiouni, "The Development of Anti-Riot Legislation," *The Law of Dissent and Riots,* ed. M. Cherif Bassiouni (Springfield, Ill.: Charles C Thomas, 1971), p. 358.

trol of riots and other violent civil disorders, including the acquisition of riot control equipment."[60] That particular emphasis was given to riots can be seen both in the language of the Act and in the fact that 75 percent of the cost for police riot programs would be paid for out of federal funds, compared to 50–60 percent in most of the other law enforcement programs. Dramatically, given the usual slowness of the federal funding apparatus, nearly $4 million in initial grants to 40 states for riot prevention, detection, and control had been made by the end of the first month of operation. According to the first annual report of the LEAA, appropriations were made for the following riot-related activities: (1) police communications (42 percent), (2) police equipment (23 percent), and (3) community relations efforts and training (35 percent). Special granting authority allowing for this quick response had been provided by Congress.[61] Major police support programs have been administered by the federal LEAA, which began on a full scale in 1969 and succeeded the old Office of Law Enforcement Assistance. The fiscal 1969 budget for the support operation came to $63 million and was followed in fiscal 1970 by a budget of $268 million; subsequent funding was expected to see a significant increase, to at least half a billion dollars a year. Thus, measured in terms of dollars disbursed over a short period of time, the federal law enforcement response to ghetto rioting and other civil disturbances does seem to have been perhaps the most substantial reaction at any level of government.

Moreover, in the 1969–1970 deliberations of Congress, additional bills directed against blacks and other minorities who might engage in militant action were proposed, including one bill that would have allowed preventive detention of dangerous defendants for months before trial. Thus Congressional support

---

[60] The anti-crime Act is reproduced in Subcommittee on Criminal Laws and Procedures, U.S. Senate Committee on the Judiciary, *Hearings: Federal Assistance to Law Enforcement,* June 24–July 30, 1970. The quote is from p. 6.

[61] The first annual LEAA report is reproduced in ibid., pp. 379ff.

for repressive reactions to collective violence on the part of minority Americans continued into the 1970s.

The Law Enforcement Response: The State Level

With hundreds of millions of federal dollars flowing down the LEAA pipeline to the newly created state task forces and planning agencies that were responsible for developing comprehensive plans and administering the block grants (grants accounting for most of the funds granted under the program) serious problems in the operation of the program at state and local levels soon began to emerge. To illustrate, one careful assessment of the 1969 state plans found that 79 percent of the federal money which in theory was supposed to go to all segments of the criminal justice system actually was being channeled into police-dominated programs. The state planning agencies had indicated weak initial concern for the problems of their court and correction facilities.[62] Moreover, the police-related programs which were being funded out of federal money and under state supervision offered little in the way of significant innovations which might improve police-community relations. Indeed, most of the police expenditures appeared to go for communications equipment and hardware, including riot control gadgetry. Almost humorous were expenditures for riot control hardware made by public officials in communities with no significant student or minority populations.[63] Moreover, only 8 percent of the grants were spent on police-community relations programs; few police departments made expenditures for the "grievance resolution mechanisms" or "neighborhood participation" programs even

[62] Advisory Commission on Intergovernmental Relations, "Making the Safe Streets Act Work," reproduced in Subcommittee on Criminal Laws and Procedures, U.S. Senate Committee on the Judiciary, *Hearings: Federal Assistance to Law Enforcement,* June 24–July 30, 1970, p. 216.

[63] National Urban Coalition, *Law and Order II* (Washington, D.C., n.d.), p. 14.

recommended by the 1968 Omnibus Crime Act.[64] While numerous other serious problems with the LEAA program have been delineated elsewhere, it is important to note that perhaps the most serious problem at the state and local level was that cited in a National Urban Coalition report: "Participation in the planning process was limited to a narrow group of officials, criminal justice professionals, and local government representatives—the same people who administered the system in need of reform."[65]

In addition to the role of the state planning agencies in supporting municipal police actions in the area of riot prevention, intelligence, and control, state legislatures also responded with dozens of new laws designed to facilitate the law enforcement response to ghetto rioting. Heavily influenced by the 1965 Los Angeles riot, at an early point in time the California state legislature rushed to conduct hearings on antiriot bills and in July 1966 added to its penal code the following section:

> 404.6. Every person who with the intent to cause a riot does an act or engages in conduct which urges a riot or urges others to commit acts of force or violence, or the burning or destroying of property, and at a time and place and under circumstances which produce a clear and present and immediate danger of acts of force or violence or the burning or destroying of property, is guilty of a misdemeanor.[66]

The inclusion of this penal code provision was considered an "urgency measure" by the legislators; thus it went into effect immediately. Both this antiriot law and the lengthy hearings which preceded it in the California legislature indicated concern both with conservative theories of rioting (particularly "agitator" theories) and repression-oriented cures for rioting.

After the passage of this important law, one of the first major

[64] Ibid.
[65] Ibid., p. 3.
[66] Quoted from a printed copy of Section 404.6 of the California Penal Code in the authors' possession.

attempts to legislate against rioting, numerous state legislatures followed the lead of California and conducted hearings on anti-riot bills and passed a variety of riot-related laws, including statutes on incitement to riot, on police power to take antiriot action such as curfew and cordoning activities, and laws prescribing punishment for riot participation. According to the *Automated Statutory Reporter* between 1966 and 1969 the following northern and western states seriously considered or passed riot-related legislation: Ohio, New York, New Hampshire, Delaware, California, Oklahoma, Arizona, Pennsylvania, Michigan, Kentucky, and Massachusetts.[67] Southern states considering or adopting antiriot legislation were Alabama, Florida, Texas, Georgia, Tennessee, South Carolina, Virginia, Arkansas, and Mississippi. While this list is doubtless incomplete, it does indicate that at least 20 states took legislative action, in part a response to ghetto rioting. Particularly striking in this list is the presence of most southern states, whose laws on rioting sometimes were coupled with legislation on various types of civil disobedience, nonviolent as well as violent. In addition to legislation designed to increase law enforcement authority and capability, several states also passed laws for indemnifying persons suffering riot losses or facilitating the provision of riot insurance, legislation of particular benefit to ghetto area businessmen.

The Law Enforcement Response: The Municipal Level

Examination of both federal and state responses to ghetto rioting in the last decade buttresses the argument that municipal law enforcement has become the major focus of public attention in regard to both riot intelligence and riot control, for federal and state agencies of government have directed many of their actions, fiscal and otherwise, toward supporting local police programs. With this substantial outside aid local law enforcement

[67] These figures were taken from 1967–1969 issues of the *Automated Statutory Reporter* (Pittsburgh: Automated Law Searching, 1967–1969).

efforts have given substance to the overall assessment of a Violence Commission task force report that since the mid-sixties "most major police departments have made marked progress in strengthening their riot control capabilities."[68] The same conclusion would also seem to be true in regard to many smaller urban police departments as well.

Even a relatively early assessment of the actual law enforcement response in 20 cities which had riots in 1967, conducted only a few months after the ghetto rioting had subsided, found that nine of the cities had already taken measures to strengthen their ability to control future outbreaks of rioting. At least five cities had moved to boost police riot control capability by developing a riot control plan, new communications centers or command posts, implementing training programs, or purchasing riot control equipment. In addition, four cities had reportedly made plans to utilize counterrioters in the event of future riots.[69]

In the years which followed the massive riots of the mid-sixties many more police departments in cities across the country took action to reinforce and strengthen their riot control capability. The extensiveness of this municipal law enforcement response can be discerned in an important *Municipal Yearbook* article on police departments and civil disturbances, an article which had not appeared in the yearbooks prior to 1969. According to the *Yearbook* figures, between 1966 and 1969 there was an 8 percent increase in the number of local police departments with riot and crowd control training, with a 9 percent increase indicated for cities with populations over half a million.[70] By 1969 no less than three quarters of the 1,267 cities reporting had some type of riot and crowd control training for their law enforcement personnel. Moreover, it should be noted that such figures as these do

[68] Campbell, Sahid, and Stang, *Law and Order Reconsidered*, p. 319.
[69] *Report of the National Advisory Commission on Civil Disorders*, p. 347.
[70] Horace S. Webb, "Police Preparedness for Control of Civil Disorders," *Municipal Yearbook: 1969* (Washington, D.C.: International City Management Association, 1969), p. 320.

not indicate the increased emphasis on riot control training which occurred even in those departments that had had in-service programs alluding to riots before 1967. By 1969 substantially more attention was given to problems of rioting in most in-service programs in urban police departments. Thus examination of the topics covered in riot and crowd control training courses in 1969 in cities over 100,000 in population revealed that those receiving the greatest emphasis were the use of tear gas, police discipline, the role of the police officer in riot situations, arrest procedure, laws limiting police procedure, riot situation characteristics, and crowd psychology. Increases in the number of these municipal police agencies which had purchased certain types of riot control equipment—including smoke-producing equipment, gas masks, riot batons, and bayonets—also conveyed the increasing stress on riot control training and preparedness.[71]

Other specific steps taken by municipal law enforcement agencies included the development of riot control manuals and riot control plans. Between 1966 and 1969 there was a 45 percent increase in the number of cities across the country reporting that they had developed riot plans and a 25 percent increase in the number reporting that they had prepared or secured riot control manuals. These increases were primarily for cities below 250,000 in population, for in both 1966 and 1969 most (80 percent) of the 50 largest cities had formalized plans and control manuals. By 1969, therefore, over half of all United States cities with populations of 10,000 persons or more had formal riot plans.[72]

Perhaps the most important organizational innovation undertaken by many local police agencies was the development and utilization of special police squads. Spurred by military advocates of special antiriot task forces, the number of departments with some of these highly trained and mobile riot squads (termed "light striking forces" and "sniper control teams") increased significantly between 1966 and 1969. The overall increase was 31

[71] Ibid., pp. 322–327.
[72] Ibid., p. 321.

237

percent, although the greatest increase was for cities below 250,-000 in population. By 1969 paramilitary police units—resembling the counterinsurgency teams developed in Department of State programs for foreign export—were now a permanent fixture in nearly half of these municipal law enforcement agencies in the United States. Moreover, in a really comprehensive analysis of local responses of this type, which we cannot provide here, one might analyze a variety of tactical developments other than the ones just noted. Other repression-oriented actions have included the passing of numerous ordinances providing city executives with greater power to establish curfews and cordon off areas, increasing the number of police informers in ghetto areas, and establishing police department programs in several cities to instruct civilians in the protective use of firearms.[73]

Thus in the last decade a major local response to ghetto rioting, as well as to pressures generated by other types of collective violence, has been the law enforcement or repressive response. This governmental reaction was not simply that of the federal government, for it inevitably encompassed local and state agencies as well. Some observers have attributed the apparent decline in the intensity of ghetto riots in the 1968–1970 period to the improved police crowd control training and riot control equipment that resulted from governmental actions. According to the International City Managers' Association there were fewer massive riots because

> city administrations and police departments have become more adept at handling potential riot situations. While riot potential was greater in 1968 than in 1967, the triggering events were rapidly controlled and large-scale disorders thus were avoided.[74]

[73] Ibid. See also Robert L. Allen, *Black Awakening in Capitalist America* (New York: Doubleday Anchor Books, 1970), pp. 199–200.

[74] Quoted in Urban America, Inc., and the Urban Coalition, *One Year Later*, pp. 69–70.

The Aftermath of Rioting: The Establishment Response

Other analysts have stressed the relatively greater restraint of police forces in handling the 1968 riots, accenting the successful results of a certain amount of police permissiveness in some areas.[75] Indeed, the question of the character of the law enforcement response to rioting during the phase of actual police interaction with rioters has provoked a debate over police restraint and permissiveness, particularly over the shooting of looters and the beating of members of crowds. Although some have preferred to accentuate the need for greater police restraint and discipline in dealing with rioters, others of a more conservative bent have argued that such permissiveness will never be a satisfactory solution, for "property rights are the oldest of human rights, antedating even other civil rights, and they must be upheld if a stable society and public support of law and order is to be maintained."[76]

Social and Economic Reform: The National Response

Although many have been impressed by the significant progress made by various government law enforcement agencies in augmenting the riot control capability of local police forces, and some have called for even greater stress on the law enforcement response, other observers have been critical of what they view as an overemphasis on just one aspect of the twofold approach to riot solutions accentuated by several recent riot commissions:

Following the Kerner Commission, there has been considerable development of riot-control weapons and programs in urban areas, without similar efforts, recommended by the Commission, to meet underlying and legitimate grievances. From the evidence, it appears that it has been found more expedient to implement recommendations for control than

[75] Ibid., pp. 68–70.
[76] Applegate, *Riot Control—Materiel and Techniques,* p. 66.

recommendations for altering the social structure. There is little evidence that a call for social reform, on the one hand, and for the development of sophisticated riot-control techniques and weaponry, on the other, will not suffer the same fate today.[77]

Moreover, in the Urban America and Urban Coalition report on post-1967 developments in responses to riots, entitled *One Year Later,* a similarly pessimistic conclusion was reached. Reviewing governmental actions in such important areas as poverty, education, and housing, the report concluded that most actions and programs to meet ghetto problems and grievances had been, depending on the area, too limited, underfunded, or nonexistent.[78]

Specifically, what were the more or less immediate reactions of government and private organizations at the national level both to public discussion of possible social and economic reforms, which might meet ghetto grievances, and to the reform recommendations of government-created riot commissions? While one is faced in assessing reforms, as in evaluating law enforcement actions, with the possibility that the reforms reflected more than the pressures of collective violence in urban ghettos, many actions taken by federal, state, and municipal governments seem related to ghetto riot developments. For example, in the months between the long hot summer of 1967 and the publication of the *Report of the National Advisory Commission on Civil Disorders* several cities which had experienced riots received new or renewed federal attention. Examining surveys of the postriot aftermath in 20 cities, the National Advisory Commission reported that by the end of 1967 there were "at least 10 examples, in eight cities, of Federal programs being improved or new Federal programs being instituted."[79] This would seem a fair proportion of

---

[77] Skolnick, *The Politics of Protest,* p. 343.

[78] Urban America, Inc., and the Urban Coalition, *One Year Later,* especially pp. 114–118.

[79] *Report of the National Advisory Commission on Civil Disorders,* pp. 86, 346.

the cities that were examined. Yet closer inspection suggested that these responses may have reflected an ongoing process of renewal as much as a specific response to ghetto rioting; thus, in six of the 10 cases the "response" was the approval of Model Cities programs by the Department of Housing and Urban Development (HUD). The other examples mainly involved the development or expansion of Office of Economic Opportunity (OEO) programs.

It is also interesting to note that a similar pattern of response emphasizing HUD and OEO programs may well have characterized the federal government reaction after riots in years other than 1967. For example, a study of the nation's four largest cities found that Los Angeles had received the least antipoverty money per poverty-stricken family prior to the summer of 1965; however, after the outbreak of collective violence in Watts, Los Angeles suddenly soared to the top of the list in the per capita amount of OEO money received.[80] In addition to the increased OEO funds, several organizations and agencies in Los Angeles ghetto areas received aid from other federal agencies. Yet Bullock notes that increased funding had its limitations:

> The mention of Watts in a proposal for a government contract or grant had a magic effect, as funds began to pour into special programs and facilities in the area. Expenditures were actually scanty in proportion to the size of the problem confronted, but they were much greater than all previous public spending.[81]

Inspection of the available data on federal funding suggests that responses to riots of this type necessitated local cooperation with the federal government, even local initiative, in bringing

[80] J. David Greenstone and Paul E. Peterson, "Reformers, Machines, and the War on Poverty," *City Politics and Public Policy,* ed. James Q. Wilson (New York: Wiley, 1968), pp. 287–288.

[81] Paul Bullock, ed., *Watts: The Aftermath* (New York: Grove Press, 1969), p. 51.

these programs to fruition. Moreover, examination of this HUD and OEO funding flow also suggested to us that it might be useful to raise some comparative questions. That is, was there a *distinctive* acceleration of government aid to riot cities, or was federal economic aid to nonriot cities increasing as well? Did the intensity and magnitude of rioting, or even the number of riots per city, relate directly to increases in federal expenditures? And, if there was such an increase across the board, did it reflect a general preventive concern in regard to future rioting? These questions indicate that much additional research on postriot responses by government is needed. For example, a study of cities that had riots for a period of time before and after the riots, compared to cities that did not have riots in the same period, might begin to elucidate some of these issues; yet another study might focus on the intensity of rioting, comparing cities with serious riots to those that did not have collective violence of serious consequence.

Although to our knowledge no one has yet undertaken such systematic research, one exploratory analysis touching on some of the aforementioned questions has been made available to us. In an interesting attempt to assess the riot aftermath response of several federal government agencies and programs—and indirectly the responses of local governments as well—Button examined increases in HUD and OEO expenditures to 40 cities randomly selected from the 1967 riot cities enumerated by the National Advisory Commission.[82] Initially, inspection of the percentage increases in federal support through the HUD and OEO programs for the 40 riot cities revealed that about half saw an increase greater than the national OEO and HUD budget increase for all counties and cities in that five-year period, while half saw less of an increase than the national figure, or even a decrease in funding for local programs.

[82] James Button, "The Effects of Black Violence: Federal Expenditure Responses to the Urban Race Riots," unpublished manuscript, University of Texas at Austin, January, 1972.

The Aftermath of Rioting: The Establishment Response

Moreover, using measures of riot intensity and the number of riots as independent variables, and percentage increases in several federal fiscal aid programs for two and one half year periods before and after the 1967 riots as dependent variables, he found that there was no significant relationship between riot intensity and increases in total HUD and OEO expenditures for these 40 riot cities. This was also found to be the case when population size of the city was controlled for. There was one exception to this pattern when specific HUD and OEO programs were examined: increases in VISTA funds (an OEO program) were significantly related to the intensity of the 1967 riots studied, even when the population size of the city was held constant. The more severe the riot, the more likely a city was to receive a sizable percentage increase in VISTA aid in the period studied. Virtually the same pattern was discovered when the overall intensity of rioting in each city for a longer period, the five years between 1963 and 1968, was computed, a measure taking into consideration both the number of riots which occurred (ranging from one to six) and the intensity of each specific riot. No significant relationship was found between HUD and OEO expenditure increases and this measure of rioting. Again the only exception was for VISTA funding. These results thus suggest that the federal government, and perhaps local governments as well, did not respond in any systematic way to the intensity of the riots in this period, with the exception perhaps of the VISTA program, among the least important in terms of dollars of the programs examined.

One tantalizing finding did appear when the simple number, rather than intensity, of riots per city in the 1963–1968 period was examined in relation to the flow of HUD and OEO funds. Using this measure as the independent variable, one significant relationship did appear when size of city population was controlled: between increases in overall HUD funding and the measure indicating frequency of ghetto rioting. Although this was the only relationship found to be significant, it did intimate that the number of riots a city endured might have had a some-

243

what greater effect in generating significant jumps in federal expenditures than the intensity of rioting. So far, however, exploratory research has provided only weak evidence for a link between government expenditures in specific cities and ghetto rioting. Yet one still might speculate that ghetto rioting had a very significant influence on the general level of HUD and OEO funding, with administrators perhaps feeling that such aid increased ghetto stability in nonriot as well as riot cities. In fact, federal expenditures in programs such as these did see a general increase over the 1960s.

Other federal actions that appeared to be linked in a more general way to ghetto rioting often had a modest appearance and seemed to lack long-term commitment to eradicating ghetto problems. In response to riot commission recommendations and presidential directives, a number of federal agencies were required to "look into" recommendations for reform and asked to take action. Indeed, the President reacted to the *Report of the National Advisory Commission on Civil Disorders* by asking each member of his Cabinet "to study it and analyze every recommendation to determine (1) which proposals were already being carried out, (2) which would be covered by our 1968 legislative program, and (3) which had not yet been adopted."[83] Although the scope of federal agency activity was seriously limited by the unwillingness of the Administration to fight Congress for the billions the Bureau of the Budget estimated would be required to implement the Commission's recommendations, several agencies other than HUD and OEO did take some action in general response to ghetto rioting, although the actions often did not distinguish between riot and nonriot cities.

Among the most important of these actions were those involving the Small Business Administration (SBA). Spurred by the growing interest of some prominent government and corporate executives in creating a managerial and entrepreneurial class in

[83] Johnson, *The Vantage Point,* p. 172. See also p. 173.

ghetto areas, the Small Business Administration expanded its efforts by trying to secure new black borrowers, particularly by "lowering equity requirements (which in 1968 could be less than 15 percent), guaranteeing up to 90 percent of bank loans, and developing counseling programs in cooperation with volunteer groups such as the Service Corps of Retired Executives (SCORE) and Minority Advisors for Minority Entrepreneurs (MAME)."[84] This increased interest among white leaders, both inside and outside the federal government, in a class of black capitalists often appeared to be motivated by concern over ghetto rioting and concomitant urban instability. It was hoped that a buffer group would serve as a preventive in regard to future ghetto revolts and "thereby as a means of social control by disseminating the ideology and values of the dominant white society throughout the alienated ghetto masses."[85]

Likewise, concern for ghetto stability and riot prevention was the driving force behind expansion of ghetto activity in the riot aftermath by a number of large national corporations, although other motives such as a sense of corporate responsibility or a desire to secure a share of the ghetto market were also involved. Indeed, when it comes to issues like these, it is difficult to disentangle government and private efforts, as there has been much cooperation between sectors. A common pattern was for a black-controlled corporation to be established in an important ghetto area and funded by federal grants or loans. Coupled with this is the aid of a large national corporation, which provides such things as advisory personnel and an outlet for the goods produced. In other cases large corporations have set up branch plants in ghetto areas, usually with subsidies in the form of federal training programs, or have provided a new pool of financial resources for loans to improve ghetto housing and businesses. A

---

[84] Tabb, *The Political Economy of the Black Ghetto,* p. 47.

[85] Robert L. Allen, *Black Awakening in Capitalist America* (Garden City, N.Y.: Doubleday Anchor Books, 1970), p. 212.

list of the important examples of these diverse corporate efforts would include the following: (1) a black organization called FIGHT in Rochester, New York, supported by Xerox Corporation; (2) a black-controlled container corporation in San Francisco aided both by Crown-Zellerbach Corporation and the Bank of America; (3) branch plants set up by Aerojet-General in a Los Angeles ghetto and by Avco in a Boston ghetto; (4) the announcement of Chrysler Corporation that a few million dollars of its assets would be deposited in black-controlled banks in several ghetto areas; (5) the action taken by the Prudential insurance company in Newark to provide millions of dollars in loans for ghetto businesses; and (6) the announced intention of the American insurance industry to support ghetto improvement projects to the tune of a billion dollars.[86]

As yet, the effects of these various government and private actions on critical ghetto problems of low wages and unemployment have not been fully assessed. The data available to us, however, indicate that the impact has been limited, in part because of the extraordinarily difficult character and tremendous scope of ghetto employment and business problems, and in part because of fluctuations in the general economy. Even with federal subsidies the costs of retraining ghetto workers forced numerous private operations into the red, a result that both explains the distinctive involvement of large corporations in ghetto projects, corporations that can absorb heavy losses, and also accounts for the tendency to withdraw from such operations when a recession occurs. And Small Business Administration loan programs for minority businessmen have run into serious difficulty because of rising loss and default rates and have apparently been scaled down as a result.[87] Moreover, a serious weakness in these various black capitalism efforts is that they have been too individualistic. Apparently, only a limited number of ghetto blacks among the

[86] Ibid., pp. 223–225.
[87] Tabb, *The Political Economy of the Black Ghetto*, pp. 46–51, 73–74.

millions in economic need have been aided through such programs.

Reform reaction to ghetto revolts seems to have been more substantial in the executive branch of the federal government than in the legislative branch. Congress responded to the 1968 report of the National Advisory Commission mainly by setting up several investigating committees. Some, like the U.S. Senate Permanent Subcommittee on Investigations (McClellan Committee), were interested mainly in agitator and conspiracy theories and in repression solutions to ghetto violence; others, such as the Congressional Joint Economic Committee, did explore the possibility of major economic reform. In September 1968 a Joint Economic Committee report was issued examining the employment recommendations of the National Advisory Commission.[88] As with several in-house investigations of this type, the conclusions and recommendations of the report were actually weaker than those of the Commission and again reflected the traditional dependence on extending pre-existing government approaches: a call for more aggregate demand in the private sector, for better adult education and training programs, for the removal of discrimination in employment, for an increase in the training of ghetto entrepreneurs, and for the revitalization of central cities. Again the analysis had a vague but essentially liberal cast, yet no real innovations of consequence were being proposed. Nor were proposals forthcoming to spend the billions that would be necessary to deal with these proposals in a serious manner, much less to implement the National Advisory Commission's far-reaching proposal for millions of new jobs.

In addition, a review of congressional bills enacted during the 1965–1970 period leads to the conclusion that Congress took relatively little reform-oriented action in these years, especially action

[88] Joint Economic Committee, U.S. Congress, *Employment and Manpower Problems in the Cities: Implications of the Report of the National Advisory Commission on Civil Disorders* (Washington, D.C.: U.S. Government Printing Office, 1968).

which reflected a serious concern for the ghetto conditions underlying rioting. Congressional debates, in fact, often stressed that rioters should not be "rewarded." In the 1966–1968 period Congress frequently either failed to support remedial legislation that had been proposed by the President or funded reform programs at relatively meager levels. After 1968 a policy of "benign neglect" seemed to prevail in both the executive and legislative branches. Some legislation was passed providing for summer youth and school breakfast programs, a carefully defined model cities program was provided with modest funding, and some additional civil rights legislation became law. Conceivably, congressional support for a continuation of tokenism or gradualism in the area of minority aid may have been reinforced by ghetto rioting, but no major restructuring of the economy or polity to meet black needs was envisioned in the many business-as-usual legislative actions that emerged from Congress in this 1965–1970 period.

Social and Economic Reform: The State Response

Most state action that can be linked closely with the aftermath of ghetto rioting seems to have taken the form of either riot investigation, including riot commissions, of antiriot legislation, or of involvement in fiscal support for local law enforcement agencies. State inaction in terms of social and economic reform was actually fostered and encouraged by recent reports of major government riot commissions that virtually ignored the possible role of state governments, and suburban governments as well, in alleviating the burden of the black residents of riot-torn ghettos in the various states. Thus while state leaders sometimes indicated that they understood the conditions faced by black Americans and might support reform programs, even visiting ghettos and calling for reforms, relatively little in the way of concrete state programs directed at riot-spawning conditions was developed. On occasion, state service centers were established in ghetto areas (such as that set up in Watts after the 1965 riot there) to provide ghetto residents with better information on and access to existing state employment and welfare programs. On the whole, however, major action in pursuit of goals other than law enforcement and general investigation goals was left to government and private authorities at the federal and local levels. As far as we have been able to discern, there were few major exceptions to this generalization about state inaction.

One possible exception occurred at the level of state government in New Jersey. Although President Johnson was able to withstand the pressure for widesweeping reform that emanated from the two national commissions he appointed, New Jersey's chief executive was not quite as successful. After the submission of a final report, most riot commissioners have seen their transitory organizations evaporate quickly, and few have continued to exert any significant influence in the direction of implementing the recommendations they disseminated. However, a few of the commissioners who served on the New Jersey Commission had some impact on the subsequent actions of the governor who appointed them:

> In New Jersey, for example, Governor Hughes was threatened by individual members of the commission with public criticism if he continued his failure to respond. Shortly thereafter, the Governor and his staff received members of the commission and in an all-day session virtually wrote the Governor's special message to the legislature.[89]

This surprisingly progressive message included most of the reform-oriented recommendations of the riot commissioners—reportedly coming to more than $126 million for urban problems. A few other states, particularly those with more liberal administrations, also saw some movement on the part of governors and legislative leaders toward reform-oriented legislation. Apparently

[89] Lipsky and Olson, "Riot Commission Politics," 20.

this movement dissipated as the time between the present and the summer of the most massive riots (1967) increased.

Social and Economic Reform: The Local Response

In addition to the heavy emphasis on law enforcement capability to respond to rioting, what was the reaction of local government and private agencies to the collective violence within their boundaries? Though information on local reform-oriented responses and corresponding material on state actions have not been systematically recorded, and what we have collected is doubtless incomplete, available data indicate there was in the aftermath period some attempt, however ephemeral, in many cities to make a start on ameliorating ghetto conditions. In this section we will focus on riot responses more or less limited to the local level; of course, many of the private and public actions discussed in previous sections on state and national responses had a local focus and entailed local cooperation, participation, or initiative.

Perhaps the first municipal response to receive significant publicity was that of public and private agencies to the 1965 Watts riot. In the aftermath of that riot, after consulting with the mayor and other local and state officials, the Los Angeles Chamber of Commerce sponsored a program to hire unemployed persons from the Watts area. Later, influenced by the Los Angeles Commission report on the riot calling for permanent action on employment, dozens of companies enlisted in a program of the Management Council for Merit Employment, Training and Research, a nonprofit organization created to help business corporations employ more black workers. By May 1967 nearly 18,000 residents of the South Central Los Angeles area had reportedly been employed by this program, although it was not clear to what extent the circulated estimate included duplications and black workers who had simply shifted from one job to another.[90]

[90] H. C. McClellan, Letter to authors, May 26, 1967.

The Aftermath of Rioting: The Establishment Response

In addition, a 1967 follow-up report by the Los Angeles Commission reported on some further actions by public officials. Reportedly, in the two years since the Watts riot new facilities had been established for job retraining, a new Health Services Center had been opened in the ghetto area, and the County Health Department had expanded its services in disadvantaged areas.[91]

However, the follow-up report also noted for the years between 1965 and 1967 that relatively little in the way of significant changes had occurred in educational facilities for minority children, that the unemployment rate among blacks had not materially decreased, that new police programs consisted mainly of in-house processing of citizen complaints against the police department, and that the major transportation recommendations of the earlier Commission report had not been followed. Thus, this report indicates that while some initial steps had been taken by local officials, much remained to be accomplished. Perhaps indicative of the basic philosophy underlying much recent writing about ghetto reforms were the individualistic values reflected in the follow-up report of the Los Angeles Commission. The introduction argues that "basic changes in the societal order have never been achieved quickly" and that the Negro himself must shoulder "a full share of responsibility for his own well being"; and "work and study" were suggested as the keys to the future advance of black Americans.[92]

Turning to municipal actions taken in the aftermath period following on the long hot summer of 1967, one finds somewhat more available material than in the case of riots which occurred before and after that summer. Examining in some detail the responses of 20 cities with riots in 1967, the National Advisory Commission investigated not only the actions of control agencies attempting to prevent or contain future outbreaks but also offi-

[91] Governor's Commission on the Los Angeles Riots, *Staff Report of Actions Taken to Implement the Recommendations in the Commission's Report,* August 18, 1967, pp. 7–11.
[92] Ibid., pp. 12–13.

cial actions directed toward social and economic reform. The general conclusion of the Commission in regard to these postriot consequences was that "despite some notable public and private efforts, particularly regarding employment opportunities, little basic change took place in the conditions underlying the disorder."[93] More specifically, looking at the local problems of police-community relations, employment, housing, education, recreation, ghetto representation, grievance machinery, and municipal services, the National Advisory Commission found that only a minority of cities had taken significant remedial action in each of these areas. The first three grievance areas just listed were considered to be of high intensity, an estimation made on the basis of the evaluations in postriot interviews with ghetto residents.

In the aftermath of rioting 8 of the 20 cities evaluated had taken action in the police-community relations area.[94] While there was obviously an element of riot detection and control even in these police department actions, on balance there was some concern expressed for reforming the character of police relationships to local communities. In most cases, however, these actions were relatively limited, encompassing the establishment or expansion of community relations programs in police departments, the creation of a few store front police offices, and active recruitment or promotion resulting in the addition of a few more black officers. As we have noted previously, some of the federal LEAA grants in the years after the 1967 riots also went for similar police-community relations projects, although in general there has been a strong tendency for these local police-community projects to concentrate on instructing the community about the police rather than the reverse, and "on assigning functions to the police which could better be performed by City Hall."[95] One

[93] *Report of the National Advisory Commission on Civil Disorders,* p. 84.

[94] Ibid., p. 85.

[95] National Urban Coalition, *Law and Order II,* p. 14.

other basic weakness in expanding along traditional lines, appointing special community relations officers, is that most of the actions of the regular policeman on the beat are left relatively unaffected and remain under the control of white authorities; yet it is these police-community contacts on the beat that have been perhaps the most critical in generating riot-precipitating police incidents.[96]

Looking toward the goal of getting potential rioters off the streets, 9 of these same 20 riot-torn cities had made some attempt in the postriot period to improve the employment situation of blacks residing in their boundaries, including both public actions and business efforts. These actions included accelerated efforts urging employers to hire more ghetto residents by local human relations commissions, the inauguration of limited job training programs, and two "crash" programs to find several hundred new jobs, a strategy that originated in Los Angeles after the 1965 Watts riot.[97] Yet none of these employment programs seemed to have been on the scale of that in Los Angeles, and all appeared to involve only modest extensions of traditional approaches to the eradication of poverty. In addition, nine cities among those examined by the National Advisory Commission also saw some local government action to expand local housing programs in the riot aftermath. These actions included setting up an urban renewal complaint office in a ghetto, approving applications for the development of some new public housing units for local blacks, the passing of a weak fair housing ordinance, and actions taken by a few local housing authorities to disperse new public housing projects. Again the governmental actions taken in the aftermath of rioting were quite modest and along traditional lines.

Looking at municipal efforts to meet black grievances at what

[96] David Perry and Paula Sornoff, "Street-Level Administration and the Law: The Problem of Police-Community Relations," *Criminal Law Bulletin,* 8 (January–February, 1972), 43–61.

[97] *Report of the National Advisory Commission on Civil Disorders,* pp. 345–346.

were considered lower levels of intensity, the National Advisory Commission found that out of the riot cities examined, 5 had taken steps to meet some educational grievances, 4 had tried to improve recreational facilities, and 4 had moved to refurbish municipal services in riot areas. In addition, 2 cities reportedly appointed new human relations commissions, and 4 saw a little progress in the area of black representation in local government.[98]

Among the most significant postriot efforts at the municipal level in the aftermath of the 1967 riots were made in Detroit, Michigan. Following on the temporary relief provided by charity organizations to riot area residents—a common reaction in numerous riot-torn cities—came signs of more substantial community action. While new organizations were formed in a few riot cities, "Detroit's answer was the New Detroit Committee, a joint enterprise of Cavanagh and Romney."[99] Although less than 20 percent of the Committee was composed of black residents, the Committee members did press for greater black participation in the rebuilding of ghetto businesses and stores and for open housing legislation. A few programs in the area of employment were also inaugurated, in part under the influence of the New Detroit Committee, and with the aid of local business and industry a relatively large number of ghetto residents apparently found jobs. Steps were also taken to improve the educational system. However, at the same time other government action suggested that these reforms would only be temporary or token. On the one hand, the state legislature refused to cooperate on several of these municipal programs; on the other, even greater stress on law enforcement and police control could be seen in the proposal that several million dollars be allocated by the city government for new riot control material.[100] In terms of dollars the control effort seemed to outweigh the reform effort.

[98] Ibid., pp. 85–87, 344–346.
[99] Hubert G. Locke, *The Detroit Riot of 1967* (Detroit: Wayne State University Press, 1969), p. 103.
[100] *Report of the National Advisory Commission on Civil Disorders,* pp. 84–85.

The Aftermath of Rioting: The Establishment Response

Further examination of the pattern of overall response in the area of reform in these 20 riot cities indicated that there were four somewhat different patterns of municipal reaction.[101] To determine these patterns we first grouped city responses into three levels, based on the intensity of the relevant grievances as estimated by the National Advisory Commission.[102] Employing the Commission criteria, three difficulties (police-community relations, employment, and housing) were considered high intensity grievances, the next two grievances (education and recreation) were regarded as possessing moderate intensity, and three other issues were viewed as of low intensity. Municipal attempts to resolve problems after a riot were thus characterized according to the intensity of the relevant ghetto grievances.

Examination of this information disclosed four different community reaction patterns. The six cities that took action to reduce grievances at all three levels might be termed "highly responsive cities." Municipalities that acted to ameliorate conditions at only two levels were labeled "cities with mixed responses." Five cities that made an effort to resolve only the most intense grievances were termed "somewhat responsive"; and three "unresponsive" cities generally did not move to improve local conditions. With only a few exceptions, usually reflecting unsystematic response patterns contained in the mixed response category, the reactions of the cities seemed to conform somewhat to the pattern of a Guttman-type scale. Not surprisingly, communities were most likely to respond to highly intense grievances, considerably less likely to react to moderately intense problems, and least apt to act on complaints of low intensity. Such evidence not only appeared to corroborate the National Advisory Commission criteria for grievance intensity but also

[101] This section reporting a reanalysis of Commission data draws heavily on research published elsewhere. See Harlan Hahn, "Civic Responses to Riots: A Reappraisal of Kerner Commission Data," *The Public Opinion Quarterly,* 34 (Spring 1970), 101–107.

[102] *Report of the National Advisory Commission on Civil Disorders,* pp. 81–87, 345–347.

pointed up clear distinctions between the cities. The differences between the cities were most notable at the extremes. After the 1967 riots Elizabeth, New Jersey, was involved in seven programs to reduce local dissatisfaction; Dayton, Detroit, and Tampa each participated in five; and Atlanta adopted four. On the other hand, Bridgeton and Jersey City apparently took no remedial action after experiencing riots. Yet it was clear from examining the information at hand that even those municipal governments which responded in numerous ways to local ghetto violence did so either with modest expansion of traditional programs or with operations which at best would provide temporary relief.

Given these variable response patterns, we explored a related question of some interest. Why did some municipalities respond to the 1967 riots by attempting to meet some local grievances, while others took little or no ameliorative action? Unfortunately, the research conducted by the National Advisory Commission on the 20 cities with riots in 1967 did not attempt a close investigation of all variables. However, by carefully inspecting statements regarding incidents in each of the 20 cities before, during, and after the local riot, we found it possible to assign the communities to rough but discrete categories. Exploratory examination indicated that neither the size of the city nor its regional location appeared to have any marked effect on the local remedial response to ghetto violence; and analysis of several other demographic features also did not reveal any close associations with postriot innovations. Furthermore, the severity of the disorder as rated by the Commission did not seem to be related to the actions taken by municipal governments in the aftermath of riots. Similar to the federal funding responses to riot cities discussed earlier in this chapter, responses which might be considered local responses as well, the activities of municipal governments after riots did not reflect a simple response to the level of pressure generated by the intensity of the rioting.

Analysts of riots have sometimes raised the issue of the structure of municipal governments, proposing that the less centralized and the more accessible this structure, the less the likelihood of rioting. Exploring the proposition that structure may influence ability to respond to civil riots with programs to alleviate ghetto conditions, we found that most of the highly responsive cities had a mayor-council system with at-large elections and a four-year mayoral term. On the other hand, cities with mixed responses tended to have a strong mayor-council form, district or ward elections, and a short term for mayor. A manager-council plan, a four-year mayoralty term, and district or ward elections were most prevalent among the somewhat responsive cities. Finally, the most unresponsive cities seemed to be governed by a weak mayor-council structure, a combination of ward and at-large elections, and mayors with short terms. While exceptions to these generalizations were evident in each category, certain parallels between the forms of local government and the level of responses were intriguing.[103]

Perhaps the ability of governments to respond to a social upheaval such as a riot has been influenced less by the process of easy access to decision-makers than by features of the system that facilitate centralized and unified action and allocation of certain resources. Cities that responded to riots by taking a relatively large number of actions tended to have greater centralization of authority and less direct citizen access, at least at the level of municipal government. Of the available governmental characteristics the method of electing councilmen seemed very critical, signaling perhaps that ward or district representation may substantially interfere with a local government's ability to respond in traditional welfare ways in the few months following a riot. Apparently the most significant responses to ghetto riot-

[103] In addition, city councils in the more responsive cities processed more complaints than those in the less responsive cities; and certain official actions taken during the 1967 riot might have been linked to government structure. The use of neighborhood counterrioters, for example, was authorized before riots began in five of the six most responsive cities. They were merely condoned in three of the six cities with mixed responses and in three of the five somewhat responsive cities. In the three unresponsive cities they were either not recognized or absent.

CHAPTER 5

ing emerged in cities with powerful elected representatives and strong central governments.[104]

However, in examining official actions in the riot aftermath it is important to keep in mind the character and extent of most municipal reactions—expanding pre-existing programs somewhat and accentuating traditional approaches to ameliorating ghetto conditions. And the relatively short time span under examination by the National Advisory Commission may also have been an important factor. While the more centralized city governments were more likely to take some action in the few months after the 1967 riots, so far as we can tell they were just as unlikely as other cities to explore truly innovative or far-reaching reforms, including many such reforms proposed by government riot commissions.

After the assassinations during the first half of 1968 there seems to have been a sharp decline in white concern with ghetto problems and a new emphasis on law and order. While there was some discussion and investigation of government and private responses after the 1965 and 1967 ghetto upheavals, relatively little specific information appears to have been recorded on local reform-oriented activities in the wake of riots in the 1968–1971 period. Perhaps such a lack of information and investigation emphasizes the general lack of significant local action to meet the numerous ghetto grievances. The brief accounts of local reactions to riots that are available would seem to corroborate this contention, for where official action was taken it was directed at short-lived or modest expansion of pre-existing programs or attempts at rebuilding burned-out areas. For example, one review

[104] This finding appears inconsistent with the analysis by Lieberson and Silverman of earlier twentieth-century riots which concluded that cities experiencing a riot were more likely to have at-large representation and a high mean population per councilman than cities that did not have a riot. See Stanley Lieberson and Arnold R. Silverman, "The Precipitants and Underlying Conditions of Race Riots," *American Sociological Review*, **30** (December 1965), 887–898.

of local actions in the months immediately following the 1968 riot in Washington, D.C., turned up the temporary charity activities to aid displaced victims of rioting.[105] New organizations were also created in the aftermath of the Washington riot. Based on the planning of government and private agencies, the Ford Foundation provided $600,000 to set up a Community Reconstruction and Development Corporation to aid in rebuilding efforts, particularly the rebuilding of burned-out stores. Also established was a new Economic Development Committee which set out to find risk capital for new and restored black businesses both inside and outside riot areas. In spite of these auspicious activities, however, not much in the way of concrete results could be cited five months after the riot:

> The city's five-month attempt at a dialogue—in the schools, in public meetings on rebuilding burned-out streets, in angry statements from black activists about the police—has brought out some of the problems and alienation that lay behind the rioting.
>
> But, in August, the question remained whether the nation's capital would be able to do an effective job of coping with the conditions that caused the riots to occur.[106]

As with most postriot actions by local municipalities, significant social and economic reform in Washington was at best still a promise rather than a reality which the black residents of the riot-torn areas could presently experience. Indeed, as time passed, city officials across the nation seemed to become adept at accentuating the need for federal or state action to remedy municipal problems, to the virtual neglect of extensive or innovative local action, even though the predominant black grievances had a local focus.

[105] Ben W. Gilbert et al., *Ten Blocks from the White House* (New York: Praeger, 1968), pp. 217–219.
[106] Ibid., p. 222.

CHAPTER 5

Conclusion

While the multifaceted response of government at local, state, and federal levels was not always solely in response to ghetto rioting, since the rioting and collective violence of other groups may have played a role in many of the government decisions we have examined, it does seem clear that numerous official actions reflected the pressure of recent violent events that have occurred in America's urban ghettos. While some of the changes and reforms might have occurred in the natural progress of events, without the spurring effect of ghetto violence, other actions by officials in the government sector—and in the private sector as well—perhaps would not have taken place had it not been for the actions of black Americans intent on attempting to force changes in their urban milieu. Commissions, with their sometimes useful functions, would not have been appointed, and certain social and economic reforms, however limited in effect, would not have taken place or would have been slower in coming. However, certain law enforcement reactions also might not have occurred. In general, one cannot fail to be impressed more by the scope and intensity of the law enforcement or control response than by the relatively limited character of the social and economic reforms which came in the aftermath of rioting.

Close scrutiny of the many leaders and officials who have been involved in postriot activities, particularly those involved in riot commissions, suggests the conclusion that a management approach to social problems may have come to the forefront.[107] Perhaps limited to the curative approach of liberals to rioting (for conservatives seem unconcerned with reform), the management emphasis is mirrored in the view that the established social, economic, and governmental arrangements are basically satisfactory and that emergent social problems are a result of more or less minor flaws in the functioning of those arrangements.

[107] Platt, "The Politics of Riot Commissions, 1917–1970: An Overview"; Currie, "Violence and Ideology: A Critique of the Final Report of the Violence Commission."

The Aftermath of Rioting: The Establishment Response

Proper management, proper tinkering with the existing system, will lead to an eradication of such problems, however persistent they may be. However, while presumably well-intentioned officials proceed with refurbishing existing institutions and structures, the collective violence spawned as a result of flaws in society must be quickly and efficiently repressed. Thus the persistent coupling by several riot and violence commissions of a reform perspective with a counterinsurgency perspective aimed at "managing" collective violence out of existence with the efficient use of control forces and control technology seems explicable.

Yet the twofold approach to solutions for ghetto rioting founders on the assumption that "reform measures have about the same prospect of gaining executive and legislative support as control and firepower measures."[108] Our review of historical and contemporary materials on government responses to ghetto rioting indicates that this assumption is not warranted. When faced with crises, urban governments have usually had limited financial (and other) resources at their disposal. The resources that are available will tend to flow into the areas where there is the least resistance—and strengthening law enforcement capabilities appears to be the most welcome response of government to crises from the perspective of white powerholding groups. Only limited reforms are likely to occur in American cities as long as those in power do not wish a significant reallocation of power and resources to take place. Thus we were not greatly surprised at the conclusions of a research report on the state of American cities that crossed our desk as this book was going to press:

Our basic finding is that, despite the widely accepted Kerner [1967–1968 National Advisory Commission] finding that one major cause of the ghetto disorders of the 1960's was the shameful conditions of life in the cities, most of the changes in those conditions since 1968—at least in the cities we visited—have been for the worse.

108 Skolnick, *The Politics of Protest,* p. 343.

- Housing is still the national scandal it was then.
- Schools are more tedious and turbulent.
- The rates of crime and unemployment and disease and heroin addiction are higher.
- Welfare rolls are larger.
- And, with few exceptions, the relations between minority communities and the police are just as hostile.

In short, the expressions of sympathy and concern that the Kerner Report elicited from a number of those who, privately or publicly, wield the power that governs the United States, did not signify that they were willing to take the drastic action necessary to make American cities livable again.[109]

[109] Commission on the Cities in the '70's, *The State of the Cities* (New York: Praeger, 1972), p. 5.

Ghetto Resident Views in the Aftermath of Riots

Although there are many perspectives from which one can assess the character, meaning, and effects of ghetto rioting during the last decade, one of the most important vantage points would seem to be that of black citizens residing in communities that have experienced serious riots. One straightforward method of gaining an improved understanding of the urban violence of recent years, therefore, might consist of asking the black Americans who were affected by ghetto revolts for their reactions to and evaluations of what occurred in their communities. While the residents of ghetto areas that saw collective violence included individuals who participated actively in rioting as well as those who were uninvolved, the opinions and views of both groups could provide the foundation for a penetrating interpretation of ghetto riots. An outbreak of collective violence results in a series of important events that might well have an immediate and powerful effect on those who live in the vicinity of the rioting. Although not all of the residents of a ghetto participated in the violence, at least they were placed in a closer position than most other commentators to assess the conditions that spawned rioting and to distinguish between purposeless and politically meaningful objectives. Consequently, principal attention is focused in this chapter on the perspectives of black urbanites, especially those residing in the strife-torn Detroit ghetto whose lives were interrupted, in many cases profoundly influenced, by rioting.

CHAPTER 6

The Detroit Uprising

During the last decade of collective violence on the part of black Americans perhaps the most serious instance of rioting was that which enveloped a large area in Detroit, Michigan, between July 23, the day when an after-hours club in Detroit's ghetto area was raided by the police, and August 1, when the curfew was lifted and the last government troops were withdrawn. Perhaps no greater evidence of the critical importance of this riot in recent American history can be given than the unique assessment recently provided in the memoirs of the white southerner who was President during the long hot summers of the years between 1963 and 1969:

> As the mask of black submission began to fall, the countless years of suppressed anger exploded outward. The withering of hope, the failure to change the dismal conditions of life, and the complex tangle of attitudes, issues, beliefs, and circumstances all led to the tragic phenomena known as "the riots"—"the long hot summers."
>
> Rioting in Detroit provided one of the worst instances— so bad, in fact, that the events of July 24–28, 1967, will remain forever etched in my memory.[1]

Following this intriguing evaluation is an extended discussion of the Detroit riot, with particular emphasis on the role of government in riot development and suppression. Indeed, the Detroit riot was the *only* riot singled out for comment by President Lyndon Johnson in nearly six hundred pages of detailed reflections on important political events of the 1960s.

As we have noted previously, the major riot that occurred in Detroit was triggered by a large-scale but relatively routine police raid on a "blind pig," an after-hours liquor establishment in the Twelfth Street ghetto area. The ensuing collective violence on

[1] Lyndon Baines Johnson, *The Vantage Point* (New York: Holt, Rinehart and Winston, 1971), pp. 167–168.

the part of black rioters and government control forces was extraordinarily severe and destructive. Ultimately this instance of violence would be one of the relatively small number of riots that passed through all of the important phases of rioting delineated in a prior chapter—escalating from the final precipitant to the state of siege. By the end of this week-long riot, the governer of Michigan had declared a state of emergency and had committed all the police forces and National Guardsmen at his disposal to control the expanding riot situation, the President of the United States had federalized the National Guard and ordered in several thousand federal paratroopers, several millions of dollars in property damage had been inflicted, and the grim riot statistics had risen to 43 persons dead, at least 324 persons injured, and 7,231 persons arrested for riot-related activities.[2] When these facts and figures are compared to those of other serious riots—such as those in Los Angeles, Newark, Chicago, and Washington—the Detroit riot does indeed seem the most serious episode of collective violence on the part of black Americans and white control forces in the recent history of the nation.

Opinion Surveys of Ghetto Residents

In spite of many gaps and omissions public opinion surveys of ghetto residents constitute an important source of information about popular reactions to urban violence. While a number of pollsters and researchers have attempted examinations of black and white attitudes toward ghetto riots by means of opinion surveys, relatively few have paid much attention to the significance of the timing of such polls. To illustrate, numerous postriot surveys of ghetto residents were conducted several months after the riot occurrence, a condition that perhaps raises in its most cogent form the issue of *post hoc* rationalizations of riot events by ghetto

[2] Ibid., pp. 167–172; *Report of the National Advisory Commission on Civil Disorders* (Washington, D.C.: U.S. Government Printing Office, 1968), pp. 47–61.

residents.³ That is, to an unknown degree community discussion and dissection of a riot may have had some effect on the perspectives on rioting and rioters which circulated in ghetto areas, especially the views prevalent several months after the violence. While we do not regard this problem as serious in most cases, particularly since postriot perspectives among blacks—whatever their development or construction—tell observers much about the jelling of black political consciousness, it is important to note that the principal source on which the discussion of ghetto views in this chapter is based is a postriot survey conducted in the central Twelfth Street area immediately after the 1967 Detroit riot.

Shortly after the violent and destructive uprising there, a "modified probability" sample survey of 270 residents of the Twelfth Street ghetto area was completed. The basic evidence presented in our subsequent discussion is drawn from analysis of the resulting interviews.⁴ Other survey materials will be cited

³ See Nathan Cohen, "The Los Angeles Riot Study," *The Los Angeles Riots,* ed. Nathan Cohen (New York: Praeger, 1970), pp. 1–40; Angus Campbell and Howard Schuman, "Racial Attitudes in Fifteen American Cities," *Supplemental Studies for the National Advisory Commission on Civil Disorders* (Washington, D.C.: U.S. Government Printing Office, 1968), pp. 11–12.

⁴ All blocks in the critical Twelfth Street area were stratified on the basis of a composite index of socioeconomic status derived from the median value of owner-occupied dwelling units, average monthly rent, and the proportion of substandard or dilapidated units reported by the 1960 housing census. Blocks were selected randomly within each stratum rather than within the entire area. Quota assignments for each block in the Detroit survey were based on the age and race of residents over 21 years of age. The Detroit sample included 270 black and 37 white residents, comparable to the racial characteristics of the area recorded in the census. Although interviewers and respondents in Detroit were matched by race, 37 white respondents have been eliminated from this report of the Detroit study. The authors wish to express their appreciation to the University of Michigan for a special grant which supported the Detroit Survey. Some of the evidence and data in this chapter were earlier presented in Harlan Hahn, "The Political Objectives of Ghetto Violence" (Paper presented at the 65th meeting of the

Ghetto Resident Views in the Aftermath of Riots

where relevant. Both because of its importance as the earliest postriot survey and because of its accessibility we will also give some emphasis to the data collected in a survey of New York's Bedford-Stuyvesant ghetto immediately after the 1964 riot there.[5] Since urban ghettos are by no means homogeneous entities, the opinions of these urbanites do in fact reveal some conflict or disagreement concerning riot interpretation. Even so, the similarity of views on certain crucial riot issues is perhaps the most impressive aspect of the survey data. By examining ghetto beliefs and perspectives, it may be possible to identify what the rioting was intended to accomplish as well as the impact and consequences actually produced.

American Political Science Association, New York, September 2–6, 1969).

[5] We are indebted to Paul B. Sheatsley and the National Opinion Research Center for collecting the Bedford-Stuyvesant data analyzed in this chapter. The data cited here have been drawn from interviews with a "block quota" sample of the residents of New York's Bedford-Stuyvesant ghetto shortly after the July 1964 riot there. The sample can best be described as a probability sample with quotas. Fifty blocks were systematically selected with probability proportionate to size. Four respondents were assigned in each block. On the basis of census data, 89 men and 111 women were required in the sample; of the women, 52 had to be employed, 59 not employed; of the men, 24 had to be aged eighteen to twenty-nine, the others thirty or older. All persons eighteen years of age or older were eligible for an interview, provided they resided in the dwelling unit. No more than one person in any household was interviewed. The quota controls ensured a proper representation of men and women and sufficient employed females and younger males—the most common biases of quota samples. Although race was not specified, all respondents were black; all interviewers were black.

The precipitating event of this riot was a typical one, involving the shooting of a young black ghetto resident by a white policeman. The riot began in Harlem and soon spread to Brooklyn's Bedford-Stuyvesant section, then occupied by approximately 400,000 blacks. The two riots together lasted six days, involved approximately 8,000 persons, and resulted in 118 injuries and 465 arrests, two thirds of the latter occurring in the Bedford-Stuyvesant ghetto.

CHAPTER 6

The Causes and Character of Ghetto Riots

Why have riots occurred? Generally speaking, assessments of the sources of urban unrest offered by ghetto residents in Detroit and elsewhere have been similar. Analysis of a question in our Twelfth Street survey about causes of riots revealed that 86 percent of the black residents in Detroit mentioned socioeconomic deprivation or racial discrimination as the underlying cause; only a few (8 percent) identified the raid on the "blind pig" as one of "two or three main reasons for the trouble." Moreover, an indication of the specific character of deprivation and discrimination grievances can be seen in yet another Detroit survey sponsored by the Urban League. In that poll black respondents were presented with a lengthy list of possible causes of the ghetto violence. The five most frequently selected causes were police brutality, overcrowded living conditions, poor housing, lack of jobs, and poverty, each of which was viewed as having "a great deal" to do with the rioting by at least 44 percent of the respondents.[6] Not surprisingly, when persons in our Twelfth Street survey were asked about possible remedies to avert further rioting, the overwhelming majority stressed the need for programs to end discrimination and alter basic ghetto conditions. Thus, most of these ghetto residents appeared to regard the collective violence which occurred in Detroit as a reflection of the general problems such as discrimination and deprivation that confront black people in virtually all communities, rather than as a unique product of special local grievances.

These findings on ghetto resident views of conditions underlying the Detroit riot are broadly similar to the data reported from other surveys of riot communities. For example, an early poll after the 1964 riot in the Bedford-Stuyvesant ghetto of New York City asked black residents about the "real cause" of that riot. While 36 percent of the ghetto residents emphasized discrimination and deprivation, 38 percent referred more specifically to the final precipitating incident—a police shooting of a Negro

[6] Detroit *Free Press,* August 20, 1967, p. B–4.

boy—in similar negative terms.[7] Moreover, a survey conducted by University of California researchers disclosed that 64 percent of the persons living in the curfew area in Watts said that discrimination and deprivation complaints were responsible for the violence there, and an additional 26 percent cited general hostility, hate, or vengeance directed at whites.[8] Yet another poll of Watts residents found that 58 percent of the black residents cited economic problems, 20 percent reported racial humiliation, and 24 percent referred to police actions as the "real cause" of the riots there.[9] On the whole, these ghetto resident perspectives seem to corroborate what a study of actual riot participants in Newark and Detroit found: "the continued exclusion of Negroes from American economic and social life is the fundamental cause of riots."[10]

Nevertheless, the interpretations of urban violence offered by persons who actually experienced a riot, such as those residing in the Twelfth Street area of Detroit, stood in marked contrast to the prevailing opinions of white citizens and governmental leaders, who have tended to ascribe the blame to more personalized causes—such as outside agitators, criminals, or black extremists—rather than to the overarching social, economic, or governmental structure of ghetto society. For example, in one

[7] Many of the figures in subsequent discussions of the Bedford-Stuyvesant survey have been taken from Joe R. Feagin and Paul B. Sheatsley, "Ghetto Resident Appraisals of a Riot," *Public Opinion Quarterly*, 32 (Fall 1968), 352–362. Other figures are based on unpublished tabulations.

[8] T. M. Tomlinson and David O. Sears, *Negro Attitudes Toward the Riots* (Los Angeles: UCLA Institute of Government and Public Affairs, 1967), p. 13.

[9] John F. Kraft, "The Attitudes of Negroes in Various Cities," *Federal Role in Urban Affairs,* Hearings before the Subcommittee on Executive Reorganization of the Committee on Government Operations, Part 6, U.S. Senate, 89th Congress, 2nd Session, September 1, 1966, pp. 1387–1388.

[10] Nathan S. Caplan and Jeffrey M. Paige, "A Study of Ghetto Rioters," *Scientific American,* 219 (August 1968), 21.

major national survey conducted shortly after the 1967 riots the largest proportion (45 percent) of white Americans identified "outside agitation" as one of the "two or three main reasons" for the violence.[11] Only 16 percent spoke of racial prejudice; just 14 percent mentioned poverty as a possible cause for the riot. Furthermore, a 1968 survey of several thousand white residents in more than a dozen major cities revealed that the two most frequently cited causes of the riots were "looters and other undesirables," cited by 34 percent of the respondents, and "black power or other radicals," suggested by 26 percent.[12] In contrast, a comparable survey of black residents in the same cities revealed views similar to those of earlier Watts and Detroit polls. No less than 49 percent emphasized discrimination, 23 percent referred to unemployment, and 23 percent stressed bad housing as major sources of collective violence. These views on causes of riots perhaps exemplified the continuing, perhaps increasing, polarization of black and white perspectives on urban issues.

Thus, among black citizens there has been striking unanimity of opinion concerning the broad reasons lying behind the outbreak of ghetto revolts. In cities throughout the country conditions reflecting the unequal distribution of power and wealth, such as the lack of jobs, overcrowding, substandard housing, unequal police practices, and poverty have been identified as principal sources of urban dissidence. One of the most significant features of the problems mentioned by ghetto residents, however, is that most are amenable to governmental amelioration. Since conditions of deprivation and powerlessness have been sustained and perpetuated by governmental actions, public officials possess corresponding means of reducing or eliminating those grievances. By presenting their views in a manner that could not be ignored, black rioters seemed to confront public leaders with

---

[11] *Newsweek,* August 21, 1967, pp. 18–19; see also, Harlan Hahn and Joe R. Feagin, "Rank-and-File Versus Congressional Perceptions of Ghetto Riots," *Social Science Quarterly,* 51 (September 1970), 361–373.

[12] Campbell and Schuman, "Racial Attitudes in Fifteen American Cities," p. 48.

the urgency of their demands and with the need for new methods to meet their grievances.

Evidence from several areas that have seen rioting indicates that the majority of ghetto dwellers explicitly thought that ghetto riots had a definite purpose or objective. A majority of the inhabitants of the Twelfth Street area in Detroit agreed that the riot represented purposeful activity rather than meaningless cr pathologically destructive behavior. Fifty-three percent of the Detroit sample felt that the most important objective of the people who started the riot was "calling attention to their needs," 38 percent thought they were "just taking things and causing trouble," and 8 percent failed to express an opinion on this issue. While the violence reflected broader goals than publicizing local grievances, expressions of discontent have been regarded as a necessary initial step to the attainment of larger objectives. These perceptions provided a means of distinguishing people who regarded the riots as signifying rather narrow or self-serving personal ends and those who considered them as representing justifiable collective aspirations and objectives.

Although this question was one useful means of identifying those Detroit residents who were sympathetic to the riot and rioters, it was the only question in the Twelfth Street survey that yielded somewhat less emphasis on protest and political objectives than has been found in some other polls. For example, in a postriot survey in Watts 62 percent of the residents agreed that the riot there was a "Negro protest"; in addition, just over half of these respondents and a similar proportion of a sample of black persons who had been arrested in the riot unequivocally stated that the collective violence had "a purpose or goal."[13] When the Watts residents were requested to describe the purpose or goal of the riot, 41 percent defined it as an attempt to call attention to the problems faced by black citizens, 33 percent

[13] David O. Sears and T. M. Tomlinson, "Riot Ideology in Los Angeles: A Study of Negro Attitudes," *Social Science Quarterly,* **49** (December 1968), 489.

271

viewed it as an expression of accumulated hostility or rage, and 26 percent explicitly regarded it as a means of gaining specific social and economic changes or improvements.[14] A similar question was posed in the survey after the 1964 Bedford-Stuyvesant riot, which asked, "What do you think they (the rioters) were trying to do or to show?" The replies indicated that more than half of the New York residents felt that the rioters intended to demonstrate their opposition to discrimination and deprivation. A 1968 survey conducted by Campbell and Schuman in 15 major cities across the country also reported that 58 percent of the black respondents saw the riots as "mainly a protest . . . against unfair conditions" rather than as simply "a way of looting"; an additional 28 percent viewed them at least partially as a protest.[15]

Yet, as Campbell and Schuman have noted, the term "protest" may be a key one.[16] The use of such a term in the fixed-response questions used in a number of surveys of ghetto residents may have obscured the even more direct political purpose seen in ghetto riots by many black urbanites. As a few surveys have suggested (for example, the Watts survey), many who were affected by a serious riot saw it as more than protest simply aimed at calling attention to black grievances, as in fact a means of forcing specific changes in the existing arrangements, whether in regard to police practices, economic exploitation, or government practices.[17]

Moreover, another series of questions in our 1967 Detroit survey touched on the issue of selectivity in the attacks and looting of rioters. Two thirds of the residents of the Twelfth Street area

[14] Ibid., p. 496.

[15] Campbell and Schuman, "Racial Attitudes in Fifteen American Cities," p. 47.

[16] Ibid., p. 62.

[17] See E. L. Quarantelli and Russell Dynes, "Looting in Civil Disorders: An Index of Social Change," *Riots and Rebellion,* ed. Louis H. Masotti and Don R. Bowen (Beverly Hills: Sage Publications, 1968), p. 134.

Ghetto Resident Views in the Aftermath of Riots

said that "most of the stores that people tried to burn were owned by whites"; only 28 percent said that "it didn't make much difference." Over half of the Twelfth Street area residents stated that local stores were burned because "the owners deserved it"; only 38 percent ascribed the burning to other reasons. Personal involvement in the riot, at least in the corona of bystanders often surrounding the rioting crowds, was related to the view that the burning reflected important political motives. While two thirds of the people who reportedly had been outside during the riot believed that the stores in Detroit were burned "because the owners deserved it," 52 percent of those who stayed inside attributed the burning to other reasons. While the assaults on ghetto merchants may have represented a rather primitive form of retribution, the violence in Detroit seemed to contain relatively little evidence of random or irrational behavior, at least from the vantage point of a majority of these ghetto residents. And research in other ghetto areas has suggested that this perspective was not limited to Detroit residents.

Perhaps surprisingly, an important feature of the mood in the Detroit ghetto after the 1967 riot was a strong sense of inevitability. When the residents of the Twelfth Street area were asked if they felt the "trouble could have been avoided" or if they thought "it had to happen sooner or later," 57 percent endorsed the belief that the violence was inevitable; just over one quarter said that it might have been averted. By reporting that they did not believe that the disorders could have been avoided, the majority seemed to accept an almost deterministic view of the rioting. Why did they adopt such a perspective? Perhaps the sentiments of the Twelfth Street residents were strongly influenced by the belief that those in power would remain inactive in dealing with the broad range of critical ghetto problems until they were spurred by collective violence. Some may also have felt that only an attempt at violent tactics by black Americans would provide the feedback necessary to persuade the violence-oriented among them of the ultimate futility of violence. In any event, in 1967 the Detroit respondents appeared less optimistic than those blacks interviewed after the Bedford-Stuyvesant riot in 1964; in that early survey the responses of those questioned reflected less of a sense of inevitability about rioting.[18] But even in that 1964 survey the possibility of more riots had been considered by many ghetto residents, prophetically, nearly 60 percent of those ghetto residents estimated that additional riots in other northern cities were either "very likely" or "fairly likely."

Thus, in the Twelfth Street survey a large proportion of ghetto residents accepted the almost deterministic belief that the outbreak of violence could not have been avoided, given the continuance of "business as usual." When the respondents were asked why the riot had to happen or how it could have been avoided, most cited basic inequities such as the lack of equal rights, job discrimination, or police practices. Moreover, most of those who felt that the violence reflected a type of ghetto protest did not believe that the trouble could have been avoided. While 63 percent of those who viewed the rioters as merely "taking things and causing trouble" said that the riot could have been prevented, two thirds of the respondents who considered the rioting as an attempt on the part of dissidents to "call attention to their needs" thought it was unavoidable. The implications of this relationship seem relatively clear. Since most of the residents who felt that the riot could have been avoided regarded it as purposeless theft or senseless troublemaking, they might well have supported increased repressive measures to stop the outbreak of rioting. Yet those who saw rioting as an attempt to call attention to basic ghetto needs, and felt that rioting was inevitable, seemed to lack faith in the ability of existing leaders and programs to meet those needs without further impetus.

In addition, a majority of the residents of the Twelfth Street area apparently did not regard the riot as a sudden or unpremeditated expression of discontent. Fifty-seven percent said that "most of the people who started the trouble in Detroit had been thinking about it for a long time," while only 30 percent felt

[18] Feagin and Sheatsley, "Ghetto Resident Appraisals of a Riot," 360.

that "they got the idea all of a sudden." The riot was seen as the product of conscious consideration rather than of impulsive reactions. Moreover, a sizable minority (37 percent) of the Detroit respondents stated that "most of the people who started the trouble were mainly organized" rather than "acting on their own." Such opinions, however, do not constitute evidence that the riot was produced by any type of planned conspiracy to riot prior to the outbreak of the violence; that is, the term "organized" can have several different meanings. As we have emphasized elsewhere, "preliminary analyses of those responses have indicated that organization was intended to mean 'directed activity' and that perceptions of the lack of spontaneity referred to long-standing grievances."[19] It seems that the events that marked the start and the development of ghetto revolts revealed instances of co-ordinated activity; participants in those events often contributed to the pursuit of collective aims by cooperating in various endeavors. While the circumstances that preceded the outbreak of violence could not be described as the product of an organized conspiracy—a view also rejected by the National Advisory Commission on Civil Disorders—the opinions of these ghetto residents indicated that interactions among local persons during the violence also could not be accurately characterized as reflecting totally disorganized, autonomous, or isolated behavior.

Perspectives on the Use of Violence

In a number of ghetto resident surveys, including those administered after riots, a small but extremely important segment of the black community has expressed commitment to the position that violence is (or will be) necessary in the struggle for black progress and equality. For example, in our Detroit survey one in six among those interviewed stated that violence rather than peaceful protests was the "more effective way for Negroes to get

[19] Harlan Hahn, "The Kerner Report and the Political Objectives of Civil Disorders," *Social Science Quarterly*, 50 (December 1969), 755–756.

what they want"; and a question about the "faster way" of achieving black goals saw a significant increase in ghetto resident support for violence—to one third. Indeed, the comparatively large number of people in the Twelfth Street ghetto who were willing to accept violence as other tactics became ineffective may have partially accounted for the scope and destructiveness of the 1967 Detroit riot.

The intensity of the Detroit insurrection may have been fueled by a growing conviction in large urban ghettos over the last two decades that violence was a necessary, and perhaps the only remaining, means of promoting widely shared needs and aspirations. Furthermore, this advocacy of violence by the Detroit respondents seemed to be associated with a view of rioting which stressed attainment of important political or protest purposes rather than with a perspective emphasizing troublemaking and disruption. While most Twelfth Street residents who preferred peaceful protests thought that the rioters were "just taking things and causing trouble," an overwhelming proportion of those who favored violence believed that rioting was a meaningful way of calling attention to ghetto needs.

In addition to the Detroit survey findings, several other surveys have disclosed broadly comparable results on ghetto support for violence. In the 1964 Bedford-Stuyvesant survey, respondents were asked if "Negroes will be able to get equal rights, better jobs, and such, by using nonviolent means" or if they will "have to use violence." Of those interviewed 17 percent expressed the view that violence would be required. Another survey in the Watts area of Los Angeles found that 12 percent of the black residents there had come to view violence rather than negotiations or nonviolent protests as the most effective method of achieving black advancement.[20] Similarly, in a subsequent 1968 survey of black citizens in more than a dozen major urban areas 15 percent advocated violence instead of nonviolent action as

---

[20] Tomlinson and Sears, *Negro Attitudes Toward Riots,* pp. 23–24.

"the best way for Negroes to gain their rights."[21] Black proponents of violence, therefore, generally have comprised a small but significant fraction—ranging from 12 to 17 percent—of the population in the large urban ghettos where serious riots have occurred. In addition, as we noted in an earlier discussion of the basic conditions underlying riot development, a few national surveys of black Americans in all areas of the country have suggested that the proportion of black Americans believing that violence might be necessary to win equal rights apparently grew from 21 to 31 percent between 1966 and 1970.[22]

Despite this limited overt advocacy of violence as a tactic, however, the approval of violence expressed by approximately 12–17 percent of urban ghetto residents over the last decade has represented a serious danger to the continuing viability of the existing political framework. As the riots have demonstrated, overwhelming commitment to violence by a minority group has not been required to create the groundwork for a serious uprising. Although the ghetto revolts probably would not have occurred if an even more general condoning or understanding of collective violence had been totally absent in black communities, the presence of even a small group of people who were convinced of the need for violence provided a sufficient base for the outbreak of rioting, particularly in the larger ghetto areas where relatively small percentages mean large numbers. The results of ghetto surveys, as well as the results of ghetto riots, reveal that a predisposition to sanction violent tactics for attaining desired goals has been widely distributed in the highly segregated black pockets of urban areas across the United States. Such sentiment raises a serious question concerning whether or not a democratic community can continue indefinitely without introducing major changes in its political arrangements to accommodate the legitimate strivings of such dissident minorities.

[21] Campbell and Schuman, "Racial Attitudes in Fifteen American Cities," pp. 51–52.
[22] "Black America, 1970," *Time,* April 6, 1970, p. 29.

In addition to those who directly support violence as a tactic, many cities have included black citizens who were not at a given point in time overt advocates of violence, but who were potentially susceptible to the lure of collective violence—particularly as alternative strategies failed. Support for this speculative contention is reflected in the often favorable attitudes of ghetto residents toward the impact of collective violence on the civil rights struggle. In our 1967 Detroit survey no less than 62 percent of the blacks interviewed felt that the rioting would be helpful rather than harmful to the struggle for equality. Moreover, this perspective emphasizing the benefits of collective violence seemed to reflect a negative view of the pre-existing governmental structure. To illustrate this point we can note that whereas 59 percent of the Detroit respondents with confidence in *prior* government efforts to solve local problems also believed that the rioting would have a harmful effect on civil rights progress, more than three quarters of those who distrusted such governmental efforts felt that the rioting would aid their cause. In this Detroit ghetto politically disillusioned black citizens were the most likely to express a belief in the efficacy of riots as a means of securing equality and freedom, but most of their neighbors who remained loyal to existing governmental structures felt that the violence would damage black efforts to gain equal rights.

Although the figures are not as striking as those in the Twelfth Street survey, other polls in the period between 1965 and 1969 have found significant support for a view of the actual and potential impact of rioting which sees it as beneficial to the black cause. In a postriot survey in Watts 38 percent of the black citizens in that section of Los Angeles felt that the violence had advanced civil rights, 30 percent saw no difference, and 24 percent stated that it had been harmful.[23] A national poll in 1966 discovered that 34 percent of black Americans believed that the riots had helped the cause of civil rights, 20 percent said that

[23] Sears and Tomlinson, "Riot Ideology in Los Angeles: A Study of Negro Attitudes," p. 490.

they had been disadvantageous, and 46 percent either were unde-cided or saw no appreciable difference.[24] In a 1968 survey of black attitudes conducted in 15 major cities approximately one third thought the riots had aided civil rights progress, one fourth stated that they were harmful, and the remainder reported mixed emotions.[25] A subsequent national survey in 1969 revealed that 40 percent of black adults expressed the opinion that the riots had been helpful, while only 29 percent asserted that they had hurt civil rights.[26] While many black Americans doubtless pre-ferred to adopt other approaches in seeking significant structural change, the events that occurred after the outbreak of rioting in the early 1960s made it increasingly difficult to deny that collec-tive violence might conceivably be an effective means of achiev-ing what earlier methods had failed to accomplish. Perhaps most important, on the basis of numerous postriot surveys one can conclude that in the years after the Watts riot in 1965 only a minority of those blacks interviewed—never more than a third—viewed rioting as unequivocally harmful to the quest for equal-ity. This implicit condoning of violence doubtless contributed to subsequent riot development.[27]

A related issue which can be raised at this point is the ques-tion of actual participation in collective violence by those en-capsulated in America's black ghettos. In a supplemental report to the National Advisory Commission on Civil Disorders, two social scientists delineated what they term the "riffraff theory" of riot participation, a theory developed by numerous public offi-cials in their immediate responses to ghetto rioting.[28] In addition

[24] William Brink and Louis Harris, *Black and White* (New York: Simon and Schuster, 1967), pp. 67, 264–265.

[25] Campbell and Schuman, "Racial Attitudes in Fifteen American Cities," pp. 48–49.

[26] "Report from Black America," *Newsweek,* June 30, 1969, p. 23.

[27] A 1964 survey in a few ghettos found that the proportions viewing riots as beneficial ranged from 39% to 63%. Gary T. Marx, *Protest and Prejudice* (New York: Harper & Row, 1967), p. 32.

[28] Robert M. Fogelson and Robert B. Hill, "Who Riots? A Study of

to a stress on rioters as the dregs of society, the common riffraff perspective often encompassed the view that those who rioted were but a small raffish minority, at most 1–2 percent of the local black population. However, in several surveys residents of riot-torn ghettos were questioned about actual riot involvement, and the percentages reporting riot participation have run substantially higher than this 1–2 percent. For example, Sears and McConahay calculated the number of blacks residing in the 46-square-mile curfew area of the 1965 Watts riot in Los Angeles. Using information from sophisticated questions on riot participation from a random sample survey of adults in that curfew area, they estimated that 15 percent of the black population had been active in the rioting, altogether approximately 30,000 persons.[29] Even allowing for a tendency on the part of some respondents to exaggerate or fabricate riot participation—a tendency perhaps offset by the countervailing effect of covering up riot participation for fear of police detection—this participation is much higher than that proposed by most public officials, including prominent California leaders who commented publicly on the rioting in Los Angeles.

Nor was the Los Angeles riot atypical. On the basis of a Detroit survey the National Advisory Commission reported that "approximately 11 percent of the sampled residents over the age of 15 in the two disturbance areas admittedly participated in rioting."[30] Based on our sample survey in the critical Twelfth Street area of the Detroit ghetto, we have elsewhere estimated those who were active in some fashion in the rioting at perhaps one third. This figure is based on activity attributed to various groups in the community by persons who were themselves mem-

---

Participation in the 1967 Riots," *Supplemental Studies for the National Advisory Commission on Civil Disorders* (Washington, D.C.: U.S. Government Printing Office, 1968), pp. 229–231.

[29] David O. Sears and John B. McConahay, *Riot Participation* (Los Angeles: UCLA Institute of Government and Public Affairs, 1967).

[30] *Report of the National Advisory Commission on Civil Disorders,* p. 73.

bers of those groups.[31] Moreover, drawing heavily on postriot surveys of participation in violence, as well as on census data and riot arrest figures, Fogelson and Hill have estimated that the following percentages of eligible riot area residents (those aged 10–59) participated in several 1967 riots: (1) Cincinnati, 4 percent; (2) Detroit, 11 percent; (3) Newark, 15 percent; (4) Grand Rapids, 16 percent; (5) Dayton, 26 percent; (6) New Haven, 35 percent.[32] While the data on which these participation figures are based are problematical and incomplete, such approximations seem considerably better than more speculative guesses reflecting only the bias of the evaluator. Again, postriot surveys provide partial evidence for an alternative perspective on ghetto rioting, one that takes into consideration the rather significant percentages of ghetto residents who were discontented enough with existing arrangements to riot. One might also note that two or three national surveys conducted in the 1960s included a hypothetical question asking those black Americans interviewed if they would join a riot. Affirmative replies to such an inquiry have ranged from 10 to 15 percent in the polls.[33]

Actual riot participation was not the only form of self-reported involvement by ghetto residents during the outbreaks of violence. In addition to those involved in the looting, arson, and attacks on the police, there were many more out on the streets as (active?) onlookers. For example, in the 1967 Detroit survey 61 percent of the respondents reported that they themselves had gone into the streets to see what was taking place during the riot. In the survey of riot zone residents in Watts, 31 percent were found to be active spectators, those who reported that they had seen the crowds on the streets and the looting and burning of stores. This was in addition to the 15 percent who by self-report were actively in-

[31] Harlan Hahn, "The Political Objectives of Ghetto Violence" (Paper presented at the annual meeting of the American Political Science Association, New York, N.Y., September 3, 1969), p. 14.

[32] Fogelson and Hill, "Who Riots?" p. 231.

[33] Brink and Harris, *Black and White,* pp. 67, 266–267; "Report from Black America," *Newsweek,* June 30, 1969, p. 23.

volved in the rioting.[34] However, in the earlier 1964 survey after the Bedford-Stuyvesant riot this proportion of active spectators was smaller. As one might perhaps expect, given the relatively smaller area encompassed by the rioting in New York in 1964, only 22 percent of the residents there admitted that they had seen any of the rioting which occurred on the city streets; and 16 percent said another member of the family had witnessed the violence.

Moreover, ghetto resident estimates of the number of rank-and-file black citizens of riot areas who participated in the rioting have generally been higher than those of many outside observers. But this is not to say that ghetto resident estimates are invariably the same. To illustrate, when the black respondents in the Twelfth Street area were asked to estimate the proportion of local residents who had participated in the 1967 Detroit uprising, 32 percent of the respondents estimated that at least one quarter of the area residents had participated, 26 percent estimated the proportion at one in ten, and only 17 percent indicated that fewer than one in ten actively participated. The rest were uncertain. After the 1965 Watts riot, ghetto respondent estimates of area participation also varied significantly, with the mean estimate of those interviewed being 20 percent of the local citizens.[35] In the 1964 Bedford-Stuyvesant survey respondents were not asked to calculate the specific proportion of rank-and-file citizens who participated. However, six in ten felt that "a great many" or "quite a few" took part in the riot there; only a quarter suggested that "not many at all" had been involved. Given these data, one is not surprised to learn that—also contrary to the riffraff theory—black respondents in several ghetto surveys have also emphasized that the proportion of those who rioted included a broad spectrum of rank-and-file residents, not just criminals, teenagers, and extremists.[36]

---

[34] Sears and McConahay, *Riot Participation,* pp. 1–10.
[35] Ibid.
[36] For example, see Feagin and Sheatsley, "Ghetto Resident Appraisals of a Riot," 358.

Ghetto Resident Views in the Aftermath of Riots

Views on the Police

Some of the most interesting responses in the 1967 postriot survey in Detroit were prompted by a hypothetical question that attempted to tap the reflexes of the community toward potential precipitating events. One situation presented to Twelfth Street respondents involved "a policeman beating up someone from the neighborhood." Since serious ghetto riots have often been ignited by an incident involving police action, the replies provided a relatively clear indication of the proportion of ghetto dwellers who might react to a precipitating event with conduct conducive to the outbreak of violence. Only 44 percent stated that they would follow the conventional protest procedure of filing a formal complaint. In response to the police misconduct situation 18 percent were uncertain about their probable action, or said they would ignore the incident. The remaining replies fell into two categories: "going to other people for help" (27 percent) and "waiting around to see what happens" (10 percent). These latter responses implied lack of confidence in the local police and indicated behavior that has frequently been associated with the start of black riots. The potential for incidents that might trigger the eruption of rioting in the Twelfth Street area seemed relatively high.[37] Furthermore, in the Detroit survey reactions to the hypothetical instance of law enforcement malpractice were found to be associated with assessments of general police practices. While 62 percent of the residents who said they had positive images of police practices prior to the 1967 uprising also said they would respond to the police beating by filing a complaint with the police department, a majority of those who had unfavorable views of police actions said they would respond in a potentially provocative manner by waiting around or securing the help of other residents.

In the Twelfth Street survey yet another major issue was the police handling of the massive 1967 riot. In previous chapters

[37] See also the merchant incident discussed in Campbell and Schuman, "Racial Attitudes in Fifteen American Cities," 52–53.

we have noted the negative view that many ghetto residents have taken in regard to both routine police services in the ghetto and police harassment and malpractice. We have also seen the major role that encounters between the police and ghetto residents have played in the buildup to serious rioting.[38] It is not surprising, therefore, that the repressive tactics of police forces in quenching the flames of ghetto revolt have been criticized by ghetto residents. In the postriot survey only a fifth of the residents of the Twelfth Street area expressed an unequivocally favorable opinion of police handling of the Detroit uprising. Three quarters said that the performance of the police during the rioting was either "not good" or "poor"; half believed that the force applied by police officers and soldiers to end the disturbances was "too strong." Nearly one third of the Detroit respondents claimed that policemen treated people even worse during the riot than they had previously. Perhaps the most disquieting finding of the Detroit survey, however, concerned assertions that police personnel had been engaged in illegal activities in various phases of the violence: no less than 81 percent of the residents of the Twelfth Street area related that they had heard reports that some policemen were involved in looting or burning stores during the riot. Moreover, evidence from other ghetto surveys also indicates that police activities during riots may have intensified local disrespect for and negativism toward law enforcement officers. For example, in the 1964 Bedford-Stuyvesant survey 61 percent of the black respondents there said that they disapproved of the behavior of the New York police commissioner during the riot there, and 49 percent expressed a similar judgment about the conduct of policemen. Only 18 percent and 39 percent, respectively, approved of the actions of the police commissioner and policemen.

[38] Harlan Hahn and Joe R. Feagin, "Riot-Precipitating Police Practices: Attitudes in Urban Ghettos," *Phylon,* **31** (Summer 1970), 183–193; see also Harlan Hahn, "Cops and Rioters: Ghetto Perceptions of Social Conflict and Control," *American Behavioral Scientist,* **13** (May–June–July–August 1970), 761–779.

Ghetto Resident Views in the Aftermath of Riots

While the actions of numerous law enforcement officers and officials during ghetto revolts apparently exacerbated the problem of re-establishing police authority in the aftermath period, many ghetto residents were prepared to accept relatively firm riot control measures by law enforcement agencies, provided that basic restraint in the use of counterforce was exercised and that police violence, brutality, and malpractice were held to a minimum. The failure of police agencies to recognize such ghetto sentiment concerning riot control may be linked to a prevalent belief among law enforcement officers that persons living in a riot area would not support any type of large-scale police riot action short of the absolute withdrawal of police personnel. Perhaps surprisingly, this police supposition was not entirely supported in the results of our 1967 Detroit survey. When the Twelfth Street respondents were asked to assess why the police had actually been unable to control the rioting during its initial stages, two thirds suggested that "they were not allowed to use enough force," while the other third stated that "they were outnumbered by the crowds." However, a closer investigation of these responses indicated that some respondents—those who felt that the police had been hesitant to use large-scale force in the early stages and that police treatment of local citizens did not worsen during the riot—tended to favor relatively firm riot control strategies during the early phases of violence. In addition, the emphasis on police self-restraint was found to be closely associated with the expectation that relations between blacks and the police would improve after the riot. Police restraint, therefore, may have formed an important basis for support among some blacks for certain types of riot control measures. The results of this survey suggest that a substantial proportion of the persons who had experienced a major riot approved of both a display of strength and relatively firm measures to control violence, provided that strict restraints were imposed on police behavior.

CHAPTER 6

Some Other Views

While the 1967 Detroit riot seemed to represent a relatively direct attack on both white merchants and police forces, the respondents in the Twelfth Street survey did not feel that the violence there would have a major impact on interpersonal relations between rank-and-file blacks and whites in that area. Among the black respondents interviewed, 57 percent of whom believed that race relations before the riot had been "very good" or "good," two thirds thought that the relations between white and black residents of the area would be "about the same" after the violence and 15 percent predicted that the two groups would "get along better than before." In assessing the Detroit riot, which may have encompassed the first significant cases of integrated looting in urban history, more than three quarters of the residents in the Twelfth Street ghetto area perceived that the blacks and whites who had actually been involved in the rioting were "fighting on the same side"; fewer than one in ten felt that rank-and-file blacks and whites were involved in interracial fighting. Moreover, even in the 1964 Bedford-Stuyvesant survey the findings on this issue were roughly similar. Among the Bedford-Stuyvesant residents who said that they had white friends or acquaintances, for example, nine out of ten did not believe that the riot would change these relationships in any way.

Despite the deprivation and oppressive conditions that had prompted the riots, therefore, in the aftermath of violence the black residents of numerous riot-torn neighborhoods exhibited a significant degree of optimism about the future. Further evidence of this continuing optimism can be seen in a series of questions in the Twelfth Street interviews. Respondents were presented with the Cantril Self-Anchoring Striving Scale. They were asked to indicate on a ladder containing ten rungs—the top of which rerpesented "the best possible life" and the bottom its opposite —the present, past, and future positions of themselves, of whites as a group, and of blacks as a group.[39] Although the scales did

[39] For a discussion of the construction and use of this scale, see

not yield particularly direct or consistent associations with aspects of riot behavior such as participation and attitudes toward violence, they did provide a useful measure of the existing perspectives and future aspirations of these ghetto residents at the end of the long hot summer of 1967. When the respondents compared their present position with an ideal way of life, one quarter ranked themselves toward the bottom of the ladder, just over half placed themselves in an intermediate position, and only one fifth rated themselves at or near the top. Perhaps more important, most respondents felt that they would actually improve their lot in the next five years. A large plurality also believed that black people as a whole would experience similar progress. Moreover, most of these Detroit respondents not only expressed an optimistic faith that they would soon be approaching the status enjoyed by the white population, but they also foresaw their rate of progress as surpassing that of whites in the future. This continuing optimism of black Americans has also been seen in other surveys. For example, even in the early Bedford-Stuyvesant survey 59 percent of the respondents thought that conditions in the area would get better in the future, 22 percent thought that they would be about the same, and only 12 percent guessed that they would be worse. Nationwide surveys in the mid- and late-sixties have found a similar pattern of hope and confidence in future advancements for black Americans.[40]

Although the residents of the Detroit ghetto interviewed after the 1967 riot voiced generally optimistic views of the future, the survey did disclose important criticisms of existing governmental programs. For example, even the reputedly innovative projects developed through the antipoverty program in Detroit were regarded by the Twelfth Street residents with a considerable

---

Hadley Cantril, *The Pattern of Human Concerns* (New Brunswick, N.J.: Rutgers University Press, 1965). The index was arbitrarily divided into scores of 1 through 3, 4 through 6, and 7 through 10.

[40] For example, see Brink and Harris, *Black and White,* and the numerous surveys reported in *Newsweek* in the 1960s.

amount of skepticism. More than 40 percent of the survey respondents stated that they disapproved of the antipoverty program; just over one third reported that they approved of it. The
rest of those interviewed were undecided. Another indication of
the political discontent that prevailed in the Twelfth Street area,
therefore, can be glimpsed in these negative and equivocal evaluations of established approaches to ghetto problems. In rejecting
the existing antipoverty strategy many seemed to be calling for
the creation of new and even more radical structural arrangements for solving ghetto problems. Moreover, opposition to the
current program was found to be concentrated among persons
who appeared to favor more radical political goals. While 55
percent of the residents who supported "peaceful protests" to
achieve civil rights progress agreed with the antipoverty program,
three quarters of those who endorsed violence disapproved of it.
For many black Americans, therefore, the advocacy of violence
as a means of gaining political objectives may not have been
associated with a simple desire to augment existing social and
economic policies such as the antipoverty program. These residents of a black ghetto that had experienced a major riot did not
simply wish to gain increased support for traditional "liberal"
welfare programs. Rather, many seemed to be seeking basic
changes in the structure of the political process that had designed
and enacted those programs.

Several other studies have indicated that criticism of these
antipoverty approaches may have been greater in the Twelfth
Street area of Detroit than in other parts of the country. In the
survey conducted after the Watts riot less than 12 percent of the
black respondents expressed unfavorable attitudes toward any of
the local agencies or plans sustained by the "war on poverty."[41]
A national poll of black citizens in 1966 found that two thirds of
those interviewed felt that antipoverty plans would be "more

[41] David O. Sears, *Political Attitudes of Los Angeles Negroes* (Los
Angeles: UCLA Institute of Government and Public Affairs, 1967),
pp. 11–12.

helpful than harmful to Negro rights," while 31 percent were not sure.[42] Later, a 1968 survey conducted in 15 cities disclosed that three quarters of those blacks interviewed believed that the existing antipoverty program had done a "good" or "fair" job in those communities.[43]

However, the Detroit respondents seemed somewhat less critical of their mayor, especially his actions during the 1967 riot, than ghetto residents elsewhere. In the 1968 survey of black urbanites in 15 cities only 47 percent conceded that their local mayor was "trying as hard as he can" to solve urban problems.[44] Similarly, in the survey several months after the Watts riot two thirds expressed unfavorable evaluations of Los Angeles Mayor Sam Yorty, reflecting discontent with Yorty's indifference to the black population.[45] In addition, in the Bedford-Stuyvesant survey 44 percent of the respondents said that they disapproved of the actions of the New York mayor during the riots in New York; only 40 percent unequivocally approved of his conduct. Yet 56 percent of the residents of the Twelfth Street area in Detroit assessed Mayor Jerome Cavanagh's handling of the violence there as "very good" or "good," while 36 percent expressed critical judgments of his actions.

Even though a relatively large percentage of ghetto residents voiced general approval of the conduct of Detroit Mayor Cavanagh, at least of conduct during the Detroit uprising, a sizable minority (22 percent) of the residents of the Twelfth Street area also reported that they would favor a movement to have the Detroit mayor recalled from public office. Although the recall drive had been started several months prior to the riots by conservative white leaders who felt that the mayor was lax on the law-and-order issue, it was supported by some black citizens who perhaps

[42] Brink and Harris, *Black and White,* pp. 242–243.
[43] Campbell and Schuman, "Racial Attitudes in Fifteen American Cities," pp. 41–42.
[44] Ibid., p. 41.
[45] Sears, *Political Attitudes of Los Angeles Negroes,* p. 8.

entertained hopes for major changes in the local governmental structure. Among blacks the objections to the Detroit mayor in this ghetto community tended to emanate from the radical sphere rather than from the right. For example, over three quarters of the black representatives who sought civil rights progress through "peaceful protests" wanted Cavanagh to remain in office, but the residents who favored violence were evenly divided on the recall issue.

In general, however, adults in the Twelfth Street ghetto area disclosed major signs of political disaffection. When the Detroit respondents were asked to evaluate the actions and perspectives of government before the riot, 78 percent subscribed to the view that government leaders were "just interested in keeping things quiet"; only one fifth believed that government officials "were really interested in solving the problems that the Negro faces in this city." Thus, only a minority of these ghetto residents believed that government had been seriously attempting to solve local problems before the collective violence flared. Furthermore, these attitudes were found to be related to black perceptions of riot objectives. Three quarters of the respondents who believed that government had been trying to solve local problems before the riot started felt that the collective violence represented a way of stealing and troublemaking, but two thirds of those who had been critical of prior governmental efforts viewed the riot favorably as a means of calling attention to the basic needs of black Americans. In this sample at least, negative views of the prior political situation were linked more often than not to a perspective on collective violence which had a relatively radical political cast.

In addition, postriot surveys of self-reported rioters conducted by the National Advisory Commission on Civil Disorders in both Detroit and Newark after the 1967 riots revealed a striking lack of confidence in political institutions and leaders. The following excerpt from the final report of the National Advisory Commission also illustrates the relationship between political dissatisfaction and riot orientation:

Ghetto Resident Views in the Aftermath of Riots

In the Newark survey, respondents were asked how much they thought they could trust local government. Only 4.8 percent of the self-reported rioters, compared with 13.7 percent of the noninvolved, said they felt they could trust it most of the time; 44.2 percent of the self-reported rioters and 33.9 percent of the noninvolved reported they could almost never trust the government.

In the Detroit survey, self-reported rioters were much more likely to attribute the riot to anger about politicians and the police than were the noninvolved.[46]

Moreover, despite the negative evaluation of government actions prior to the Detroit riot, the respondents in our Twelfth Street survey also expressed hope that the ghetto area would become an increasingly influential area, even more autonomous and self-governing in the period following on the riot. Perhaps the clearest statement of the political objectives of many ghetto residents was contained in the Twelfth Street responses to a series of questions about attitudes toward government structure and action. On the one hand, they were relatively optimistic about the actions of white authorities in the postriot period; the riots seemed to instill a belief that ghetto residents would not continue to be neglected by white authorities. While 61 percent of the residents believed that the needs of the area would receive more attention from city officials, 31 percent guessed that they would get about the same amount of attention as before the riots, and only 3 percent said they would obtain less attention. On the other hand, most also expected greater rank-and-file participation in local decision-making. The feeling that local people would enjoy increased opportunities for political participation after the collective violence, for example, was indicated by three quarters of the ghetto residents who said they would have "more to say about what should be done in this neighborhood." One

[46] *Report of the National Advisory Commission on Civil Disorders,* p. 77; see also Sears, *Political Attitudes of Los Angeles Negroes,* p. 20.

fifth felt that they would participate to the same extent as before. Finally, in reply to a direct and strongly worded question about whether the people in the area would have "more power, less power, or about the same amount of power than they did before the trouble started," nearly half stated that they expected more power, one third estimated that they would have about the same amount of power, and only 3 percent anticipated less power. As Conant has emphasized, these aspirations and expectations have not been unlike the persistent objectives of white citizens:

> The demands themselves are, in the main, forms of control and influence which whites are quite used to having and exercising. What appears to be a demand for separation is really a demand for local self-government, which is a cherished tradition in white America. . . . To put it another way, whites want to run their own schools, have their own police departments, determine land uses, and all the rest. So does the black community.[47]

The attitudes of Twelfth Street residents toward major issues affecting their relationships to existing political arrangements after Detroit's riot—including ghetto resident participation, recognition, and power—further suggest that collective violence in the last decade has had political overtones.

Although the responses to the three questions just discussed imply a hope that the Detroit ghetto would become an increasingly autonomous and self-governing area, the residents expressed somewhat greater optimism about the prospects for increased rank-and-file participation in local decisions than they did about receiving more attention from city officials. This relative lack of confidence in public officials reflected a continuing and basic distrust of established governmental processes. Even more strik-

[47] Ralph W. Conant, "Black Power: Rhetoric and Reality," *Urban Affairs Quarterly*, 4 (September 1968), 23.

ing than the modest differences in their responses to these questions, however, was the prevailing hope for major structural changes to improve the relationship between black citizens and government. Surprisingly, only a minority of the residents felt that existing political arrangements would remain essentially unchanged after the revolt, and even fewer thought that they would grow worse. For many, experience with a serious riot evoked expectations that the political objectives of ghetto violence would be fulfilled.

The violence that took place in predominantly black sections of many cities not only reflected an intense reaction to the deprivation and state of powerlessness that had been imposed on black Americans by white society but also seemed to encompass a direct and purposeful attempt to promote increased local independence and control of ghetto communities.[48] While the attitudes of most Twelfth Street residents concerning the consequences of the massive Detroit riot—such as in regard to local participation and recognition—suggested the rioting was motivated basically by

[48] One manifestation of relatively radical political goals that existed in the Twelfth Street area after the riot can be seen in the lack of support found for the traditional integration principles among a significant minority of residents. In response to a question about the best means of achieving racial progress 71 percent of the black respondents argued that "they should integrate with whites." Most of the others took a separatist stance. By contrast, only 11–13 percent of the ghetto residents in national surveys, including rural blacks as well as urban ghettoites, have approved of the basic ideas of separatism. (See Marx, *Protest and Prejudice,* p. 108.) Significantly, the black "separatists" in the Twelfth Street area were more than twice as likely as those who were integration-oriented to express a distrust of government, to reject the antipoverty program, to say that the riots had not harmed the civil rights movement, to advocate violence as the fastest means of achieving progress, and to claim that owners deserved the burning of their stores. By rejecting the ends of integration, many black residents of this area may have been seeking to withdraw from the political supervision of the white public and political leaders. For a further discussion, see Harlan Hahn, "Black Separatists: Attitudes and Objectives in a Riot-torn Ghetto," *Journal of Black Studies,* 1 (September 1970), 35–53.

political objectives, a fundamental expression of their aspirations was conveyed by views of the prospects of gaining enhanced power. In attempting to ascertain the objectives of the recent collective violence on the part of black Americans, one might find some support for a political interpretation of that violence in a relationship between assessment of rioters' actions in protest terms and an emphasis on increased ghetto power after the upheaval. Analyzing the Twelfth Street data, we found that an orientation toward rioter actions in protest terms was indeed likely to be associated with the belief that ghetto residents would enjoy increased power and influence afterwards. While 59 percent of the residents who perceived the riot as a form of protest expected the area to have more power, over half of those who thought the rioters were merely "taking things and causing trouble" predicted the area would have the same or less power. The approval of violence as a means of securing civil rights progress was also linked to the conviction that this ghetto area would gain increased power. Sixty-three percent of the respondents who felt that the rioting would help the civil rights movement anticipated more power, but 56 percent of those who viewed the violence as harmful to civil rights foresaw the same or less power for the neighborhood. In addition, 68 percent of the people who would support violence as a tactic estimated that they would have more power, but 52 percent of those who favored "peaceful protests" believed that the area would possess similar or declining power after the riot. Expressions of support for violence and for rioters and their goals, therefore, seemed to be associated with more optimistic political expectations for the area in the postriot period.

Conclusion

The survey of the Twelfth Street area in Detroit after the major riot there failed to uncover any significant evidence of an apolitical desire on the part of black ghetto residents to withdraw from decision-making activities. Black Americans there exhibited strong dissatisfaction both with existing political arrangements and with agencies of social control, although it seems likely on the basis of evidence from several sources that the structure of local power and authority rather than the democratic political process itself was a primary source of their dissidence. By expressing demands —and hope—for expanded political involvement and participation, persons living in this ghetto area seemed to adopt the perspective that the goals of black Americans reflect the desire to restructure the existing political framework in urban areas. This modification of established arrangements not only was regarded as a practical necessity to facilitate significant local involvement in the process of governing but also was seen as necessary for an end to the neglect of their problems by government officials and agencies.

Although such aspirations and expectations have been investigated in only a few surveys of areas that have experienced ghetto uprisings, they probably have been reflected in many forms of contemporary violence. As an important staff report to the National Commission on the Causes and Prevention of Violence concluded:

> Almost uniformly, the participants in mass protest today see their grievances as rooted in the existing arrangements of power and authority in contemporary society, and they view their own activity as political action—on a direct or symbolic level—aimed at altering those arrangements. A common theme, from the ghetto to the university, is the rejection of dependency and external control, a staking of new boundaries, and a demand for significant control over events within those boundaries.[49]

Inspired in part by the growth of a collective sense of community, the 1967 riot that brought convulsions to the Twelfth Street

[49] Jerome Skolnick, *The Politics of Protest* (New York: Simon and Schuster, 1969), p. 7. Italics omitted.

CHAPTER 6

area of Detroit can be viewed as representing a demand for increasing independence and self-regulation to satisfy the needs and
aspirations of the ghetto residents—a demand conspicuous in the
Twelfth Street responses to numerous questions about the causes,
character, and aftermath of perhaps the most massive riot in the
recent history of the American city.

The Continuing Struggle
for Black Power

Careful investigation of the history of intergroup relations in American society reveals a series of conflicts between a variety of racial and ethnic groups. Often highly structured and intricate, the relationships between a multiplicity of old and new immigrant groups arriving in waves on the urban scene have ranged from harmony to violent conflict. Older immigrant groups frequently enjoyed a relatively advantageous economic, social, and governmental position vis-à-vis groups that arrived more recently. The continuing struggle of new groups to move up within the existing system, to increase their power at the expense of those groups already established, has periodically led to urban conflict. While this struggle has varied in intensity, it has inevitably been linked to the protective reactions of those already dominant in power:

> Whenever a number of persons within a society have enjoyed for a considerable period of time certain opportunities for getting wealth, for exercising power and authority, and for successfully claiming prestige and social deference, there is a strong tendency for these people to feel that these benefits are theirs "by right." The advantages come to be thought of as normal, proper, customary, as sanctioned by time, prece-

dent and social consensus. Proposals to change the existing situation arouse reactions of "moral indignation."[1]

In their historical and contemporary pursuit of equality in American society black migrants to cities have repeatedly encountered white groups and their agents firmly entrenched in a persisting structure of power, arrangements sanctioned by time, white consensus, and elaborate rationalizations. Moreover, the built-in inertia in this structure of urban power has been particularly resistant to change in response to demands of black Americans, because in their case "differences in power, wealth and prestige coincide with relatively indelible symbols of collective membership, such as shared hereditary physical traits."[2] The physical distinctiveness of black Americans, together with such factors as their relatively late arrival in the waves of urban migration, has made the black quest an extraordinarily difficult task.

Once in the cities, black urbanites have had the chance to view the operation and consequences of urban white domination up close, the exploitative slumlords and ghetto businessmen, the discriminatory real estate and lending institutions, the constant surveillance and periodic brutality of ghetto police, the omnipresent penetration of a variety of social workers, the privileged status of white employees in urban businesses, the expropriation of ghetto resources by white racketeers and politicians. Some have even described the ghetto as oppressed by a foreign army of occupation bent on rule in neocolonial fashion.[3] Thus whatever form the black struggle for equality has taken, opposition has arisen, since many whites have a great deal to lose if a significant shift in the status quo should occur.

[1] Robin M. Williams, "Prejudice and Society," *The American Negro Reference Book,* ed. John Davis (Englewood Cliffs, N.J.: Prentice-Hall, 1966), p. 728.

[2] Ibid.

[3] William K. Tabb, *The Political Economy of the Black Ghetto* (New York: Norton, 1970), p. 30.

The Continuing Struggle for Black Power

In the recent history of American race relations the pursuit of self-determination by blacks has included the formation of new ideologies or the resurgence of old concepts, often embedded in organizations of great importance. Not the least of these have been ideas summed up by phrases such as "community control" or "black power," the latter phrase having provoked an unusual amount of white reaction. While frightened whites have often equated the words with the specters of criminal violence and hate, the ideas lying behind the words seem to have stimulated hope rather than fear in many, if not most, black Americans. Why established groups in society should have difficulty in understanding the quest of another group for power may seem hard to understand. However, one explanation may lie in the fact that white groups have seldom described their own struggles for power and influence in "white power" terms. Perhaps more important, white power has been a fact of life for most white groups in urban areas for some time. While most whites take the status quo in the government and the economy for granted, many blacks do not:

Whites (especially those who live in homogeneous jurisdictions) take the basic values of local government for granted. Blacks do not. Whites disagree on precise spending priorities, and they grouse about tax increases; but they do not question the system itself. Blacks do. Whites chuckle over bureaucratic inefficiency, but they assume that the objectives being sought are proper. Blacks do not. Whites are fundamentally satisfied because they sense that the institutions of American government have been shaped by men like them, for men like them. Blacks are not, because they do not.[4]

[4] Alan A. Altshuler, *Community Control* (New York: Pegasus, 1970), p. 192.

CHAPTER 7

Rioting and the Struggle for Black Power

Against this backdrop of entrenched white groups in control of urban institutions we have seen the acceleration and oscillation of the black struggle for power in recent years. As we have noted previously, this dramatic struggle for self-determination has historically taken a variety of forms and will doubtless in the future manifest itself in many guises. In the sixties and so far in the seventies the black cause has encompassed not only legal action and electoral politics but also nonviolent demonstrations and civil disobedience. Moreover, a dramatic shift in the level of the struggle was seen in the early sixties in the increased willingness of black Americans to act violently, in concert and offensively, against white oppression in ghetto areas. Up to this point in time, the collective violence engaged in by black Americans has ranged from relatively small-scale skirmishes with the police, to massive rioting against property and the police, to warlike situations involving an extensive exchange of gunfire between black snipers and white policemen. In earlier chapters we noted that the escalation of rioting in hundreds of cities had a significant impact on the attitudes and actions of white Americans—and particularly on the actions of white leaders and officials in regard to law enforcement. However, ghetto riots not only precipitated a white reaction; they also fostered or facilitated the development of new self-conceptions, ideologies, leaders, and organizations among black Americans.

Perhaps one of the most important of these developments, which can be viewed both as growing out of ghetto rioting and as reflected in ghetto rioting, was the stirring of a positive self-conception among many in black communities across the country. In the last decade or so we have witnessed the emergence of a significant number of what Caplan has termed "new ghetto men." The new ghetto man believes that he can and must control his own present and future. He is a black man resolutely dedicated to the eradication of exploitation and oppression by open confrontation with white America, even to the point of collective violence if that is necessary.[5] Here then is a man who contradicts traditional white stereotypes of the black man: allegedly lazy, shiftless, docile, and unwilling to protect his own or his family's interests.

Evidence on the character and characteristics of new ghetto men may be found, to take one example, in the research literature on ghetto rioters. As we have noted previously, rioters were not simply the riffraff, the criminals, the deviants in urban ghettos; in fact, they were actually drawn from many segments of the black community. Nor did they seem politically unsophisticated or fatalistic about their future. Thus, Caplan's review of research on rioters and other black militants noted that generally they were politically more active, more likely to vote, more critical of responsiveness of local authorities, more distrustful of politicians, more knowledgeable about political affairs, and more likely to see anger at politicians as a cause of rioting than their less active counterparts.[6] One analyst even concluded that ghetto rioters have represented the "cream of urban Negro youth in particular and urban Negro citizens in general."[7] Moreover, the impact of this increased emphasis on black pride and black potency will doubtless be felt for many years to come as the black man's "political, social, and economic efficacy is not aligned with his new and increasing sense of personal potency."[8]

In addition to reflecting and stimulating a resurgence of black pride and a willingness to engage in open confrontation, ghetto rioting also appeared to play a stimulating role in the development of new black spokesmen and leaders, who increasingly gave

[5] Nathan Caplan, "The New Ghetto Man: A Review of Recent Empirical Studies," *Journal of Social Issues,* **26** (Winter 1970), 59.

[6] Ibid., p. 69.

[7] T. M. Tomlinson, "The Development of a Riot Ideology among Urban Negroes," *Racial Violence in the United States,* ed. Allen D. Grimshaw (Chicago: Aldine, 1969), p. 229. This passage was called to our attention by a comment in Caplan, "The New Ghetto Man," 60.

[8] Caplan, "The New Ghetto Man," 71–72.

emphasis to the quest for black *power*. The actions of those black rioters who plundered white businesses and property and attacked white policemen can be viewed as attempts not only to protest conditions but also to force a restructuring of power arrangements and gain expanded participation in the urban decision-making process. Thus the actions of these dissident blacks seem to have played an important role in accelerating the "black power" movement, which surfaced dramatically in the mid-sixties.[9] While other factors, such as the continuing failure to gain significantly by means of integration approaches, were also important in the development of new black power leaders and groups, the dramatic actions of blacks rioting across the country for self-determination were of paramount importance.

Black power advocates early articulated the demands and desires of many rioting in ghetto streets and explicitly communicated to a wider audience the questioning of civil rights ideologies and tactics accentuating integration and nonviolence. From their vantage point black power advocates were aware that the old black leadership with its exclusive commitment to nonviolence and integration seemed to be losing its grip on certain segments of the black community, for "none of its so-called leaders could go into a rioting community and be listened to."[10] From this perspective, language giving exclusive stress to nonviolence and integration was seen as narcotizing the black community.[11] Moreover, black power leaders were among the first to articulate and publicize the idea of community control, black domination of governmental and economic institutions in ghetto areas, a concept already implicit in the attacks of rioters against selected ghetto targets and in the seizing of control in large areas of ghettos during riots, if only for short periods of time. Proclaimed and elaborated by emergent black leaders such

[9] Chuck Stone, *Black Political Power in America* (rev. ed.; New York: Delta, 1970), p. 25.

[10] Stokely Carmichael and Charles V. Hamilton, *Black Power* (New York: Random House Vintage Books, 1967), p. 50.

[11] Ibid., p. 51.

as Stokely Carmichael and H. Rap Brown, the term "black power" came to symbolize for many not only black pride but also community control and self-determination.

Not surprisingly, the increasingly conspicuous and articulate black power advocates were seized upon by many white American as a major "cause" of ghetto rioting. In the minds of many whites advocacy of black power quickly became linked to the use of offensive violence by black Americans and nestled well with theories of riot causation which saw outside agitators and un-American radicals as the primary igniters of specific instances of ghetto violence. However, the inappropriateness of such theories was suggested by the simple fact that many serious ghetto riots had occurred in dozens of cities prior to the articulation of the black power concept by Stokely Carmichael in Mississippi during the summer of 1966.[12] Thus it makes more sense to view the burgeoning of the black power movement as a consequence of rioting, which in effect stimulated significant changes in black spokesmen. It is also important to note that the arguments of the emerging black power leaders initially related to the use of violence only in self-defense—although their remarks were often taken out of context by the mass media.[13] However, as more riots occurred, and particularly after the massive riots in Detroit and Newark in 1967, advocates of black power were all but forced to speak of the possibility of revolutionary violence and guerrilla warfare on the part of black Americans in the quest for community control.

At least as important among the effects of ghetto rioting as the stimulation of black pride and the fostering of black power advocates was the triggering of a new awareness of the necessity for and effectiveness of concerted effort, of militant group action in pursuit of black goals. While this awareness was not new for some black Americans, ghetto rioting did seem to accelerate the

[12] See Stone, *Black Political Power in America,* pp. 17, 24–25.
[13] Robert Allen, *Black Awakening in Capitalist America* (Garden City, N.Y.: Doubleday Anchor Books, 1970), pp. 249–250.

commitment of black urbanites to collective attacks on the existing structure of urban power and authority: "What is also new is that blacks, increasingly concentrated in central cities, see that change is possible if they fight for it, and that appeals for justice are not nearly so effective as black-organized and black-led struggles to force concessions."[14] Indeed, this growing awareness of the importance of solidarity may have been one of the most significant consequences of the ghetto revolts in the 1960s, confrontations that made it conspicuously evident "what manifestations of solidarity could accomplish and demonstrated that power could be massed if individual blacks were more solidary."[15]

The Meaning of Decentralization

What the aims of the new ghetto men who rioted, the emergent black power advocates, and many of the new militant organizations seemed to boil down to was a demand for alteration of the existing arrangements of power and authority in cities and a demand for significant control by ghetto residents over the institutions which effectively dominated their lives. By the late sixties, therefore, decentralization and community control had become critical issues.

The demands of community control advocates have often included the restructuring of extant patterns of governmental power and authority—in effect, demands for governmental decentralization. In recent literature on American cities the phrase "governmental decentralization" has had a variety of meanings. For example, for some it has meant simply the redistribution of significant authority within a given government agency from the highest level to lower administrative levels. Supporters of administrative decentralization thus seem to want increased authority for the existing arms of bureaucracies already in local

[14] Tabb, *The Political Economy of the Black Ghetto*, pp. 129–130.
[15] Peter H. Rossi, "Urban Revolts and the Future of American Cities," *Cities Under Siege*, ed. David Boesel and Peter H. Rossi (New York: Basic Books, 1971), p. 421.

communities, for field officers, those who can still be controlled by their superiors if they should get out of line.[16] However, this decentralization is not what most black advocates of community control have had in mind.

Yet another meaning that has been attached to decentralization relates to the structure of the central governments in urban areas. If city councilmen are elected on a ward or district basis, rather than at large, the city government would be considered relatively decentralized in this sense. Short terms of office for mayors and city councilmen would also be assessed as indicators of governmental decentralization. As we noted in a previous chapter, governmental decentralization of this particular type apparently had a negative effect on the ability of some cities to respond quickly after ghetto riots. Examination of riots in 20 cities which had riots in the summer of 1967 disclosed that cities that initiated a relatively large number of remedial programs were more likely to have at-large elections, a strong mayor-council system, and longer terms of office for elected officials than localities that were less responsive—at least in the immediate aftermath period.[17] Thus, the choice of alternatives presented by the decentralization of governmental authority obviously may not be as easy as it may seem at first glance. Whereas in many situations centralized municipal governments might yield some short-term and tangible benefits for black urbanites—the enactment or expansion of traditional remedial programs along liberal lines—the enhanced prospects for community control and self-determination produced by a decentralized city governmental structure might well result not only in substantially increased black confidence in public authority, but also over the long term in more substantial gains in power and material benefits.

Nevertheless, calls for community control emanating from ghetto spokesmen, as well as community actions in accord with

[16] Altshuler, *Community Control,* p. 16.

[17] See Harlan Hahn, "Civic Responses to Riots: A Reappraisal of Kerner Commission Data," *Public Opinion Quarterly,* 34 (Spring 1970), 101–107.

a community control model, have not placed primary emphasis on this particular meaning of governmental decentralization. Community control advocates have had in mind not only greater black representation in the highest decision-making institutions at the citywide level by means of ward-type electoral procedures but also greater representation and participation at all levels of governmental boards (for example, school boards and county commissions), agencies, and public bureaucracies (for example, welfare and police bureaucracies).[18] Moreover, social and economic institutions have also been encompassed within the proposals for community control. From the developed community control point of view various ghetto businesses and landlords, as well as contractors and industries operating within ghetto boundaries, must ultimately come under greater if not exclusive control of black urbanites.

Advocates of Community Control

While proposals for community control have stimulated growing debate and interest among black Americans, so far few exhaustive plans for local autonomy have appeared. Nor has a community control plan been implemented on a large scale. Despite this, a number of supporters of restructuring governmental and economic power and authority in urban areas have begun to elaborate their ideas and examine the ramifications of the community control perspective.

Among the first to articulate and detail proposals for black self-determination and community control was Stokely Carmichael. Beginning in the summer and fall of 1966, elaborations of Carmichael's challenging black power ideas appeared in a number of speeches and periodicals; these ideas were carefully developed and worked out in a subsequent treatise with Charles V. Hamilton, entitled simply *Black Power*. As a first major step in the quest for increased power, these two authors stressed

[18] Altshuler, *Community Control,* pp. 14–15.

The Continuing Struggle for Black Power

the need to develop even more blacks who will be "new ghetto men," adopting a self-conception which accentuates pride in the group and emphasizes the ability to control actively one's own destiny:

> Black people must redefine themselves, and only *they* can do that. Throughout this country, vast segments of the black communities are beginning to recognize the need to assert their own definitions, to reclaim their history, their culture; to create their own sense of community and togetherness.[19]

That this redefinition process was well under way even as they were writing—particularly among young black adults—could be seen in the continuing willingness of blacks to engage in open confrontation with established white authorities across the country. Among the next important steps in the process of "political modernization" for black Americans were included the questioning of certain American institutions and values, the search for new forms of political strategy and structure, and the attempt to extend black participation in the urban decision-making process.[20] The questioning of old institutions and values relates to such things as rejecting the notion that one-way integration or assimilation into white America should be the basic goal of black Americans. Searching for specific new structures, in the view of Carmichael and Hamilton, refers to the need to put the structures which control the everyday lives of black Americans into the hands of black Americans:

> Black people have seen the city planning commissions, the urban renewal commissions, the boards of education and the police departments fail to speak to their needs in a meaningful way. We must devise new structures. . . . If this means the creation of parallel community institutions, then that must be the solution. If this means that black parents must

[19] Carmichael and Hamilton, *Black Power,* p. 37.
[20] Ibid., p. 39.

307

gain control over the operation of the schools in the black community, then that must be the solution. The search for new forms means the search for institutions that will, for once, make decisions in the interest of black people. It means, for example, a building inspection department that neither winks at violations of building codes by absentee slumlords nor imposes meaningless fines which permit them to continue their exploitation of the black community.[21]

Carmichael and Hamilton further argue that blacks must develop even more innovating organizations among themselves—modeled after groups like the Lowndes County Freedom Organization—in order to mobilize themselves more effectively.

Anticipating some of the criticism of their proposals to increase black power, Carmichael and Hamilton explicitly reject the view that black power ideas could be accurately described as racism in reverse, for "racism" means for them exclusion on the basis of race for the purpose of exploiting a subordinate group.[22] In their view black power does not entail white exploitation, only full black participation in the structure of American power arrangements. The black power thrust is seen simply as an attempt to extract black Americans from the manacles of subordination. Thus, although the ideas expounded by Carmichael and Hamilton had important historical precedents, such as the earlier writings of Malcolm X, *Black Power* was one of the first articulate statements of the resurgent black drive for self-determination and community control.

Since the mid-sixties many black spokesmen and writers, as well as rank-and-file ghetto residents, have contributed to the development of black power and community control ideas. A list of names of those leaders and writers whose actions, speeches, and writings have contributed significantly to this development would doubtless include such men as H. Rap Brown, Huey New-

[21] Ibid., pp. 42–43.
[22] Ibid., p. 47.

The Continuing Struggle for Black Power

ton, Bobby Seale, Eldridge Cleaver, Floyd McKissick, LeRoi Jones, Harry Edwards, and Dick Gregory—to mention only a few of the names that quickly come to mind.[23] While we cannot here trace out the broad range of arguments which have been made and the conceptual developments along black power lines which these and other black Americans have accelerated—a task worthy of book-length treatment—it is appropriate to note that there has been much stimulating and heuristic debate in the black community, as well as outside, over the concepts associated with black power.

To take one example illustrating the value of much of the criticism by other black writers, in a recent work entitled *Black Awakening in Capitalist America,* Robert Allen has criticized Carmichael and Hamilton for excessive vagueness in their delineation of the precise strategies blacks ought to follow in their quest for self-determination. Yet Allen has obviously been influenced by their ideas and proceeds to lay out in somewhat more specific terms a community control strategy. Paralleling the thought of other black power advocates, Allen views community development and control strategy as a transitional program that will bridge the gap between the present and the time when mass revolution will be possible. Liberal reformism is rejected, and the search for a transitional strategy culminates in an emphasis on the idea of a "cooperative commonwealth."[24] Drawing heavily on ideas outlined by DuBois several decades earlier, Allen concludes that a planned communal system without internal classes is required and favors such specific developments as consumer unions, the cooperative organization of black professionals, and black-controlled schools and businesses.[25] At the very least, at-

[23] See Floyd B. Barbour, ed., *The Black Power Revolt* (Boston: F. Porter Sargent, 1968), pp. 61–199; H. Rap Brown, *Die Nigger Die!* (New York: Dial Press, 1969); Robert Scheer, ed., *Eldridge Cleaver: Post-Prison Writings and Speeches* (New York: Random House, 1969).

[24] Allen, *Black Awakening in Capitalist America,* p. 275.

[25] W. E. B. DuBois, *Dusk of Dawn* (New York: Schocken Books, 1968), pp. 208ff.

tempts "to implement this program should increase the organization, and consequently the fighting ability, of the black community."[26] One new black organization is seen as drawing on the entire black population, as linking blacks not only nationally but also internationally. Termed a "militant political party," this new organization would use any workable strategy from legal action to collective violence:

> Under the aegis of a militant political party—a party which acts not as an occasional vote-getting machine but as a continuously functioning governing instrumentality—diverse activities, from efforts to establish rank-and-file labor union caucuses to struggles for community control of local schools, can assume a cohesiveness and meaning, independent of their immediate success or failure. Within the framework of the party, these activities can become integrated into a unified strategy for winning black self-determination.[27]

Perhaps the most specific and systematic review of the demands by black activists and black power advocates for greater participation and community control has so far been provided by Alan Altshuler. Focusing more or less on governmental issues, Altshuler summarizes the specific agenda of black power spokesmen as follows:

> (1) devolution of as much authority as possible to neighborhood communities; (2) direct representation of such communities on the city council, the board of education, the police commission, and other significant policy bodies; (3) black representation at all levels of the public service in far more than token numbers; (4) similar representation on the labor forces of government contractors; and (5) the vigorous ap-

[26] Allen, *Black Awakening in Capitalist America,* p. 279.
[27] Ibid., p. 280.

plication of public resources to facilitate the development of black-controlled businesses.[28]

Viewed more generally, the black thrust for community control is perceived as embracing the idea that government must abandon neocolonial control of ghetto life and develop an orientation toward aiding black Americans in their attempt to gain meaningful power. Thus black-dominated school systems would probably do far better than white-controlled school systems in preparing ghetto youth; doubtless they could do no worse. Black-controlled police departments might well begin to change black attitudes toward law enforcement agencies and provide the meaningful cooperation of black communities in the pursuit of criminals. And crimes of concern to black communities would be investigated, rather than just those of concern to white urbanites. Since white policemen have played a major role in precipitating and accelerating ghetto violence in hundreds of American cities, it is not difficult to believe that black-controlled police forces could substantially reduce black grievances against police practices.[29] Under community control arrangements, therefore, a variety of white workers in ghetto agencies and bureaucracies would be forced either to leave the ghetto or to work under the direct control of local black authorities.[30]

Yet Altshuler's analysis gives little attention to the specific alterations envisaged by some community control advocates in regard to the restructuring of power in nongovernmental areas of urban life. That is, some who have reviewed the arguments of black power advocates, as well as the arguments of blacks rioting in the streets, have distilled important contentions in regard to other social and economic institutions which impinge on the lives of ghetto residents. Thus a number of spokesmen have demanded that black power and authority must also be increased

[28] Altshuler, *Community Control,* p. 14.
[29] See ibid., pp. 199–216.
[30] Richard E. Rubenstein, *Rebels in Eden* (Boston: Little, Brown, 1970), pp. 149–150.

within these institutions. Perhaps the most important impact of expanding the control of ghetto residents in these areas would be to drive out those who currently benefit from the inequality of resources and power dramatized in oppressed situations of ghetto residents. Indeed, this would seem to be what many ghetto rioters actually had in mind. Absentee landlords preying on the ghetto would be forced to leave and seek a livelihood elsewhere. Resident rather than absentee ownership of ghetto housing would doubtless mean increased management skills and better ghetto housing for many ghetto residents. Exploitative white store owners would have to retire or relocate their businesses.[31] Business enterprises and property would be turned over to black ownership, preferably ownership by community-oriented organizations.[32] Channeling credit through community-controlled lending institutions might result in significant changes in ghetto credit operations.[33] Community ownership would be quite different from programs of black capitalism or corporate relocation, preferred more recently by white leaders as a way of defusing the future potential for ghetto violence.[34] Actions would be made cooperatively and would be directed so as to benefit the community at large, not just individual entrepreneurs.

If many of these proposals were in fact implemented, the specific benefits to black urbanites of redistributing power and authority in both governmental and nongovernmental institutions seem fairly obvious. However, more general benefits to the black community are also of great importance. Even the first major steps in the direction of expanded community participation and self-direction might well lead to further black solidarity and organization, to more experienced leaders, and to a better understanding of the operations of bureaucracies, councils, and agencies previously inaccessible. In summary, then, increased

[31] Ibid.
[32] Ibid., p. 149.
[33] See Altshuler, *Community Control,* pp. 199–216.
[34] Tabb, *The Political Economy of the Black Ghetto,* p. 58.

autonomy "would provide an arena in which blacks might engage their energies and experience power."[35]

Given the vigorous reaction of many white Americans to the simple phrase "black power," one might have anticipated that much white criticism would be directed at the character and workability of ideas about community control and local autonomy for ghetto residents. Thus some analysts have viewed steps toward community control as steps in the direction of extreme racial separatism and the acceleration of black and white polarization. Yet others have feared that the assumed general urban consensus on basic values would be destroyed. Some have argued that substantial ghetto autonomy would only increase existing corruption in cities. Yet others have worried that local control for blacks would work against the basic need of metropolitan areas for a centralized government which can deal effectively with area-wide problems. In addition, some white and a few black observers have argued that blacks do not have the basic resources, particularly economic resources, to sustain local autonomy successfully. And some have seen community control as leading to a cycle of guerrilla warfare and retaliatory white violence. While it is not our purpose here to dissect these particular objections and provide detailed answers for each one—Altshuler has already done that in his book *Community Control* —we would like to note briefly certain weak or fallacious lines of reasoning implicit in many of the prevailing critiques of ghetto autonomy proposals. Following the suggestions of Rubenstein,[36] we would argue that a number of the more important criticisms of community control ideas stem largely from three major misconceptions about current power and authority arrangements in American cities: (1) the urban consensus misconception, (2) the equivalence-of-values misconception, and (3) the lack-of-white-control misconception.

Criticisms indicating concern over the intergroup friction which

[35] Altshuler, *Community Control*, p. 199.
[36] Rubenstein, *Rebels in Eden*, pp. 153–159.

might arise from community control often reflect the urban consensus fallacy, the notion that peaceful negotiation and consensus are the warp and woof of urban politics. From the earliest period American cities have endured intergroup and interethnic friction, competition, and conflict, frequently to the point of collective violence. Intercommunity conflict over resources and power within urban boundaries has been part and parcel of the history of American cities. The rising of black Americans against the social, economic, and governmental status quo has been basically similar to the rising of many white immigrant groups before them and has already generated friction. Thus cities have seldom, perhaps never, operated according to the consensus model. Cities have not operated solely as a collection of equal groups peacefully negotiating their differences, for powerless groups have also played a role, not only as the colonized or subordinated but also as a constant source of disequilibrium and intergroup conflict.[37] Certainly from the point of view of established white groups and their agents already in power increasing black control over local councils, schools, police, and other important institutions may mean increased friction and ultimately power losses for established groups. However, this process is neither new nor unfamiliar to either the powerful or the powerless.

A somewhat related misconception can be seen in attacks on ghetto autonomy proposals which suggest that, since blacks and whites alike value highly such critical things as personal security and family protection, blacks and whites in fact have no basic value differences. Thus it has been suggested that at a fundamental level blacks must also value the "law and order" currently effectuated only by the existing and reputedly neutral central governments of cities. In this view community control of the local police, to take one important example, would mean chaos. One problem with this perspective is that there have long been major differences in the "law and order" goals desired by black and white Americans, as anyone familiar with the police literature is

[37] Ibid., p. 156.

aware. Since existing law enforcement and criminal justice systems already embody the goals and concerns of those white groups which had previously risen in power within the urban political system, it would be disingenuous to believe that blacks do not value and expect similar alterations. Even initial steps toward community control would in fact require the embodiment of some critical black goals in existing bureaucratic structures.

Arguments that accentuate the view that community control for blacks will necessarily mean placing new and similar control in the hands of white communities, particularly the suburbs, mirror yet a third misconception about present-day urban life. Explicitly or implicitly, such arguments suggest that present power and authority arrangements, in both government and economic sectors, already entail serious limitations on most white communities within urban areas. From this perspective the "extension of community control principles to the white community will therefore lead to a weakening of the position of minorities."[38] In some respects such arguments seem less than frank, in that most (but certainly not all) distinctive white groups in cities already have a significant measure of control over most urban institutions of concern to them, including those whites residing in suburbs—at the very least most white groups can influence the actions of those in government and corporate establishments if they so desire.[39]

One further argument against community control as a viable solution to the problems of black Americans might also be noted here. Some debate has centered on the problem of the lack of black capital and monetary resources viewed as requisite for the building of local autonomy for black urbanites. Indeed, an awareness of this problem has led some black power advocates to call for white reparations to help build up the economic resources for community control, presumably to be provided with

[38] Ibid., p. 157.
[39] Ibid., pp. 157–158.

no strings attached either by the governments or by the private corporations involved. One important proposal for reparations was the famous Black Manifesto, presented to white church groups in 1969; reparations of a half billion dollars were asked in return for centuries of black exploitation, the money to be used for black community control and self-determination efforts.[40] In addition, some have proposed massive federal government aid to facilitate the development of black economic power.[41] One demand has been for a federally funded program, paralleling the WPA of the Depression, designed to provide jobs at fair wages for all blacks in need.[42] Given such reparations, the black struggle for community control would obviously be expedited and the problem of economic resources might gradually be overcome, although the issue as to who would ultimately have control over the funds supplied might still remain to be resolved. Alternative avenues might also lead to new resources; for example, community corporations could be financed by selling stock in the corporations both inside and outside ghetto communities. However, even with no significant increase in the economic resources available, the black quest for community control would be more difficult but still not impossible. In the past, increasing the internal organization and solidification of a minority group has often stimulated the awareness and consolidation of its available resources and thus its level of mobilization. The struggle itself has a valuable payoff, for, as Bluestone has argued,

> while the creation of a black economy in the ghetto may not lead inexorably to a viable economic base—competitive with the staunchest of white enterprise—the act of striving toward an inner city economy yields a powerful tool for organizing the black community into a coherent political force

[40] Tabb, *The Political Economy of the Black Ghetto,* pp. 141–142.
[41] See Tabb, *The Political Economy of the Black Ghetto,* p. 59.
[42] Ibid., p. 141.

capable of extracting concessions on jobs, housing, income, and dignity from the government and the corporate establishment.[43]

An Aside on Federalism

While critics of community control approaches do not always make their underlying suspicions entirely explicit, they often seem to intimate that the nonviolent and violent black struggle for increased power and local autonomy is somehow un-American or foreign to the traditional working of the American system. At the very least, there seems to be an unwillingness on the part of many observers to think out the implications of certain fundamental American principles and traditions for the situation and problems of black Americans. Thus the black struggle for self-determination, reflected not only in ghetto rioting but also in the concomitant development of the black power and community control movement, may well have been engendered or stimulated by the historically circulated principles of American federalism.

The American experiment in federalism drew heavily on the idea that freedom depended on small governmental units and maximum possible autonomy for such jurisdictions. Following Montesquieu, many of the founding fathers were inclined to the view that citizen self-rule and freedom would endure "only in the small republic, where the interest of the whole was easier to grasp, where conspiracies were easier to guard against, and where each individual had a large enough share of responsibility to inspire political virtue."[44] Thus, the final version of the Constitution of the United States gave only specified and restricted

[43] Barry Bluestone, "Black Capitalism: The Path to Black Liberation?" *The Review of Radical Economics* (Ann Arbor, Mich.: Union for Radical Political Economics, May 1969), p. 53. The quote and the citation are taken from Tabb, *The Political Economy of the Black Ghetto,* p. 57.

[44] Altshuler, *Community Control,* p. 97.

powers to the national government. As a framework for the allocation of governmental responsibilities, the federal system has
constituted the basic context within which many major social
problems have been generated, debated, and resolved. Perhaps
most important, over the centuries of its existence the nature and
operation of federalism has been one of the most persistent and
explosive sources of conflict in United States history. The federal structure of government seldom has separated public officials
into tightly sealed compartments, each intent on performing his
own distinctive mission; but it has frequently produced serious jurisdictional altercations between national, state, and local
groups and governing officials. Many of the nation's most divisive
disputes—including the one which nearly tore the country asun-
der during the Civil War—basically have evolved as clashes over
opposing conceptions of local autonomy and self-determination.

Residents of the United States since the earliest years, black
Americans may have been profoundly influenced by their distinctive experiences within the federal system. During most of
United States history federalism was employed as an instrument
for the repression of black citizens. The doctrine of "states'
rights" and the corollary principle of "interposition" were exercised to prevent the national government from intervening in
local governmental affairs in such areas as southern racial practices, thus reinforcing and sustaining white domination in the
South. As a result, white voters in the South maintained more
or less exclusive control over the local and state institutions that
controlled the lives of most black southerners. In part to escape
the devastating effects of this local tyranny and to seek greater
opportunities to participate in the critical decisions affecting their
lives and futures, increasing numbers of black migrants fled the
South and relocated in northern and western cities. Arriving
expectantly in the North, black citizens there encountered a new
form of local control and power inequality that seemed to be at
least as constrictive and oppressive as the system they had left
behind in the South. Through such practices as residential encapsulation and economic discrimination, reinforced by violence

and other collective action on the part of established white groups, black residents of northern cities were effectively denied the advantages of full partnership.

Despite the endemic local problems that plagued black Americans in the North as well as in the South, the historic Supreme Court decisions on school desegregation and subsequent civil rights legislation for a time focused attention on the national government. Aware of the oppression that they suffered as a result of local autonomy by whites, many black citizens for a time seemed to regard national rather than municipal or state government institutions as the major hope for ameliorating the troublesome conditions confronting them. Yet the national legislation and court decisions, triggered in part by nonviolent protest demonstrations on the part of black Americans, appeared to yield only a few lasting benefits for ghetto residents, particularly in the North. In ghetto areas the effects of local institutions buttressing pervasive discrimination impeded national efforts to promote equality, not only in employment, education, and housing, but also in a variety of important municipal services. Discriminatory governmental policies tied into local economic discrimination and local residential segregation often appeared relatively immune to the influence of national regulation. To many blacks local social, economic, and governmental institutions also seemed impervious to the nonviolent civil rights movement and to the ideology of integration as well. Although black residents were granted the right to vote in northern cities, there as in southern cities they remained dominated by the governmental and economic strength of white majorities and sometimes manipulated by the use of imposed blacks fronting for whites. Furthermore, whites were ensuring local control of many of their communities in the future by creating separate municipalities on the fringes of the metropolitan area.

As northern and western ghettos grew in size and experience with this urban tyranny, desire accumulated for the active overthrow of dependency on outside agencies and for greater local independence and control. The unusual sense of distinctness and community that developed among black urbanites as a result of the confinement of increasingly large numbers in huge but encapsulated urban communities spurred mobilization for self-determination and augmented the ghetto resources necessary for increased local activity and control. Since the recent historical experience of many ghetto residents had demonstrated to many the problematical character of engaging solely in forms of non-violent protest and electoral politics, many black citizens appeared to be ready to employ physical force as a means of conveying their grievances and demands. The collective violence they engaged in was thus commonly directed at altering local rather than state or national arrangements. Most of the principal targets of attack during ghetto uprising—such as local businessmen and law enforcement forces, and their property—were directly linked to existing local powerholding groups. Thus the confined character of ghetto revolts may have reflected a purposive appeal for the delegation of local power and authority to the ghetto community level, although not necessarily implying the absence of broader objectives. Instead of attempting to exert an impact on the national government directly, black urbanites sought to force a redistribution of local power and authority so that they could exercise significant influence over decisions that most directly affected their lives. For many years black citizens had suffered from the use of the federal system by white voters and their leaders who utilized federalist concepts and structures to impede national intervention in state or local affairs and to maintain white domination of local institutions and agencies at the expense of black Americans. However, the black actions and demands in the sixties on behalf of self-determination, particularly including ghetto rioting, might be seen as perhaps the first major effort by black Americans to employ the principles of federalism to their own advantage.

Moreover, the nature of the federal structure may also have shaped other important characteristics of ghetto rioting. Perhaps one of the most significant features of the ghetto revolts was their localized nature. The fact that these uprisings generally remained confined to ghetto areas also may have been strongly influenced by the original designs of the founding fathers when they established the foundation of American federalism. Since the events of the eighteenth century had demonstrated that local insurrections might form a serious threat to governmental units, particularly at the national level, James Madison and other framers of the Constitution devised an ingenuous remedy for the problem. By superimposing smaller governmental units on the landscape of the country, Madison hoped to quarantine potentially disruptive movements or uprisings and to prevent them from capturing the higher level centers of authority. In a famous essay in *The Federalist Papers,* Madison wrote that "the influence of factious leaders may kindle a flame within their particular States but will be unable to spread a general conflagration through the other States."[45] Although Madison could not have predicted the growth of urban America or the outbreak of riots in the sixties, his views were highly prophetic. Since the arrangements blacks sought to change were complex and widely distributed among numerous jurisdictions, they were hindered from exploiting the support of sympathizers in other localities or from seizing the entire apparatus of government.

Federalist principles and the federal system, therefore, may have served both as an important means of preventing the potentially dangerous escalation of ghetto revolts to revolutionary proportions and also as a facilitating framework for the emergence of ghetto riots and the general black movement for local community control. After centuries of subjugation to discriminatory practices sustained in part by the actual operationalization of prevailing concepts of federalism in the American federal structure, many black Americans seemed to express a growing desire to adapt federalist principles—and traditional principles of participatory democracy as well—to their own needs. Broadly viewed,

[45] James Madison, "No. 10," in *The Federalist Papers,* ed. Clinton Rossiter (New York: New American Library Mentor Books, 1961), p. 84.

the community control movement among black Americans mirrors certain fundamental ideals of the American republic.

The Prospects for Community Control

With the resurgence of black power and community control concepts and philosophies during the 1960s, fostered by a number of important nonviolent and violent collective developments in black communities, have come many questions about the workability and likely future of proposals for increased autonomy for black Americans. Many remain skeptical about the prospects for black rejection of external dependency and seizure of a significant measure of local control. While we are only cautiously optimistic about the future and do not wish to suggest that such developments are inevitable or that they will come without great effort or difficulty, in our review of current events inside and outside urban ghettos we have discerned some signs that community control ideas are becoming grounded in concrete organizational developments. Thus the prospects for a significant measure of community control seem to be enhanced by the variety of actions already taken by blacks in the continuing process of group solidification and mobilization.

While rioting can be viewed as part of the process of group mobilization of black Americans, the apparent cessation of massive rioting by the late sixties did not mean a concomitant deceleration of the mobilization process. For example, after numerous ghetto riots black communities have seen steps taken in the direction of greater cooperative effort and organization for self-determination goals. On the one hand, cultural nationalism has flourished, an important example of which might be Ron Karenga's US group in Los Angeles, stimulated in part by the 1965 Watts rebellion. On the other hand, organizations have emerged which have gone beyond the goals of black consciousness and the creation of a new black culture. For example, in a survey of postriot developments in 20 cities the National Advisory

The Continuing Struggle for Black Power

Commission on Civil Disorders reported that new black militant organizations, many oriented toward community control ideas, had emerged in such cities as Cincinnati, Tucson, New Haven, Milwaukee, and Detroit. Organizations like the City-Wide Citizens Action Committee in Detroit stressed greater autonomy and control for the black community and were reportedly "developing plans for Negro-owned cooperatives" and had demanded "Negro participation in planning new construction."[46]

After the 1967 riot in Newark there was a significant spurt of new organizational activity. By 1968 a black united front was trying to establish black control of the city of Newark, and in that summer a Black Political Convention was held, which chose its own black candidates for mayor and city councilmen and pressed for a variety of community control proposals.[47] Similar organizational efforts were made in other cities:

> There was the Black United Front of Washington, D.C., the North City Congress in Philadelphia, the United Front in Boston, the Black United Conference in Denver, and the Black Congress in Los Angeles, to mention a few. All of these were coalitions which sought to alter power relations in the cities where they existed.[48]

Moreover, growing cooperation was evident in Washington, D.C., after the 1968 riot. A group named Build Black, Incorporated, was formed and attempts were made to get white merchants, particularly those whose stores and businesses had been attacked, to sell out to ghetto ownership. Prominent among the demands of this new group was community control of local unions, businesses, and contractors.[49] The Black United Front, founded in

[46] *Report of the National Advisory Commission on Civil Disorders* (Washington, D.C.: U.S. Government Printing Office, 1968), pp. 84–85.

[47] Allen, *Black Awakening in Capitalist America*, p. 141.

[48] Ibid., p. 142.

[49] Ben W. Gilbert et al., *Ten Blocks from the White House* (New York: Praeger, 1968), p. 216.

early 1968, pressed for black control over local law enforcement agencies and local civil rights organizations.[50]

One might also view the rapid growth of the Black Panther Party for Self-Defense as one organizational embodiment of the ideological quest for community control. Originally organized after the long hot summers of the 1964–1966 period by two "new ghetto men," Huey Newton and Bobby Seale, the Black Panther Party soon became an important organizing force in black ghettos, particularly among young black men. Spurred in part by the militancy reflected in ghetto rioting, the party had grown to at least several thousand strong by the late 1960s and had enlisted the active involvement of prominent community control advocates, among them Stokely Carmichael and Eldridge Cleaver. Attacked by conservatives and liberals alike, the party clearly articulated the goals of many ghetto rioters and developed a radical program placing heavy emphasis on a drive for increased black power. A ten-point program was widely circulated and incorporated critical goals such as (1) black housing cooperatives, (2) locally controlled education which includes black history, (3) defensive action by blacks to forestall police brutality, (4) freedom for all jailed black men, (5) trial of black people by black juries, and (6) a United Nations plebiscite of black people in America.[51] While the Black Panther Party—decimated by police harassment, arrests, and killings and torn by internal discord—now seems to be in decline, it should not be perceived as an isolated phenomenon which gained no support from the wider black community. In fact, a 1970 *Time* poll found that no less than a quarter of a representative sample of black Americans openly admired the Panthers a great deal.[52]

Moreover, the Black Panther Party and groups like the Student Nonviolent Coordinating Committee (SNCC), together with other

[50] Ibid., p. 219.
[51] "Black Panther Party Platform and Program," *The Black Panthers Speak,* ed. Philip S. Foner (Philadelphia: Lippincott, 1970), pp. 2–4.
[52] "Introduction," in ibid., p. xiv.

factors, played an important role in the wave of new militant organizations and self-direction efforts of black students on white campuses. One black student leader also noted that

> urban rebellion, the dismal failure of integration as a social, political and economic process, and the inability of the government at all levels to reconcile its rhetoric with its actions have all served to intensify the spirit of self-determination that pervades the entire black community, of which black students are a part.[53]

In the wake of these groups came literally hundreds of new courses in black studies and programs in colleges and universities, not to mention new black solidarity and consciousness in this segment of black America.

Another sign of the apparently growing effectiveness in organization can be glimpsed in renewed black activity in such areas as union organization and electoral politics. While the espoused goals of blacks involved in these areas have not always emphasized community control ideas, much of this new organizational activity is ultimately grounded in thinking closely related to that laid out by black power advocates. On the one hand, new black-dominated unions have emerged in the sixties, sometimes explicitly espousing the views similar to those of the Black Panthers. In recent years we have seen the emergence of new organizations of black workers, including hospital workers and garbage workers, and of welfare recipients.

Yet another manifestation of the continuing struggle for black power can be seen in new community activities directed at electing black government officials. New black electoral organizations have surfaced in the last few years in both the North and the South. While there were relatively few black elected officials in all of the nation in the early sixties, by 1971 there were over 700

[53] Robert Johnson, quoted in Allen, *Black Awakening in Capitalist America*, p. 257.

in the South and no fewer than 1,860 in the nation.[54] Organized blacks won major electoral victories in cities like Newark, Gary, and Cleveland; and losing black candidates participated in rather close elections in Los Angeles and Detroit. Although one can raise serious questions about the community control potential of such victories, at the very least they do provide greater experience in leadership and somewhat expanded power and authority for blacks in those particular cities. Furthermore, as more and more governmental offices were won by blacks, it became obvious that black voting blocs were switching from their allegiance to white candidates and black candidates chosen by white leaders to support new and often more militant black candidates.[55]

Some might argue that the prospects for expanded community control for black Americans have been enhanced by certain proposals and activities emanating from the white communities. As evidence might be cited white-supported proposals for black capitalism. However, white supporters of such an approach are particularly inclined to the notion of individual ownership, ordinarily in small businesses developed in close collaboration with outside white agencies.[56] From the black community's point of view there are very serious limitations to such linkages, for external control of the ghetto economy might only be partially altered, if at all, by increasing the number of small businesses owned by blacks.[57] In addition, small business operations are generally on the decline throughout the United States because of narrowing profit margins. Expanding the number of small businessmen in ghettos might only mean accelerating the number of bankruptcies in ghetto areas in the future. Thus advocates of community control for black Americans have severely criticized this type of individualistic or entrepreneurial approach and have argued al-

[54] *National Roster of Black Elected Officials* (Washington, D.C.: Joint Center for Political Studies, 1971).
[55] Stone, *Black Political Power in America,* p. 25.
[56] Tabb, *The Political Economy of the Black Ghetto,* p. 35.
[57] Ibid., p. 35.

ternatively that real progress for black ghetto residents as a group would necessitate communal or cooperative economic endeavors on a relatively large scale.

Perhaps more promising concessions in the direction of community control for black Americans can be seen in a few legislative proposals designed to foster such cooperative economic endeavors. A significant step in the direction of greater black control over the ghetto economy might be the community development corporations envisioned in a bill recently put forward by several U.S. senators. Such corporations would be private, nonprofit, and black-controlled and would become involved in such activities as ghetto housing projects and the ownership and development of ghetto property.[58] However, community development corporation legislation has yet to be put into effect.

Although in most cases there have been serious reversals, perhaps the most significant first steps toward community control yet participated in by some white authorities have been taken in the area of public schools—in part a result of pressure from the black power movement.[59] While no city has yet significantly decentralized its school system—placing major authority in the hands of neighborhood boards—a few state legislatures have considered or passed decentralization legislation. Perhaps the most famous of the experiments in decentralization was in the Ocean Hill-Brownsville area in New York.[60] When a black-controlled school board tried to transfer white teachers seen as blocking goals the board sought, a clash with the teachers' union resulted in the fall of 1968—a clash which the union eventually won. Unfortunately, this well-publicized clash destroyed that particular experiment and seriously crippled the school control movement. Similar pressures by teachers' unions have frustrated

[58] Ibid., pp. 52–53.
[59] Maurice R. Berube and Marilyn Gittell, "The Struggle for Community Control," *Confrontation at Ocean Hill-Brownsville,* ed. Maurice R. Berube and Marilyn Gittell (New York: Praeger Paperbacks, 1969), p. 9.
[60] See ibid.

the few other local attempts at school decentralization.[61] Although the history of school decentralization experiments has been stormy, white support for community control ideas was expressed in concrete terms, if only for a brief period of time.

Thus, while there is some apparent evidence for the argument that certain white actions have enhanced the prospects for a significant measure of community control for black communities, it does seem that the evidence is on the whole rather shaky. The now highly touted black capitalism may only be a new means of neocolonialism. And school decentralization experiments have so far failed because of the opposition of powerful white groups. Legislation of great importance has been proposed by white representatives, but significant concessions to ghetto autonomy have not been implemented. Nevertheless, it is important to note that some in white communities are at least beginning to think seriously about the *possibility* of community control in black areas, and, at the very least, the decentralization programs that have been tried and withdrawn have demonstrated the basic feasibility and potential of many of the ideas of community control advocates.

Conclusion

While there has been some grudging and vacillating white support for greater self-determination for black Americans, up to this point in time there have been no major experiments in community control in an American city. It seems evident that the efforts by most white leaders and groups have not been directed toward accelerated community control for black Americans but rather toward token reforms or "benign neglect," if not to increased neocolonial control over ghetto affairs. In the main, the commitment of most urban leaders still seems to be to white domination on the urban scene, to exploiting the poor by means

[61] See Mario Fantini, Marilyn Gittell, Richard Magat, *Community Control and the Urban School* (New York: Praeger Paperbacks, 1970).

such as urban renewal, and to providing a favorable environment for white middle-class residents and businessmen. However, it seems likely that current neglect of ghetto problems can only lead to a more turbulent urban future, for it is only when an emerging group attains significant control over its own destiny that the likelihood of further turbulence in its quest for power is substantially reduced. Thus social science research has discovered the not too surprising finding that there is a close relationship between an individual's, and his group's, participation in the structure and process of power and political satisfaction.[62]

At this critical juncture in American history the black struggle for self-determination and equality continues, and current tactics continue to range from the relatively nonviolent to the relatively violent. In the last decade we have seen new weapons added to the contemporary repertoire of black tactics, including collective violence and offensive guerrilla-type attacks by black Americans on the symbols and reality of white power in ghetto areas. Mirrored in the attacks has been a new radicalism, indicating that the idea of community control of the institutions and agencies governing black lives has been gaining militant adherents. In the wake of ghetto rioting has come a rekindled emphasis among black Americans on personal efficacy and on community control. The newly articulated demands for community control, seen in the black power movement and in the multiplication of militant organizations such as the Black Panther Party, stand in contrast to earlier demands emphasizing integration as the dominant goal. Now the goal of an increasing number is black domination of the social, economic and governmental institutions impinging on black communities, with the issue of integration with white Americans postponed for later consideration (if considered at all), at the time when black Americans have secured relative equality in power and authority with powerholding white groups.

Conceivably, in the future the goal of somewhat greater local autonomy and self-direction for black Americans may have greater

[62] Ibid., p. 231.

appeal and more to offer to white Americans than goals focusing on immediate and thoroughgoing integration. That such community control provides a viable and realistic alternative to other choices available to existing powerholding groups stems in part from the obvious failure of the conservative and liberal approaches to redressing the ghetto grievances underlying the development of collective violence. While blacks have benefited in some ways from liberal reforms, the changes which have come have been token or transitory, and always insufficient, given the seriousness and complexity of ghetto problems. Thus both the merits and the possibilities of creating increased local autonomy and self-regulation in ghetto neighborhoods have already compelled many black and white citizens and leaders to engage in an agonizing reappraisal of the fundamental inequalities in the resource and power structure of American cities. Indeed, whites may well have a lot to gain from such an agonizing appraisal, perhaps even from major concessions to the black struggle for self-determination, for increased political satisfaction in black communities might insure prevention of occurrences of guerrilla warfare or even large-scale revolution with its tremendous costs to majority and minority alike. Serious grants of increased community control, therefore, might result in much greater reliance by black Americans on the tactics of electoral politics. In this sense, then, the future of American society is clearly in the hands of white Americans: "The aim must be to persuade Negroes that playing by the rules can produce some meaningful gains."[63]

Given the apparently growing sense of efficacy and solidarity in ghetto communities, it seems very likely that black Americans will continue their struggle for power and equality and that their demands can be neglected only for finite periods of time. What distinctive tactics will characterize the black cause in the future? A number of scenarios of the future of the black struggle have already been projected for those seeking answers to this speculative question. Though some observers expect little action on the

[63] Altshuler, *Community Control,* p. 196.

part of black Americans, others have projected into the near or distant future of black-white relations an acceleration of collective violence, perhaps in the guise of sophisticated guerrilla warfare, perhaps in the form of massive rioting in a number of cities at one time. Evidence that lends credibility to forecasts of guerrilla warfare can be seen in revolts such as that in Cleveland, Ohio in the summer of 1968; in that revolt black snipers and white policemen were involved in an extensive gun battle. "And apparently alone among major outbreaks of racial violence in American history, it ended in more white casualties than black."[64] And evidence for the emergence of a guerrilla warfare alternative might also be seen in the reportedly rising number of city policemen killed in the last few years in ambush attacks "surrounded by an atmosphere of racial conflict."[65] Moreover, some analysts have even speculated that the currently rising "crime" rates in numerous central cities prophesy a continuation of black-white power conflict in yet another form of violence directed against white persons and property. In contrast to these views emphasizing varieties of violent tactics, however, other observers of the American racial scene seem persuaded that violence is less likely because of changing black views taken together with the buildup in the repressive capability of governmental police forces and have predicted that the future will see a reinvigoration of electoral politics. Yet others have forecast a new stress on non-violent tactics such as boycotts, demonstrations, or civil disobedience.

Yet these scenarios may be too restricted. Were we forced to speculate on the future of the black cause, we would be inclined to predict that attacks on existing arrangements would continue on numerous fronts and that a variety of tactics would be drawn from the now extensive repertoire of black Americans—electoral

[64] Louis H. Masotti and Jerome R. Corsi, *Shoot-out in Cleveland* (Washington, D.C.: U.S. Government Printing Office, 1969), p. xiii.

[65] See International Association of Chiefs of Police, *Annual Law Enforcement Casualty Summary: July, 1970–June, 1971* (Gaithersburg, Md.: Police Weapons Center, 1971), p. 25.

politics, nonviolent demonstrations, boycotts, civil disobedience, and various types of collective violence. In the early seventies we have already seen the application of all of these tactics in the continuing struggle for black power. One should not, therefore, expect the future of the black cause to follow one course to the exclusion of all others. Up to this point in the history of the black struggle, there have already been sudden advances and sudden reversals, intermixed with periods of relative inactivity. Given variations in the magnitude of black pressure and the character of the white response, it is probably a fail-safe prediction to suggest that the black pursuit of self-determination will continue to develop in this zigzag fashion, at least within the foreseeable future.

INDEX

Aggression. *See* Frustration-aggression

Alienation: role of, in collective violence, 16–17

Allen, Robert, 309–310

Altshuler, Alan, 310–11, 313

Antidraft riot of 1863, 73–74, 78

Antipoverty programs, 116, 287–88

Antiriot provisions of the 1968 Civil Rights Act, 230–31

Bedford-Stuyvesant riot (1964), 99
survey of residents after, 267, 268–69, 272, 276, 282

Black Americans
attitude of, toward governmental agencies, 130–32
commitment of, to the national government, 128–29, 132
gains of, before emergence of serious riots, 23
negativism of, against local police, 152–55
political tactics of, prior to ghetto violence of 1960s, 81–98
during Depression and World War II periods, 89
during years of slavery until the forties, 82–91
fifties and early sixties, the, 91–98
impact of large structural changes on, 84–85
post-World War I, 88–89

Black-controlled corporations: establishment of, 245–46

Black government officials, 325–26

Black Manifesto, 316

Black militant organizations: emergence of, 323–24

Black Muslims, 93

Black Panther Party, 324

Black perspectives 124–25, 126–34

Black Political Convention, 323

Black Power. *See also* Community control
struggle for, 297–332

Black protest activity, nonviolent, 39–40

Black United Front, 323–24

Black urbanization, 3–6
as group mobilization process, 33
impact of, on history of black political action, 84, 85, 87–88
problems of, 31–37
exploitive ghetto merchants, 35
geographic residential segregation, 31–34
preventive patrolling by the police, 36, 156–57
urban renewal, 35
white-dominated politicians and machines, 36
white landlords, 35

Boycotts, economic, 40

Brown, H. Rap, 303, 308

Carmichael, Stokely, 303, 306–309, 324

Chicago riot (1919), 90

Chicago Riot Study Committee, 206, 213, 217

Civil disobedience tactics, 39–40

Civil Disorder Clearinghouse at Brandeis University, 102–108, 136, 137

Civil disorders, 102, 105
defined, 103, 104, 135

Civil disturbances, 106–107

Civil rights progress: effect of violence on, 278–79

Cleaver, Eldridge, 309, 324

Collective political violence, 16, 18, 42–54

Index

Collective violence. *See also* Ghetto riots; Ghetto violence; Riots; Urban violence
 in American history, 60–80
 before Harlem and Bedford-Stuyvesant (1961–1964), 94–98
 effect of on civil rights progress, 278–79
 ghetto residents' position on use of, 275–82
 ghetto-specific explanations of, 24–28
 interaction issue in, 50–51
 occurrence of, in the 1960s, 40–43
 political. *See* Collective political violence
 riot preparation by authorities, and development of, 52–53
 role of civil authorities and power groups in, 16, 50–53
 social science explanations of, 12–24
 U.S. and foreign countries compared, 58–59
 weaknesses in common approaches to, 28–30
Collective violence in history. *See* Violence in American history
Collective violence in the 1960s, 99–140
 deprivation and. *See* Deprivation
 ghetto size and, 119, 122–23, 138
 government malfunctioning and, 114–15, 119
 major, serious, and minor riots, 104, 137, 182
 number of disorders during, 101–108
 number of persons involved in, 102, 103, 104, 279–81
 operational criteria for riots, 104, 137
 precipitating incidents. *See* Precipitating incidents
 underlying conditions of, 109–24, 138
Community control, 299, 304–306
 advocates of, 306–17

prospects for, 322–28
Community Control (Altshuler), 313
CORE (Congress of Racial Equality), 40, 92
 activities of, 93
Corporations, black-controlled, 245–46
Corporations, national: expansion of ghetto activity by, 245–46
Counterrioters, 166
"Creative disorder," politics of, 92
"Creative rioting," 27
Crowd formation stage in development of riot, 160–64

Decentralization, 304–306
 of schools, 327–28
Department of Housing and Urban Development. *See* HUD
Deprivation, 110, 111, 112–13, 114, 119, 122, 124, 138, 268, 269, 270
Detroit riot (1943), 90
Detroit riot (1967), 152, 153, 161, 164, 165, 173, 176–77, 189, 195, 264–65. *See also* Twelfth Street area of Detroit
Discrimination, racial, 268, 269
DuBois, W. E. B., 86

East St. Louis riot (1917), 4, 78–79, 206
Education programs, 254
Edwards, Henry, 309
Employment programs, 247, 250–51, 253

FBI report on 1964 riots, 8, 11
Federalism, 317–22
Ford Foundation, 259
Foreign countries: violence in U.S. and, compared, 58–59
Freedom rides, 92
Frustration-aggression approaches to collective violence, 17–20

Garvey, Marcus, 88–89
Ghetto "grievance bank," 149
Ghetto grievances, 255–56

Index

"Ghetto man, new." *See* "New ghetto man"
Ghetto merchants, 34, 35
    attacks on, 46
Ghetto residents: opinion surveys of, 265–67. *See also* Ghetto riots: residents' views in aftermath of
Ghetto riots. *See also* Collective violence; Urban violence
    calling in of the National Guard, 179
    causes of, according to residents, 268–75
    counterrioters in, 166
    defined, 135–37
    final precipitating incident of, 142–51. *See also* Precipitating incidents
    formation of commissions as aftermath of. *See* Riot commissions
    information transmission in development of, 164, 167–72
    law enforcement response to, 226–39
    negotiations during, 179–81
    official actions during, 183–96
    patterns in development of, 159–83
    percentage of residents participating in, 279–81
    police planning and preparations for, 185–86
    as the politics of violence, 43–54
    recurrent stages in development of, 160–83
    residents' views in aftermath of, 263–96
        on causes and character of riots, 268–75
        on confidence in local government, 290–91
        on future aspirations, 286–87
        on participation in riot, 279–82
        vs. views of white citizens and governmental leaders, 269–70
        views on the police, 283–85
    response to, that focuses on social and economic reform, 239–59

    in terms of stages of severity, 104, 182–83
Ghetto size in precipitation of riots, 119, 122–23
Ghetto violence. *See also* Collective violence; Ghetto riots; Urban violence
    remedies for, 200–205
        conservative approach, 201–202
        liberal approach, 202–203
        radical approach, 203–205
Gregory, Dick, 309
Grievances, ghetto, 255–56

Hamilton, Charles V., 306–309
Harlem riot (1964), 99, 173
Harlem riots (1935 and 1943), 89–90
"Hostile outbursts," 102, 135
Housing conditions, 268
Housing programs, 253
HUD (Department of Housing and Urban Development): programs of, 241–44

Industrialization, black: impact of, on history of black political action, 84, 85
Information transmission in development of riot, 164, 167–72
Interracial friction, 123
Isolation: role of, in collective violence, 14, 16

Job blockades, 92, 93
Johnson, Lyndon B., 200, 209, 210
    on Detroit uprising, 264
    reaction of, to final report of National Advisory Commission, 221–22, 244
Jones, LeRoi, 309

"Keynoting" in the development of crowd action, 163–64
King, Martin Luther, Jr., 39–40, 92
    assassination of, 105
    development of riots following, 161
    precipitating incidents following, 147–48

335

Index

Ku Klux Klan, 67–68, 84

LEAA (Law Enforcement Assistance Administration), 231–32
appropriations of, 232, 233, 252
problems in operation of, 233–34
Lemberg Center for the Study of Violence, 147–48
Looting stage of riot, 172–77, 272–77
Los Angeles. *See also* Watts riot
Governor's Commission on the Los Angeles Riots, 206, 217, 250–51
social and economic reforms in, 250–51, 253
US group in, 323

McKissick, Floyd, 309
Malcolm X, 308
MAME (Minority Advisors for Minority Entrepreneurs), 245
March-on-Washington threatened in 1941, 92
Mass Marches, 39
Mattick, Hans W., 214
Media, the
grievances and activities of black rioters ignored by, 195
role of, in development of riot, 167–70
Migration to the city ghettos, 87–88
Militant political party, 310
Model Cities programs, 241
Montgomery, Alabama: bus boycott in, 92

NAACP (National Association for the Advancement of Colored People), 40, 86–87, 88
National Advisory Commission on Civil Disorders, 200, 201, 206, 214, 221, 224
findings and recommendations of, 24–25, 103–104, 106, 107, 108, 114–15, 125, 145–47, 149–50, 166, 168–69, 217, 218–20, 227, 240, 247
functions of, 208
personnel of, 211–12, 213, 215–16

National Association for the Advancement of Colored People. *See* NAACP
National Commission on the Causes and Prevention of Violence, 206, 209
findings and recommendations of, 217, 218, 222–23, 236
functions of, 209
personnel of, 211–12, 214–15
National Guard, 228–29
actions of, during riots, 179, 182, 189, 193, 195
National Negro Congress, 88
"New ghetto man," 25–26, 300–301, 304
New Jersey
Governor's Select Commission on Civil Disorder, 206, 217, 218, 249
Newark riot (1967), 152, 173, 189
Newton, Huey, 308–309, 324
Niagara movement, the, 86
Nonviolent protest activity, 39–40

Office of Economic Opportunity (OEO): programs of, 241–44
Official actions during ghetto riots, 183–96
Omnibus Crime Act, 231–32, 233

Picketing, 39
Police, the, 51–52, 123, 235–36
actions of, during the riots, 184–94
actions of, as precipitating incident, 143–46, 149n., 150, 151–57
attacks on, during riot, 166, 174
brutality of, 268, 269
critical role of, 151–59
criticism of, 131–32, 139, 152
frictional interaction between ghetto residents and, 50–51
ghetto residents views of, 283–85
preventive patrolling of, 36, 156–57
riot control training for, 236–38
Political violence
in American history. *See* Violence in American history

Index

collective. *See* Collective political violence

Politics of violence, 43–54

Precipitating incident(s), 109–110, 111, 112, 113
  categories of, 143–48, 148n., 149n., 150
  chain of events as, 149–51
  final, of ghetto riots, 142–51
  police actions as, 143–46, 149n., 150, 151–52. *See also* Police, the

Race riots, 79–80

Racial discrimination, 268, 269

Relative deprivation approach to collective violence, 20–22

Reparations, white, 315–16

"Revolution of rising expectations," 21

Riot commissions
  Chicago Riot Study Committee, 206, 213, 217
  findings and recommendations of, 216–24
  formation of, 205–206
  Governor's Commission on the Los Angeles Riots, 206, 213, 217, 250–51
  Governor's Select Commission on Civil Disorder (New Jersey), 206, 217, 218, 249
  National Advisory Commission. *See* National Advisory Commission on Civil Disorders
  operation of, 212–16
  personnel of, 210–12, 213–16
  significance of, 224–26
  Violence Commission. *See* National Commission on the Causes and Prevention of Violence

Riot control, 228–32, 236–38

"Riot ideology" approach to ghetto violence, 26–27

Riot preparation by authorities, 52–53

Rioting. *See* Collective violence; Urban violence

Riots. *See also* Ghetto riots
  negotiations during, 179–81

Rumors: role of, in riots, 171n.

School decentralization, 327–28

School desegregation: 1954 Supreme Court decision on, 100

Seale, Bobby, 309, 324

Separatism, 130, 132

Sit-ins, 39, 92

Small Business Administration (SBA) loan programs, 244–45, 246

SNCC (Student Nonviolent Coordinating Committee), 92, 324–25

Social science investigators, 213–15

Southern Christian Leadership Conference, 92

Spilerman, Seymour: on riot development, 118, 119–20, 121, 123–24, 138

Strikes. *See* Labor violence

Summer riots, 107, 108

Supreme Court decision (1954) on school desegregation, 100

Tension or strain: role of, in collective violence, 13, 16

Twelfth Street area of Detroit, 153 and *n.*, 158, 176–77. *See also* Detroit riot
  survey of residents of, after riot, 266, 267, 293–94
    on antipoverty programs, 287–88
    on causes of riot, 268, 269, 271, 272–73, 274–75
    on future aspirations of residents, 286–87
    on future relations between rank-and-file blacks and whites, 286
    on local political disaffection, 290
    on opportunities for political participation, 292–93
    on participation in riot, 280, 281, 282
    on the police, 283–85
    on use of violence, 275–76, 278

Unemployment, 268

Unions, black-dominated, 325

Urban League, the, 87

337

Index

Urban renewal, 35
Urban violence. *See also* Collective
    violence; Ghetto riots; Ghetto
    violence
  popular explanations of, 6–12
    disproof of, 9–10
    outside agitators, 7–8
    recent migration from the South,
      6–7, 8
    "riffraff" or "rotten apple"
      theory, 8–9, 279–80
    "wild youngsters" theory, 10–12
  social science explanations of. *See*
    Collective violence
  weaknesses in common approaches
    to, 28–30
Urbanization, black, 3–6

Vigilantism, 66–68
Violence. *See* Collective violence
Violence in American history, 60–97
  among white ethnic groups, 72–77
  group violence, classification of, 64
  incidents of (1819–1968), 60–62
  negative violence unrelated to "con-
    structive development," 62, 63,
    64
  positive violence related to "popu-
    lar and constructive move-
    ments," 62, 63, 64
  vigilantism, 66–68
  white violence against nonwhite
    Americans, 77–80
Violence Commission. *See* National
    Commission on the Causes and
    Prevention of Violence
VISTA program, 243

War-on-Poverty, 116, 287–88
Washington, Booker T., 86
Washington, D.C.
  1968 riot, 173
  social and economic reform in, 259
Waskow, Arthur I., 79–80
Watts riot, 116–17, 152, 154, 166, 173,
    189, 241. *See also* Los Angeles
  final report on, 217
  survey of residents after, 271–82, 288
White landlords, 35
White racism, 24–25